D1317510

Emotional Health and Well-Being

Emotional Health and Well-Being

A Practical Guide for Schools

HELEN COWIE, CHRISSY BOARDMAN, JUDITH DAWKINS AND DAWN JENNIFER

P·C·P
Paul Chapman
Publishing

LB1027.5
.E468
2004x

053192018

© 2004 Helen Cowie, Chrissy Boardman, Judith Dawkins and Dawn Jennifer

First published 2004

Apart from any fair dealing for the purposes of research or private study,
or criticism or review, as permitted under the Copyright, Designs and
Patents Act, 1988, this publication may be reproduced, stored or
transmitted, in any form or by any means, only with the prior
permission in writing of the publishers, or in the case of reprographic
reproduction, in accordance with the terms of licences issued by the
Copyright Licensing Agency. Inquiries concerning reproduction outside
those terms should be sent to the publishers.

Paul Chapman Publishing
A SAGE Publications Company
1 Oliver's Yard
55 City Road
London EC1Y 1SP

SAGE Publications Inc
2455 Teller Road
Thousand Oaks, California 91320

SAGE Publications India Pvt Ltd
B-42, Panchsheel Enclave
Post Box 4109
New Delhi 100 017

Library of Congress Control Number: 2003115339

A catalogue record for this book is available from the British Library

ISBN 0 7619 4354 4
ISBN 0 7619 4355 2 (pbk)

Typeset by Dorwyn Ltd, Rowlands Castle, Hants
Printed in Great Britain by T.J.International, Padstow

Contents

Foreword   vii

About the authors   viii

Acknowledgements   x

Section 1   3

1.1   Introduction   3

1.2   The Stigma of Mental Health Difficulties   13

1.3   Why Should Schools be Involved?   24

1.4   Schools in a Social Setting   30

1.5   Why Intervene at Whole-School Level?   35

1.6   Where to Start in Matching an Intervention to your School   40

Section 2   55

2.1   Creating a School Community   55

2.2   Disaffected Young People   68

2.3   Violent Behaviours   80

2.4   Bullying Behaviours   92

2.5   Sexual Health   109

2.6   Alcohol, Drugs and Substance Abuse   120

2.7   The Socially Isolated/Children in the Asperger's/Autistic Spectrum 132

2.8   Helping Children Deal with Loss   142

2.9   Eating Problems   151

2.10   Deliberate Self-Harm   161

2.11   Attention Deficit Hyperactivity Disorder   172

2.12   Accessing Outside Help   184

Section 3   191

3.1   Predicting the Difficulties   193

3.2   Review and Evaluation   203

References   214

Index   226

Foreword

Those who read this book, either as newcomers to the field or as experienced practitioners within it, will do so at a time of change. As new initiatives permeate the educational landscape the context and impact of change has to be measured in relation to its effect on the whole child. Central to this view of learning is a holistic view of children as learners. Keeping this in sight can be difficult when practitioners are under constant pressure to have countable measures of performance. Daily we are confronted with children who self-abuse through self-harm behaviours, eating disorders, drug or alcohol abuse or we observe incidents that involve social isolation, for example racial abuse. We are also aware of cases of bullying and aggression that reaches extremes and we witness the harm inflicted on children through a range of violent acts. We cannot ignore as professionals that our classrooms are part of broader social and cultural contexts, which we are preparing children for.

The importance of promoting emotional well-being therefore is central to developing security and self-confidence. This requires practitioners to be aware of, and responsive to, the importance of personal and social well-being, encouraging children to understand their own feelings, beliefs and values within home, school and community environments. The educational process is 'sowing the seeds' of emotional well-being where children understand their emotions, and can express themselves as a valued members of the community. *Emotional Health and Well-Being* provides teachers and trainees with a practical guide to promoting positive strategies and extending good practice.

Dr Julie Shaughnessy
Roehampton University of Surrey

About the Authors

Chrissy Boardman, having worked initially in paediatrics, completed her psychiatry training and went on to lecture at the Malawian Medical School and run a private practice. She now works as a child and adolescent psychiatrist in West Dorset. She has always been actively involved in youth work: running groups for young people, drama workshops, music and dance workshops, using art with young people and helping to staff a youth drop-in centre.

Helen Cowie is a developmental and counselling psychologist currently working as Research Professor and Director of the UK Observatory for the Promotion of Non-Violence (www.ukobservatory.com) in the University of Surrey European Institute of Health and Medical Sciences. She has published widely on the subject of young people's emotional health, in particular on the effects on young people's well-being of bullying and social exclusion. She has also carried out extensive research on the positive outcomes for young people of peer support in challenging the misuse of power in relationships and in creating a helpful school ethos. She is co-author (with Peter K. Smith and Mark Blades) of the widely used textbook *Understanding Children's Development*, published by Blackwell and now in its fourth edition. With Sage she has co-authored (with Sonia Sharp) *Counselling and Supporting Children in Distress* and (with Patti Wallace) *Peer Support in Action*. She has three children, Julian, Anna and Ben, two stepsons, Sam and James, and three grandchildren, Corrie, Isabel and Haruki.

Judith Dawkins is a Consultant in Child and Adolescent Psychiatry in an independent practice in Brookwood, Surrey. She has a special interest in children who are experiencing problems at school and attention deficit hyperactivity disorder. Prior to this she was a Consultant in a Child and Adolescent Mental Health Service and a Senior Lecturer at St George's Hospital Medical School where she developed research and clinical interests in children who are bullied at school and who have other difficulties at school.

Dawn Jennifer is a Doctorate Researcher in the School of Psychology and Therapeutic Studies at Roehampton University of Surrey. Since 1999 she has worked on a number of research projects including the promotion of non-violence in schools, the promotion of positive emotional health and well-being in secondary school aged pupils, bullying in the workplace, and the use of participatory research methods with children. She is co-author (with Helen Cowie and Sonia Sharp) of 'Violence in schools: the United Kingdom' in P. K. Smith (ed.), *Violence in Schools: the Response in Europe* published by RoutledgeFarmer (2003). She is a founder member of the UK Observatory for the Promotion of Non-Violence: working with children and young people. (www.ukobservatory.com)

Photographs by Sue Jenkins and Chrissie Boardman.

Acknowledgements

APAUSE
Sue Bailey
Anna Barker
Big Fish Theatre Company
British National Temperence League (BNTL)
Box Clever Theatre
Helen Carmichael, *Leap* Confronting Conflict
Michael Dawkins
Drug and Alcohol Service for London (DASL)
Gillian Dunne, Granard Primary School
The Essex Schools Award Scheme
Carol Evans, Wirral Health Promoting Schools Scheme
Martin Evans
David Gillborn
Philip Graham
Meg Griffiths, CRISP
Sue Jenkins
Ann Kimber
Barbara Kingsley
Jean Law, The Essex Schools Award Scheme
Robert Long
Stuart Mcleod
Jenny Mosley, Ginny Sutton and Jenny Mosley's Consultancies
Paul Naylor
Derris Powell
Radcliffe Medical Press for permission to reproduce the questionnaire for teachers which appears in *Child Mental Health in Primary Care* book

Samantha Rowe-Beddoe, Pop Up Theatre Limited
Michael Rutter
Val Scott, The Essex Schools Award Scheme
Julie Shaughnessy
Southwark Black Mentoring Scheme
Anne Stewart
Sarah Stewart-Brown
Lorenzo Talamelli
John Tripp
Maggie Turner, CHIPS
Katherine Weare
Diana Whitmore
Winston's Wish
George Varnava, Author of 'Checkpoints'
Patti Wallace

We would like to thank the pupils and staff at the following schools:-
Chelmer Valley High School, in particular Rob Cowling
Greenshaw High School (Tim Buckley and his team)
Llantwit Major School
Morpeth School, in particular Laura Worsley
Ralph Allen School, in particular Kath Brownell,
St Osmunds C.E. (Aided) Middle School, in particular Rob Davies, Joy Ray and
Jan Stevens
Sandford CE VC Middle School (Geoffrey Pike and his team),
Thomas Hardyes School (Iain Melvin)

Dedications

To Amy and Jay. (Chrissy Boardman)

To Julian, Anna, James, Sam and Ben who taught me the importance of listening to the young. (Helen Cowie)

To Michael, Tim and Thomas and the schools they have attended. (Judith Dawkins)

To Flora. (Dawn Jennifer)

SECTION 1

Mental health enhances the capacity of individuals, families, communities and nations to contribute to the social networks and communities in which they exist. Young people who are emotionally healthy have the ability to develop emotionally, intellectually and spiritually; to develop and sustain personal relationships with others; to use solitude constructively and enjoy it; to develop empathy for the feelings of others; to play and learn; to develop a sense of right and wrong and address and learn from everyday conflicts and setbacks. (DfES, 2001)

Introduction

WHY DID WE WRITE THIS BOOK?

This book has developed out of our research and work as psychiatrists and psychologists, researchers and counsellors and was inspired by our collaborative research for DfES on Emotional Health and Wellbeing for all in Secondary Schools. We are passionate believers in mental and emotional health for all, and are very excited by the diversity and imaginativeness of the work going on in our schools. This book aims to share and disseminate some of this good practice. We have tried to emphasize interventions that are evidence based.

Recently, concern for the mental health of young people has been high on the political agenda in the UK through such initiatives as Sure Start, National Healthy Schools Standard, *ConneXions*, Excellence in Cities and regularly updated anti-bullying guidelines. An important theme within these policies concerns the increasing incidence of mental health difficulties among the young (Audit Commission, 1999). In this book we argue that schools have a critical part to play in preventing and alleviating the distress experienced by so many young people.

WHAT DO WE MEAN BY 'MENTAL AND EMOTIONAL HEALTH DIFFICULTIES'?

A mental health problem *can be seen as a 'disturbance in functioning' in one area of relationships, mood, behaviour or development. When a problem is particularly severe or persistent over time, or when a number of these difficulties are experienced at the same time a child is said to have a* mental health disorder. (Mental Health Foundation, 1999, p. 6)

While today's young people seem to face severe stresses that were unknown a generation ago, society still has negative and stereotyped views of mental illness and mental health problems. The sense of shame and embarrassment that surrounds the concept of a mental health disorder contributes to the fact that young people's mental health difficulties are often unrecognized or even denied (Mental Health Foundation, 1999). Only a minority of young people with mental health problems will be referred to and receive help from Child and Adolescent Mental Health Services (CAMHS). The majority will be left to deal with their difficulties on their own or with support from those around them: their family, friends, teacher or social worker. Those with internalizing disorders may become quiet or withdrawn but this is often assumed to be just a part of adolescence; those with externalizing disorders are often seen as disaffected or disruptive (Meltzer, 1999).

MENTAL AND EMOTIONAL HEALTH DISORDERS

Mental health disorders can be divided into two main types: *internalizing* and *externalizing disorders*. Internalizing disorders are those disorders in which the affected person internalizes their difficulties and becomes anxious or depressed or develops physical complaints or an eating disorder. Young people with externalizing disorders, such as conduct disorders and attention deficit hyperactivity disorder (ADHD) have behaviour problems visible to those around them. These two terms roughly equate with the educational terms *emotional and behavioural difficulties. Drug and alcohol use* can be both the result of emotional difficulties and the cause of further difficulties.

INTERNALIZING DISORDERS

Depression is one of the most common mental health disorders. Lavikainen et al. (2000) estimate that 2–4 per cent of children suffer from depression, and these rates may be two or three times as high during adolescence. Depression is characterized by sadness and misery, poor concentration, lethargy, social withdrawal, loss of interest in things and a negative view of oneself, the world and the future. Eating may be affected with the young person either eating too little or too much. Young people who are depressed may have other problems such as difficult, disobedient or even aggressive behaviour. They may also be anxious and attempt or complete suicide.

Depression seems to be caused by a number of interacting genetic and environmental factors. Social adversity and the existence of social and emotional problems among parents play a part. In such circumstances, parents may not be able to give the support that the young person so desperately needs. Since the young person is often unable to articulate their difficulties, or simply complains of 'feeling sad' or 'bored', depressive symptoms can easily be over-looked. Young people who are depressed may not pose the obvious behavioural difficulties shown by those who externalize their problems.

Suicidal thoughts are common among young people with depression, as are feel-ings of hopelessness and futility. Self-harming behaviour:

- peaks in mid-adolescence;
- occurs in 10 per cent of teenagers aged 15 and 16;
- usually takes the form of cutting;
- is four times more likely in girls than boys;
- occurs in young people who are more likely to employ poor coping strategies such as blaming themselves or drinking alcohol.

Peer relationships affect the risk of self-harming, i.e. the risk is increased by having friends who engaged in suicidal behaviour. However 41 per cent of those who self-harm seek help from friends before acting but they also report that they have fewer people in whom they can confide in comparison with other teenagers.

Death due to suicide is the third leading cause of death in adolescents (Lavikainen et al., 2000). Boys are particularly at risk. Twelve young men take their lives each week in the UK while attempted suicides by young men have nearly tripled since the 1980s; two-thirds of suicidal young men feel that they have no one to turn to for help (Samaritans, 2003). The culture of 'laddism' that requires young men to appear tough prevents many from seeking help with emotional problems. Further information is provided in Chapter 2.10.

Anxiety disorders include *generalized anxiety, separation anxiety,* as well as *specific phobias,* such as *obsessive-compulsive disorders, social phobia* and *panic disorders.* The development of anxiety in young people is accompanied in adolescence by feelings of unease and uncertainty about personal identity and body image. Separation anxiety may be manifest as excessive clinging to parents or school refusal. *Phobias* are associated with somatic symptoms such as sweating, diar-rhoea and, in some cases, panic attacks.

It is crucial that depression and anxiety are diagnosed early so that effective treatment strategies may be applied and that the key people in a young person's life, notably parents and teachers, are aware of warning signs and symptoms.

It is estimated that over one in every hundred adolescents has a serious eating disorder, such as *anorexia nervosa* or *bulimia.* If we include milder versions of the disorder, the rates are substantially higher.

■ EXTERNALIZING DISORDERS

Pupils with externalizing disorders are much more likely to be noticed in the classroom because of the disruption they cause. Aggressive behaviour is a common behaviour problem during childhood and adolescence. Both poor parental monitoring and constitutional factors, such as hyperactivity and short attention span, have been linked to externalizing disorders. The complexity of the interaction is illustrated in Box 1.1.1.

BOX 1.1.1 LEROY, A DISRUPTIVE PUPIL

Leroy comes from a family where discipline is harsh and physical. His dad always used a heavy hand in punishing Leroy for misdemeanours from as far back as he could remember. The punishments triggered outbursts of anger and aggression on Leroy's part. His mum rarely intervened to protect him for fear of violence from her abusive partner. Since he feared his father's reaction, Leroy targeted his younger brothers. His dad left home when Leroy was 3 years old and things were better for a time. However, his mum remarried and Leroy reacted angrily to his stepfather. He quickly became, in his stepfather's words, 'out of control'. Leroy became known at school as a bully to be feared. His teachers were frankly relieved when he truanted from school (as he often did) because of his intimidating and disruptive behaviour in class. After a series of extremely aggressive episodes against both pupils and teachers, Leroy was suspended from school. His academic work suffered but he did not care since he had won what he saw as 'respect' from his peer group. He became increasingly involved in a gang where his self-esteem grew. By the age of 14 he had a number of convictions for theft and vandalism. By the age of 15 he had been permanently excluded from school.

Thousands of secondary pupils like Leroy are permanently excluded from school each year. The reasons for exclusion tend to be related to general disobedience or physical aggression against staff and other pupils and the disruption of lessons (Hayden, 2002). Even though the number of exclusions decreased from 12,668 to 9,210 between 1996 and 2001, some sub-groups of young people are particularly at risk. For example, boys are significantly more likely to be excluded than girls as are Afro-Caribbean pupils. As a boy of African-Caribbean origin, living in a poor, inner-city district and in a situation of domestic violence, Leroy was especially vulnerable. The evidence suggests that understanding early childhood aggression is very important since its cost to society is great: 'A large proportion of these children remain involved throughout their lives, either in mental health agencies or within the criminal justice system. In other words, we all pay in the long run – personally, financially or both – when these children are left uncared for and their behaviour problems untreated' (Webster-Stratton, 1999, p. 27).

Recently, the advantage of involving the community in addressing the needs of young people like Leroy has been appreciated. In Box 1.1.2 we give an example of a community-based mentoring project designed specifically to help re-engage disaffected young people in education.

BOX 1.1.2 SOUTHWARK BLACK MENTOR AND INCLUSION PROJECT

This project was initially established to support black pupils excluded from school but has more recently been expanded to target any young people who are in a minority situation. It aims to help young people set personal goals, pass examinations at school and identify what is important to them in life. The scheme works by teaming each young person with a successful adult who has been trained as a mentor to rebuild the confidence of disaffected young people through a range of activities (often grounded in the context of local street culture) and by involving them in an appropriate work placement. The mentors also run group sessions on topics such as citizenship, rights and responsibility.

The advantage of this type of mentoring scheme is that pupils do not perceive it as part of school but rather as part of the young person's community. Although the Southwark Black Mentor and Inclusion Project was set up by the black community, mentoring schemes have been found to be successful in supporting other groups that are at risk of social exclusion. They can also be adapted for use within the school community to address the issue of bullying, by enhancing young people's self-esteem and clarifying career paths for participants.

ALCOHOL AND DRUG ABUSE

Rates of alcohol and drug abuse are higher in people with mental health disorders and may lead to further physical and mental health problems. Adolescence is a time when young people experiment more and engage in higher risks than children do. This in itself is a normal part of growing up. Drugs and alcohol play an increasingly central part in youth culture, particularly in urban areas. Young people may suffer harm from their own or others' drinking behaviour. Every year around 1,000 children are admitted to hospital for alcohol-related illness. There are links between high-risk drinking, permanent disability and death. Drug use has similar risks; these vary according to the drugs used (Drugscope, 2001). Drug-related damage such as dependence,

HIV, hepatitis and overdoses has a social impact and is also related to delinquency, crime, stigmatization and social exclusion. The chances of overcoming drug problems are less among people who are disadvantaged. They have fewer positive alternatives and less access to meaningful employment, housing and educational opportunities (Drugscope, 2000). Perhaps a matter of greater concern is the recent evidence showing a clear link between use of cannabis and psychiatric illness (Rey and Tennant, 2002). A longitudinal study of more than 50,000 Swedish conscripts over 15 years showed that use of marijuana in adolescence increases the risk of schizophrenia in a dose response relationship (Zammit et al., 2002). The authors also found that the risk was specific to cannabis as opposed to the use of other drugs.

RISK AND PROTECTIVE FACTORS FOR MENTAL AND EMOTIONAL HEALTH

THE CONCEPT OF RISK

Risk and protective factors relating to mental health difficulties are found at every level in society, including the individual, the family, the community and the wider social context (Rutter, 2000.). *Risk factors* are those factors that render an individual more likely to develop problems in the face of adversity; they do not in themselves necessarily cause mental health difficulties. Risk factors for having a mental health difficulty (Rutter, 2000) include:

- *family factors*: violence, abuse, neglect, discordant family relationships, being a young person who is looked after outside the family, parental psychiatric illness, inconsistent or unclear discipline, parental criminality, death and loss, rejection by parents;

- *social factors*: poverty, economic crises, deprivation, discrimination, homelessness, rejection by peers, being a member of a deviant peer group;

- *factors in the child*: low intelligence, chronic physical illness, hyperactivity, brain damage, communication difficulties, deafness, high alcohol use, drugs and substance abuse, academic failure, premature/under-age sexual activity.

Webster-Stratton (1999) points out that young people who have two or more of these risk factors are four times more likely to develop a mental health problem than other young people; those with four risk factors are ten times more likely to have a mental health problem.

There is evidence that those from African-Caribbean, Asian, refugee and asylum-seeker communities (Goldberg and Huxley, 1992) are at increased risk of mental health difficulties, with the risk being twice as high for males. The problems experienced by these young people are also commonly under-detected.

The evidence points to the need to reduce social exclusion and prejudice in society. Action is currently being taken by the Mental Health Taskforce (see Department of Health website at www.doh.gov.uk) to develop a strategy to tackle the issues surrounding black and ethnic minority mental health, and schools can play a crucial part in the movement to challenge prejudice and social exclusion wherever it happens in particular local contexts.

■ CYCLE OF DISADVANTAGE

Recent government attention, policy and guidance in the UK has focused on action to tackle the cycle of disadvantage that can trap too many families in breakdown and consequent emotional difficulties for the young people involved. The poorest families in the UK today face a lack of employment and training opportunities and bad housing; they are also more likely to fall ill and to experience mental health problems. A large body of international research indicates strong links between poverty and negative outcomes for children of all ages. Adverse outcomes include behaviour problems and difficulties with peer relationships, adjustment difficulties and delinquency, lesser likelihood of going on to further or higher education and greater likelihood of becoming unemployed as an adult. It is not simply poverty itself but the stresses associated with poverty that make it hard for parents and children to function as well as they might (for a review see McGurk and Soriano, 1998). Such stresses from the community can become part of the school ethos and make them difficult to change (Cowie and Olafsson, 2000).

Protective factors are those factors that act to protect an individual from developing a problem even in the face of adversity and risk factors such as those described above (Clarke and Clarke, 2000). This is also known as *resilience*. Protective factors include:

- *family factors*: supportive relationships with adults, small family size, material resources such as adequate family income, clear and consistent discipline, support for education;

- *social factors*: access to good educational facilities, wider support network, range of facilities available, positive policies in school for behaviour and attitudes, effective anti-bullying policies, good liaison between school and the local communities;

■ *factors in the child*: a sense of mastery, participation in activities, sports and outside interests, being a member of a non-deviant peer group, personal attributes such as good health, even temperament, positive self-esteem and intelligence or good social skills, religious affiliation.

Competence, the capacity to cope emotionally with difficulties as they arise, has been shown to be a mediating variable that predicts positive or negative outcomes in mental health; so too is the belief that others are available to offer support when it is needed. Rutter (2000) argues that long-lasting change in an individual's environment, together with a strengthening of his or her competence gives the maximum benefit. Schools play a part in this process. Much less is achieved by inputs – however effective at the time – when overall deprivation and disadvantage continue.

POSITIVE PSYCHOLOGY FOR YOUNG PEOPLE

There is a need for schools to be increasingly aware of ways in which they can create environments that support the young person's natural resilience in the face of the daily adversities of human existence. From the perspective of a positive psychology orientation (for a review see Snyder and Lopez, 2002 in Seligman, 2002), it is useful to focus on strengths, opportunities and assets rather than stressors and individual deficits. Called the sanities, these include: courage, future-mindedness, optimism, faith, interpersonal skills, hope, honesty and perseverance. Successful interventions are those that assist adolescents to focus on hope, optimism and personal growth. For example, in the Penn Prevention Program (Jaycox et al., 1994) children at risk of being depressed are taught to identify negative beliefs, to evaluate these beliefs and to formulate realistic alternatives. They also learn social problem-solving and ways to cope with conflict. Children who complete the programme are significantly more likely to be able to deal with the challenges they face in adolescence than the control group. The results of this study indicate that optimism can be taught. The effects do not wash out but are sustained. One reason for their endurance may be that the learning of skills of competency and resilience is most effective during childhood. The media can portray adolescent boys as aggressive, inarticulate individuals who may not be open to developing competency and resilience skills but Frosh, Phoenix and Pattman (2002) found that, contrary to expectation, the adolescent boys in today's society are attempting to forge new and more flexible masculine identities. The ways in which boys act as 'masculine' are contradictory and 'multiple'. Some of these versions of masculinity emphasize toughness and aggression, but they need not. All the boys in their sample engaged in thoughtful and perceptive discussions about their feelings, including fears over friendships, disappointment with parents, anger at unavailable fathers and fears and aspirations for the future. The boys often spoke poignantly about losses and also about how much value they placed on parents who attended to them sensitively and seriously, and how disappointed they were by parents who did not.

Interventions that focus on optimism and overall quality of life seem to enhance positive frames of mind for all children, both boys and girls, as well as for those with particular stressors or difficulties.

IS THERE EVIDENCE THAT WE CAN INFLUENCE EMOTIONAL HEALTH AND HELP CHANGE THESE BEHAVIOURS?

In the chapters that follow, we present a range of strategies that have been found by practitioners to help young people in distress. We have tried, where possible, to focus especially on those methods and policies that have been scientifically evaluated. While the emphasis of this book is on practice in the UK, we have cast our net widely in the international field in order to capture the best practices addressing the issue of young people's emotional health and well-being.

We aim to present a framework for educators and policy-makers to:

- promote the emotional health and well-being of young people in schools;
- create school-based policies and practices grounded in know-ledge about mental health issues relating to young people.

It is hoped that this book will assist:

- teachers and those who work directly with young people in secondary schools in the development and implementation of mental health promotion programmes within their particular context;
- policy-makers in the integration of mental health promotion within educational policies.

There is clear evidence of the effectiveness of a wide range of mental health promotion programmes. The best interventions focus on more than one factor. Certain elements seem to be crucial:

- The intervention should involve relevant parts of the social network of the target group, such as parents, teachers or family.
- They should intervene at a range of different times rather than once only.
- They should use a combination of intervention methods, e.g.

social support and coping skills.

The UK Health Education Authority (1997, p. 13) defines mental health promotion as 'a kind of immunisation, working to strengthen the resilience of individuals, families, organisations and communities as well as to reduce conditions that are known to damage mental well-being in everyone, whether or not they currently have a mental health problem'. We look to promote mental health at three levels:

- strengthening individuals or increasing emotional resilience, e.g. building self-esteem, coping or life skills;
- strengthening communities, e.g. anti-bullying strategies or after school care clubs;
- reducing structural barriers to mental health, e.g. fiscal policies to reduce inequalities.

(adapted from Health Education Authority, 1997)

The Stigma of Mental Health Difficulties

It is the stigma, and the feelings of guilt and shame, or the defensive denial, that go with it that makes people with psychiatric symptoms reluctant to seek treatment, or even to accept that their symptoms exist and might be a manifestation of mental disorder. (Kendell, 2001, p. 5).

THE ATTITUDES OF YOUNG PEOPLE TOWARDS PEOPLE WITH MENTAL HEALTH DIFFICULTIES

Although young people are accustomed to thinking about, for example, their physical health, the importance of keeping fit or taking account of the risks of unprotected sex, attitudes towards mental health seem to be different. There are two main reasons for this state of affairs. First, there is a lack of appropriate resources to support young people with mental health difficulties; second, as a society we still have negative and stereotypical views about mental illness and mental health problems. The sense of shame and embarrassment that surrounds the concept of mental health difficulty contributes to the fact that young people's mental health problems are often unrecognized or even denied. The label of mental illness is one that sticks even after the person has made a full recovery. It is harder for a person with a history of mental illness to find work, to find a partner, to get a mortgage, to emigrate or even to obtain holiday insurance.

Why are people prejudiced against those with a mental health difficulty? Hayward and Bright (1997) suggest that there are four main answers to the question: the fear that the mentally ill are dangerous; the belief that they are responsible for their illness and could somehow 'snap out of it'; the belief that there is a poor prognosis for the condition; and discomfort at the disruption to normal social interaction. Kendell (2001) argues that stigmatization is rooted in cultural attitudes towards 'madness'. Our concept of ourselves as rational beings guided by reason is threatened by people who may behave in unusual ways, may hear imaginary voices, may be occasionally violent or may express inappropriate views and emotions. People deal with these fears by using such mechanisms as mockery and social distancing in order to reduce the threat posed by others with mental health difficulties.

In 1995, the Royal College of Psychiatrists (RCP) commissioned a survey of a random sample of the adult population to estimate the degree of stigma attached to six mental disorders (Crisp et al., 2000; Gelder, 2001). The conclusions drawn from the responses of 1,737 respondents were that:

- stigmatizing opinions are frequent in the community but these opinions vary according to the disorder;

- people with schizophrenia are stigmatized by opinions that they are dangerous, unpredictable and hard to talk to, but people do not blame them for their illness;

- people with drug or alcohol addiction are stigmatized more. People expect them to be dangerous and unpredictable and more than half blame them for their condition;

- people with severe depression are less stigmatized in that few people expect them to be dangerous but more than half expect them to be unpredictable and hard to talk to;

- people with eating disorders are stigmatized the least, but one-third of people think that they are to blame for their condition and that they are hard to talk to.

The results indicate that a common feature of public opinion is that people with mental health disorders are perceived as being hard to talk to. If this view is put into practice, the outcome will be that people with mental health disorders are isolated so making it hard for the general public to understand and help them, despite initiatives like the Mind's Respect Campaign which was launched in 1997 with a mission to reduce discrimination on mental health grounds (Wilson, 2001). The authors recommend that any campaign to reduce stigma should take account of differences among disorders. In a major longitudinal study, negative attitudes in children towards mental health difficulties have been seen to persist over nearly a decade (Weiss, 1986; 1994).

Bailey (1999) reports the results of a questionnaire study of 106 young people aged 11–17 who attended a lecture at the RCP. The participants were asked to list the names that they had heard other young people call persons with a mental health problem. All implied that there was something missing or a deficit in such people, for example 'One slice short of a loaf', 'demented', 'retarded' or 'nutter'. Overall, the respondents displayed a wide range of levels of understanding and acceptance of the mentally ill. There seemed to be an urgent need to provide a programme of education to challenge the widespread use of pejorative terms and stigmatizing attitudes. Bailey considers that the challenge is for healthcare professionals to join with educators to provide programmes of education and understanding if attitudes are to change.

Armstrong et al. (2000) point out that the young people's views on mental health are relatively unexplored in the fields of healthcare and practice, despite the trend towards greater empowerment of users of health services and despite the increasing incidence of mental health problems among young people in the last decade (RCP, 1995, cited in Gelder, 2001). Young people's views matter for the following reasons:

- They are the precursors of future beliefs and attitudes.

- Negative adult beliefs and attitudes have been shown to impact on service development and on the quality of life of those who experience mental health difficulties.

- Embarrassment and stigma may prevent people experiencing mental distress from seeking out help.

- Young people's opinions are important in their own right, especially in view of their right to be heard, as recommended by the UN Convention on the Rights of the Child (CRDU, 1993, p. 6).

In the following paragraphs, we consider the limited amount of research that investigates perspectives on mental health of young people who have experienced mental health difficulties themselves, and the views of a cross-section of young people in the UK towards mental health difficulties.

PERSPECTIVES OF YOUNG USERS OF MENTAL HEALTH SERVICES

Developing appropriate mental health services for children and adolescents is a challenging task. Difficulties include the actual location of services, the approach adopted by professionals working in multidisciplinary teams, and attitudes of young people and their families towards mental health issues. The Mental Health Foundation (1999) inquiry into the emotional well-being of children and young people sought the users' perspectives. Some respondents said that it was hard for them to access services and that they found the professionals intimidating or apparently uncaring. Some also found it embarrassing or awkward to be asked too quickly to disclose details about distressing incidents in their lives. However, many *were* satisfied with the quality of the care that they received. They appreciated being listened to and cared for, and they found the professionals to be flexible and informal.

The report also recommended that schools could play a significant part in promoting children's mental health through the recognition and implementation of social and emotional education in all aspects of the curriculum and in the life of the school. Counteracting the effects of stigma would be a key aspect of such activity.

PERSPECTIVES OF YOUNG PEOPLE FROM DISADVANTAGED BACKGROUNDS

Gale and Holling (2000), as part of the Changing Minds campaign, established HEADSTUFF, a resource for 14–17-year-olds from socially disadvantaged backgrounds. They ran a series of focus groups to find out what these young people needed to know about mental health and how they would like it to be presented. There were three key findings:

- The young people's knowledge and understanding of mental health issues was very low.

- They lacked an appropriate emotional language to express themselves adequately about mental health difficulties.

- Their limited knowledge and understanding, and their lack of emotional language was in spite of their proximity with the experience of mental illness in family members or friends.

For example, in combination, the words 'mental', 'health' and 'problem' did not promote much discussion in the focus groups. By contrast, words like 'nutter', 'weirdo' and 'psycho' were meaningful and suggested a wide range of behaviours and feelings. Young people in the focus groups stated that such words implied being 'out of control' or 'unusual' or 'having a disability'. Young people were more able to accept that depression was 'being down 'cos your budgie or your gran has died' but far less likely to empathize with psychotic symptoms which they associated with 'axe-wielding murderers'. The young people in the focus groups did not think that they were stigmatizing those with mental health difficulties. In fact, they had little sense of people with such disorders, what a mental health problem meant and how it could change a person's life.

PERSPECTIVES OF A BROAD CROSS-SECTION OF SCOTTISH YOUNG PEOPLE

Armstrong et al. (2000) carried out a 16-month study exploring the attitudes and perceptions of a broad range of young people aged from 12 to 14 years towards positive mental health and mental illness. The main sample consisted of 145 young people from a variety of social and ethnic minority backgrounds who attended mainstream schools in rural, suburban and inner-city areas of Scotland. Four further groups (N = 25 participants) from Chinese and Muslim Pakistani backgrounds were recruited into the sample to ensure that the views of young people from ethnic minority backgrounds were also heard. These participants were interviewed by researchers from similar backgrounds. The researchers used focus group discussions and individual interviews to elicit the young people's attitudes. The main points were presented under five headings: understanding of positive mental health; what might make young people feel mentally healthy and unhealthy; how other people might promote young people's mental health; their own strategies for dealing with their own negative feelings and perceived differences between themselves and adults:

- *Positive mental health.* Young people from less advantaged backgrounds had difficulty in defining the term 'mentally healthy'; those from suburban schools and those from minority ethnic backgrounds referred to it as 'the absence of illness' or in terms of happiness and confidence. For some, the term was equated with 'normality' but the young people found it hard to define what they meant by normality.

- *What might make young people feel mentally healthy and unhealthy.* Key elements were family and friends, having someone to talk to, personal achievement and feeling good about yourself.

- *Promoting positive mental health.* A key theme was the role of adults to help young people feel safe, both physically and emotionally. These adults could be parents but other adults could also fill this role. Many of the participants felt that there were no professionals that they could really trust, though they specifically mentioned ChildLine as a valuable service that could be used for confidential matters. Those from ethnic minority backgrounds felt strongly that personal issues should not be discussed outside the family and that, on issues which could not be discussed with parents, members of the extended family (often close to them in age) were appropriate people to approach.

- *Dealing with negative feelings.* There were two main categories of response: reactions to angry feelings and reactions to sadness. Young people reacted to feelings of anger by taking it out on inanimate objects, on siblings or on peers, through aggressive acts, such as fighting; there were few behavioural differences between boys and girls but the boys discussed their aggression openly in the focus groups while the girls disclosed them privately on self-completion forms. Feelings of sadness, by contrast, were dealt with through internalization. Suicidal thoughts were discussed by one group; some described eating or sleeping; others spoke of talking to a trusted other, including a professional, as a coping strategy. Counselling was perceived positively by some as active coping but by others as a stigma.

- *Perceived differences between themselves and adults.* All the participants identified factors common to both adults and young people, for example, the death of friends and relatives, falling out with people and stress. However, factors distinctive for adults included job insecurity, financial concerns and worries about children. By contrast, young people's issues were often described as less important than those of adults.

The authors conclude that there are important implications arising from this study. The term 'mental health' did not appear to have much meaning for young people in this study so the authors recommend use of a different vocabulary in educational or therapeutic work with young people. They noted the relatively unsophisticated methods that young people used to deal with problems, such as bottling them up, sleeping, drinking alcohol or simply hoping that they would go away. There was also the tendency to trivialize the problems of young people in comparison with those of adults.

ATTITUDES TOWARDS SUICIDE

Eskin (1995) investigated young people's attitudes towards suicide and a suicidal classmate among 98 girl and 69 boy Swedish high school students. The Swedish sample was then compared with 167 (89 girls and 78 boys) Turkish high school students from a previous study. Among Swedish students, more boys than girls said that people have the right to commit suicide and that suicide can be a solution to some problems. More girls than boys expressed a belief in life after death. Swedish adolescents appeared to hold more liberal attitudes towards suicide than their Turkish counterparts. However, Turkish adolescents showed greater acceptance for a suicidal peer than did Swedish. Eskin (1995) argues that there is a need for educational programmes to provide basic knowledge about suicide and effective ways of dealing with suicidal peers.

In specific deliberate self-harm programmes designed to address this problem a number of issues have been raised that include:

1 Some programmes have attempted to encourage active participation of parents in the programme. However, the uptake is often poor and it remains a major challenge to access parents of young people most at risk (Nelson, 1987).

2 In a number of studies there is some evidence that students

who reported having made previous suicide attempts were more likely to show negative reactions than those who did not (Schaffer et al., 1991). Possibly it reminds them of previous feelings of vulnerability. This appears to be less true of the more supportive programmes.

3 There is a slight negative affect in some studies by boys (Kalafat and Elias, 1994; Overholser et al., 1989). Boys can see self-harm as an option following intervention that they did not before. This probably reflects an increase in their knowledge of mental health issues. It has not been shown to result in an increase in self-harming behaviour. It does, however, provide a warning for primary education programmes. It may be appropriate to look at interventions which improve basic communication skills in teenage boys so that communication channels with emotional supports are available when they are confronted with a crisis situation (Overholser et al., 1989). Appreciating that boys commit suicide more often than girls is important because boys tend to take suicide talk from their friends less seriously than do females (Kalafat and Elias, 1994).

4 There is some evidence that a proportion of teenagers will reveal that they are suicidal or have emotional problems. This suggests that a programme that combines providing information with a backup service for youngsters in distress who can be referred for individual evaluation or intervention may be helpful (Schaffer et al., 1991).

This is discussed in more depth in Chapter 2.10.

TABLE 1.2.1 HOW TO DO A MENTAL HEALTH EDUCATION PROGRAMME

Preparation
Select a key worker, e.g. PSHE co-ordinator
Research material (see resources list)
Decide on target audience
Decide on a broad-based mental health programme or specific deliberate self-harm programme

Implementation
Train the form tutors – those running the module
Arrange consent from parents
Provide information for teachers who are not involved
Set up backup for difficult disclosures
Run programme, e.g. one lesson for six weeks

Review
Assess positive and negative outcomes
Plan for a repeat the following year (as appropriate)

CASE STUDY 1.2.1 THE MENTAL HEALTH EDUCATION MODULE

In this project (grant number 1750/197) funded by PPP Healthcare Medical Trust (Cowie et al., 2002a) a personal, social and health education (PSHE) module was designed to include the following topics: depression, bullying, learning disabilities, coping with stress, eating disorders and self-harm and suicide, using teaching materials from sources that included *Changing Minds* Factsheets (RCP, 1996; 1998; 2000a; 2000b; 2000c), Chalkface packs (The Chalkface Project, 1993; 1997; 1999a; 1999b; 1999c), Independence packs (Donellan, 1998; 2000), the school module on Mental Health (unpublished) and video materials including *1 in 4* (RCP, 2000d) and *Headstuff* (RCP, 2000e), and *Don't Die of Embarrassment* (Papyrus, 2000). Details about a CD ROM, *Changing Minds*, with similar resources can be accessed on www.stigma.org/everyfamily.

In the study a letter was sent to parents informing them about the project and inviting their comments. A one-day training for form tutors was set up. Year 10 pupils participated in the Mental Health Module for six weeks during PSHE lessons. (See Table 1.2.1 for steps in how to prepare for a mental health module of this kind.)

The resource materials were rated highly by the teachers in terms of the quality of information and the variety of teaching strategies that could be used:

> *Well, I would say that we had a fantastic amount of really good information …*
> *(Form tutor)*

Overall, the Mental Health Module was considered to be a successful intervention in dealing with raising awareness of mental health problems among adolescents:

> *Before we studied this topic lots of people turned round as a natural reaction and said that if they saw someone with a disability they would say something, not to that person but to their friends. They would probably point and look. Now you don't think that person is a bit strange or that person has got something wrong with them. You sit there and you wonder why that has happened to them in their lives. You don't judge as much. (Year 10 boy)*

The key to running the Mental Health Module was the support and dedication of the form tutors who all agreed that the topic, though challenging, was essential for the PSHE curriculum. There was a strong feeling that young people need to be made aware of the underlying causes of mental health difficulties, that they need to know about where to seek out professional help and information, and that they can learn about how to offer informal support to peers in distress.

Pupils reported that they liked learning about problems of depression and suicidal impulses. They appreciated some recognition of the difficulties that they face:

I didn't find it upsetting. I found it more shocking because I actually realized that what people think of themselves can make them so distraught that they want to hurt themselves either to get the attention or to make themselves feel better ... And some people even resort to killing themselves because of what is happening in their lives. (Year 10 boy)

School staff appreciated learning to identify suicidal signs and behaviours:

schools erroneously shy away from mental health issues ... we've started addressing issues that we have never addressed before and really moving forward the skills of the tutor team ... (School co-ordinator)

The programme was generally effective in increasing students' knowledge about where to get help for their own emotional problems.

You begin the session and someone says, 'If you cut yourself up you must be mad' or 'If someone throws up after everything they eat, they must be mad'. Then I say, 'Well, I was with someone who was like that ... ' and they realize that it is real people. It's not just 'nutcases' and all the stereotypes they get into their heads. (Teacher)

WHO NEEDS TO BE INVOLVED?

In the PPP study, Year 10 pupils (180 in total) were taught the Mental Health Module by their Year 10 form tutors (seven in total).

HOW LONG SHOULD IT LAST?

It was set up to run for six weeks with the plan to repeat it in subsequent years.

COST – OVERT AND HIDDEN

Staff cover × 2 for 1 day Year 10 tutor training day	£300
Trainer for staff training day	£300
Reprographics and office costs	£100
School co-ordinator's time	Unquantifiable

POSSIBLE PROBLEMS

1 While a strength of the module is that it allows for flexibility in teaching methods, the evidence suggests that the diversity of delivery impacts on student reception of the material. Teachers reported different experiences in delivering the module. Some teachers felt uncomfortable about some subjects and underprepared: 'One of the first things I encountered ... was a certain amount of resistance, not so much resistance from

> tutors, but a feeling of inadequacy from teachers about their ability to teach this subject ... ' (School co-ordinator).
>
> 2 Other teachers who are not involved may need to know some of the content as the subject matter may appear in other lessons: 'What might be appropriate would be staff who aren't involved in delivering it knowing more about what is in the programme, I don't just mean Heads of House. If you are a Year 10 tutor you are very clear about what is involved; if you are a teacher of English, or Maths, you may not know, and there may be reasons that you would need to know what are the issues that have been discussed in PSHE' (Head of Red House).

SUMMARY

In this chapter we explore the attitudes that young people hold towards the concept of mental health difficulty. We argue that negative, stereotypical attitudes contribute to the fact that young people's mental health problems are often unrecognized or even denied. We explore some key research findings and describe one study in which negative attitudes were challenged and, in some cases, changed for the better. The implications for school practice are discussed.

RESOURCES

ChildLine, Studd Street, London N1 0QW.

Donellan, C. (series ed.) (1998) *Issues: Bullying, Vol. 13; Disabilities, Vol. 17; Mental Illness, Vol. 21; Coping with Eating Disorders, Vol. 24*. Cambridge: Independence Educational Publishers.

Donellan, C. (series ed.) (2000) *Issues: Dealing with Mental Illness, Vol. 21; Coping with Stress, Vol. 32; Self-harm and Suicide, Vol. 51*. Cambridge: Independence Educational Publishers.

Papyrus (Prevention of Suicides) (2000) *Don't Die of Embarrassment* (video film). PAPYRUS, Rossendale G.H., Union Road, Rawtenstall, Lancashire, BB4 6NE.

Royal College of Psychiatrists (RCP) (1996) *Information Factsheets: Mental Health and Growing Up*. Royal College of Psychiatrists, 17 Belgrave Square, London, SW1X 8PG.

Royal College of Psychiatrists (RCP) (1998) *Mental Illness and Stigma, Module 217*. London: Office of National Statistics.

Royal College of Psychiatrists (RCP) (2000a) *Changing Minds Booklets: Alcohol and Other Drug Misuse; Anorexia and Bulimia; Depression; Anxiety; Challenging Prejudice*. Available at www.rcpsych.ac.uk/public/stigma/htm (accessed 27 September, 2003).

Royal College of Psychiatrists (RCP) (2000b) Factsheets: *Behavioural Problems and Conduct Disorder, Factsheet 4; Attention Deficit Disorder and Hyperactivity, Factsheet*

5; *The Child with General Learning Disability, Factsheet 10; Specific Learning Difficulties, Factsheet 11*. Available at www.rcpsych.ac.uk/public/newmhgu/htm

Royal College of Psychiatrists (RCP) (2000c) *Surviving Adolescence.* Available at www.rcpsych.ac.uk/public/help/adol/survadol.htm

Royal College of Psychiatrists (RCP) (2000d) *1 in 4* (video film). The Royal College of Psychiatrists, 17 Belgrave Square, London, SW1X 8PG, www.changing-minds.co.uk (launched 10 October, 2003).

Royal College of Psychiatrists (RCP) (2000e) *Headstuff* (video film). The Royal College of Psychiatrists, 17 Belgrave Square, London, SW1X 8PG, www.chang-ingminds.co.uk (launched 10 October, 2003).

Royal College of Psychiatrists (RCP) (2002) *Changing Minds.* CD-Rom, London: RCP.

The Chalkface Project, Milton Keynes:

Ball, C. and Hartley, M. (1999) *Zero Tolerance to Bullying.*

Brown, J. and Fabey, L. (1993) *Overcoming Bullying.*

Freeman, P. and Hartley, M. (1999) *Effective Learning Through Better Classroom Behaviour.*

Naylor, P. and Eddy, S. (1997) *Equal Opportunities.*

Russell, J. and Rogers, A. (1999) *Exploring Body Images and Issues.*

Wilson, M. (2001) *Mind's Respect Campaign.* CD-ROM, pp. 415–19.

Why Should Schools be Involved?

Everyone remembers a good teacher.

'For almost a dozen years during a formative period of their development children spend almost as much of their waking life at school as at home. Altogether this works out at some 15,000 hours (from the age of five to school leaving) during which schools and teachers may have an impact on the development of the children in their care.' (Rutter et al., 1979)

Successful schools tend to have pupils who behave well, achieve their potential and are able to develop rewarding relationships with a variety of people. Schools which achieve in one of these areas tend to achieve in all three.

Rutter et al. (1979) found that the levels of achievement between schools are related to their characteristics as social institutions. Factors such as:

- the degree of academic emphasis;
- teacher's actions in lessons;
- the availability of incentives and rewards;
- good conditions for pupils; and
- the extent to which pupils took responsibility themselves

are all significantly associated with outcome differences between schools and open to modification by staff.

The cumulative effect of these variables is even greater. It is the *ethos* – the set of values, attitudes and behaviours which are important (Rutter et al., 1979). Schools that function well have a strong sense of community and loyalty. This can often reflect the community in the outside environment. However, schools made up of isolated individuals, i.e. schools where there is poor communication, an unsupportive environment and a culture of blame, tend to label both children and staff. This is often an unhelpful process. The ability of a well-functioning school is to recognize and appreciate individual characteristics, but also to encourage school allegiance and support so that it functions as a whole.

Whilst experiences at school can affect emotional well-being, young people also bring to school things that are troubling them which arise outside school. There are a number of reasons why schools should be involved with the emotional well-being of their pupils, including:

1 *Rates of psychosocial problems have increased and are common.* Rates of mental health problems in general, and psychiatric disorder in particular, have increased in the young (Mental Health Foundation, 1999). Rutter and Smith's comprehensive review of the evidence focuses on five 'psychosocial' disorders – conduct disorder, substance use, depressive disorder, eating disorder and suicidal behaviour – rates of which appear to have increased in most developed countries since the Second World War. They evaluate several possible reasons for this increase including unemployment, changes in family structure and functioning, changes in adolescent transition, changes in the pattern of 'stressors' in youth (including greater exposure to examinations) and rising expectations (in relation to educational and occupational success) (Rutter and Smith, 1995).

2 *The associated negative labels may make coping with emotional issues harder.* The Royal College of Psychiatrists, in its 'Defeat Stigma' campaign, has stated that *1 in 4* people are affected by a mental health problem at some point in their life. Unfortunately, social and personal views may delay the seeking of appropriate help and compound the isolation and difficulties experienced at the time and afterwards. This is discussed in more depth in the previous chapter.

3 *Educational stressors are an increasingly important contributory factor particularly for middle-class girls.* Schools run a balance between motivation and stress. As individuals we perform best at a low/moderate level of anxiety. However, our level of achievement drops rapidly when a certain point of anxiety is reached. As this point varies between individuals, applying global academic pressure will only benefit a proportion of the students. Some students will remain under-motivated whereas others will perform less well because their stress levels have become too high. Conscientious girls are more at risk of the latter than the 'laid back' boys.

Since the mid-1980s psychological distress has increased significantly for girls especially those from non-manual and skilled manual backgrounds. The increase in levels of psychological distress among young women may be explained by an increase in educational expectations, which together with more traditional concerns about personal identity appear to have elevated levels of stress with adverse consequences for mental health (West and Sweeting, 2003).

4 *Peer relationships are important indicators of a person's psychological health and predict their future functioning.* Peer acceptance and withdrawal are extremely important determinants of and indicators of psychopathology. As relationships with peers are crucial to a person's emotional well-being and form an important part of daily life in school, schools should be encouraged to do what they can to promote healthy positive peer relations and to assist those who are withdrawn and rejected by their peers or who misuse their power by bullying others. There is much schools can do, e.g. see chapters 2.2, 2.3, 2.4 and 2.7 for more information and examples of possible strategies to promote healthy peer relations. For a comprehensive review of the role of peer relations in psychopathology, see Deater-Decker (2001).

5 *Young people say they would approach a teacher for help.* For a number of reasons, adolescents are often reluctant to seek help and advice through traditional routes, e.g. the family's general practitioner (GP). A survey of adolescents' views of the sorts of problems, worries or difficulties that young people might have and where and from whom young people might get help, found that 80 per cent of all the adolescents surveyed (i.e. male and female) said that they would approach a teacher for help.

The most important aspects of help for both males and females, according to the adolescents, were confidentiality and to be understood, together with the advice and information provided. Girls also felt that being listened to was important as well as being able to trust the helper and the helper being approachable (Clarke et al., 2003). This is in keeping with recent recommendations advocating that young people have access to help that is outside a mental health environment, is based on trust and respect and is friendly, flexible and accessible (Mental Health Foundation, 1999).

6 *The role of the teacher is multifaceted and changing.* Teaching has always been a challenging profession. Every teacher has a number of roles including public speaker, actor, learning facilitator, curriculum planner, classroom manager, mediator, friend and surrogate parent. These roles demand a range of skills.

As well as traditional demands, teachers today also have to deal with young people who are hard to teach for a number of reasons including social factors, their emotional state, family beliefs that are anti-authority and anti-education or seeing no point in it because of high unemployment. Tiered models of mental health services have the expectation that teachers will be working at Tier 1 to help young people with emotional/mental health problems (see Chapter 2.12). A teacher is *not* a social worker or counsellor but nonetheless can be an extremely important source of support and help to a young person in distress and may be the first person they turn to.

Schools have increasing social expectations placed upon them, which lie behind some of the recent changes to the curriculum such as the introduction of lessons which incorporate citizenship.

Schools have always had some role in health education. Although the emphasis tends to be on physical health and specific topics such as drugs, nutrition and exercise, there is a growing realization that mental, emotional and social health need to be more prominent (Stewart-Brown, 1998) and that a concern for physical health should be underpinned by a concern with emotional and social matters. Emotional and social abilities are fundamental to success in life. Abilities such as emotional resilience, getting on with others, handling frustrations and managing emotions are better predictors of a successful career than is IQ (Felsman and Valliant, 1987).

7 *Academic success will be enhanced if schools promote the emotional health and well-being of their pupils.* There is considerable evidence that pupils learn more effectively (including academic subjects) if they are happy in their work, believe in themselves, like their teachers and feel school is supporting them (Aspey and Roebuck, 1997; Goleman, 1996; McCarthy, 1998). The influence works both ways: achievement in school in academic subjects is of vital importance to pupils' happiness and self-esteem (Gordon and Grant, 1997).

The importance of satisfying physical, emotional and social needs, before people can concentrate on intellectual matters, has long been recognized (Maslow, 1970). Maslow described a hierarchy of needs (Figure 1.3.1). A person's needs at the lower level must be satisfied before they can deal with the tasks of a higher level.

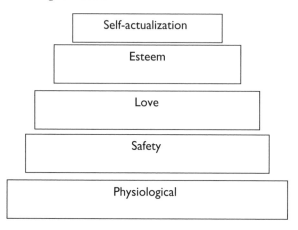

FIGURE 1.3.1 MASLOW'S HIERARCHY OF NEEDS

According to Maslow, there are general types of needs (physiological, safety, love, and esteem) that must be satisfied before a person can act unselfishly. Satisfying needs is healthy.

Physiological needs are the very basic needs such as air, water, food, sleep, sex, etc. When these are not satisfied we may feel sickness, irritation, pain, discomfort, and so on.

Safety needs have to do with establishing stability and consistency in a chaotic world. These needs are mostly psychological in nature. We need the security of a home and family.

Love and belongingness are the next needs on the ladder. Humans have a desire to belong to groups: clubs, work groups, religious groups, family, gangs, etc. We need to feel loved (non-sexual) by others, to be accepted by others.

There are two types of esteem needs. First is self-esteem which results from competence or mastery of a task. Second, is the attention and recognition that comes from others.

The need for self-actualization is 'the desire to become everything that one is capable of becoming'. People who have everything can maximize their potential. They can seek knowledge, peace, aesthetic experiences, self-fulfilment, oneness with God, etc.

For pupils, this means they need to be physically fed, well nourished, healthy and feel safe before they can achieve their full potential at school. If these needs are not met it is impossible for them to benefit from a learning environment, i.e. if a young person is being picked on he or she will not be able to work. Maslow's hierarchy of needs also holds true for staff. A teacher in an abusive relationship at home, or who is uncertain and nervous about his or her relationship with the headteacher will teach less well than if in a more secure environment.

8 *It is intrinsically a worthwhile thing to do.* Achieving (or striving to achieve) happiness, emotional health and good relationships are good things in themselves.

SUMMARY

Schools are an important influence on a young person's emotional development. They can be aware of the stresses on a student, encourage supportive peer relationships and be a stable place where a young person can access support.

Schools in a Social Setting

Change is also difficult because it is about transforming sophisticated relationships not simple behaviours, in complex classroom situations and organisational systems, whose purpose and direction are politically compounded and contested. (Hargreaves et al., 1996)

Emotional health and well-being are best understood within a social-cultural framework (see Figure 1.4.1) in which consideration is taken of a range of interacting factors. Our focus is very much on the social context within which young people either develop resilience in the face of stress and adversity or are precipitated into states of distress and disturbance.

Over the past 50 years Western Europe has seen a rise in economic prosperity but also a rise in psychosocial problems. Despite the prosperity there are still a significant number of youngsters living in poverty amongst whom the rate of mental health problems is higher.

SCHOOLS AS SANCTUARIES

Liaison with the local communities can be crucial to the success of the school and thus of its pupils. This is particularly true where there is a culture of violence in the school which spills into the surrounding community or violence in the community which invades school. Some schools are places of sanctuary where violence is outside its gates. Other schools have known violence but have now become safe places. These schools are known as violence resilient.

Schools can be oases within restless communities. To become a sanctuary within its community a school needs to develop:

- good quality of relationships within schools amongst staff and between staff and students;

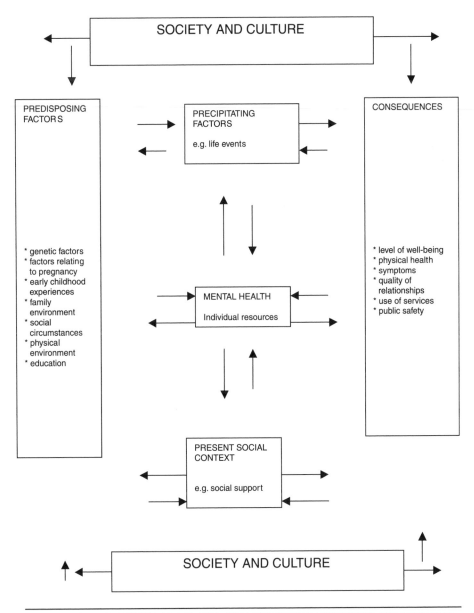

FIGURE 1.4.1 MENTAL HEALTH AS A PROCESS WITH PREDISPOSING, PRECIPITATING AND SUPPORTING FACTORS, TOGETHER WITH OUTCOMES AND CONSEQUENCES (ADAPTED FROM LAVIKAINEN ET AL., 2000, P. 38)

- good communications within schools, including staff–student communications over violent incidents;
- a range of policies and practices for dealing with violence and its potential emergence;

- an engagement with, and relationship to, the neighbourhood of the school and its communities of interest (Hewitt et al., 2002). The researchers stress that a key factor was the relationship between the school and its social setting.

SCHOOLS AS BRIDGE BUILDERS

Schools are often important bridge builders within their communities. This can be an important role. One example of this is Owler Brook Infant School.

BOX 1.4.1 OWLER BROOK INFANT SCHOOL

Owler Brook is an inner-city infant school, serving a highly transient population of whom 90 per cent have a first language other than English. Pupils' mothers were encouraged into the classroom as teaching assistants. The headteacher forged links with the local university to encourage teacher training students to develop bilingual resources as part of their course work. Five of her bilingual teaching assistants wished to take their studies further and Owler Brook became an approved outreach centre for Sheffield University.

Source: 'Local focus', *Times Educational Supplement*, 17 January 2003, p. 6.

Schools serving communities made up of differing ethnic groups are well placed to liaise between communities. Links between communities can be formed within schools.

The research literature relating to different ethnic groups suggest that, for a school to work well within its community, it needs :

- an adult *understanding of the individual needs* which concern adolescents in order to cater appropriately for them;

- a *willingness to work with parents* as genuine partners in the pursuit of a socially and academically rewarding experience for students;

- an increasing *understanding* by the adults in the school of the *political and social concerns* of students, and the *willingness and courage to address these* however uncomfortable or difficult. Teachers need to know and understand their students individually in order to assist their daily interactions and to cater for them as individuals, and also to be familiar with the wider issues that affect them. Parents are well placed to provide information on the issues which affect minority ethnic group students;

■ a *clearly articulated vision* for the schools which should be shared by the majority of staff, students, parents and the community;

■ *staff development* is important. For some schools serving different cultures an understanding and knowledge of history and culture outside the European and European-American orientations may be helpful;

■ *staff stability* is important so that the same staff are part of the vision and are there to see changes through. In addition staff stability is supportive to students;

■ the *support of the local education authority* so that efforts are reinforced, and not undermined (adapted from Pollard and Ajirotulu, 2001).

There are more formalized methods of liaison such as *mentoring* (see also Chapter 2.4). The positive benefits of this intervention have been shown to include (these results come from a paper by Tierney et al., 1993, unless otherwise stated):

For the individual

■ increasing confidence in ability;

■ improved relationship with parents;

■ improved relationship with peers;

For staff and peers

■ improved working environment;

■ increasing knowledge and understanding;

■ improved relationship with students and peers;

The negative benefits include:

For the individual

■ less likely to start using illegal drugs (46 per cent less likely that their peers to start using illegal drugs);

■ less likely to begin using alcohol (27 per cent less likely to begin using alcohol);

■ less likely to miss a class (37 per cent less likely than peers to miss a class);

■ less likely to be excluded (Truancy and Exclusions Report, 1998).

An audit of mentoring schemes in Britain was commissioned by the Commission for Racial Equality. The study found that mentoring was one of the most effective means of helping disadvantaged young people. However attempts to evaluate programmes are difficult due to the diverse nature of the programmes. Mentoring is useful, not only within cultural settings, but also with developing links with industry and future work opportunities. Local communities, industry and social structures are knowledgeable resources.

Many religious communities have established *'rites of passage' programmes.* In America therapeutic rites of passage programmes have been developed as social work interventions that seek to educate and support young people involved in self-destructive behaviours (Graham, 2002).

However, there is increasing community interest in looking at providing rites of passage type interventions for teenage boys to give them:

- a sense of identity;
- an increasing social knowledge and understanding;
- a reverence for the natural worth and dignity of one's parents, extended family, and community;
- a masculine ideal that conforms to pro-family and pro-social values;
- a philosophy that honours and facilitates continued growth and development.

In the future, schools may play a role in this type of work in liaison with their local communities.

SUMMARY

Schools have a role in:

- listening to all their pupils;
- liaising with parents representing all the groups within a community;
- increasing their knowledge and understanding of local communities which they serve.

They may be places of sanctuary within restless communities, or important links and bridge builders helping young people move towards finding their valued role within society.

RESOURCES

Dadzie, S. (1999) *Toolkit for Tackling Racism in Schools.* Stoke-on-Trent: Trentham Books.
Excellent practical manual.

CHAPTER 1.5

Why Intervene at Whole-School Level?

Both the mental health and the emotional intelligence of everyone in a school can be improved by instituting an intervention for the whole school. Issues may be highlighted by individuals but a whole-school response can generate benefits for everyone.

MENTAL HEALTH OF THE WHOLE-SCHOOL POPULATION

Schools are places of social activity: large communities which have a personality in their own right. They are inevitably involved in the mental and emotional health of their pupils. In any school of 1,000 pupils there are likely to be :

- 50 pupils with a depressive illness, i.e. seriously depressed;
- 100 who are suffering significant distress;
- 10–20 pupils with obsessive-compulsive disorder;
- 5–10 girls with an eating disorder (Young Minds, 2002).

The majority of the school is made up of young people who have reasonable mental health and resilience. These pupils may have experienced emotional distress, which though not significant enough to present as a syndrome, makes their life less fulfilling and enjoyable. Life events, such as prolonged bullying or parental separation, can tip their mental health into distress or illness. A small number of adolescents will have very good mental health and a high level of resilience. (See Figure 1.5.1.)

The cut-off point for presenting symptoms is dependent to some extent on an individual's behaviour problems, but it is also influenced by the environment.

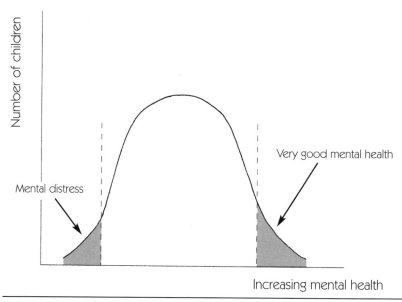

FIGURE 1.5.1 MENTAL HEALTH OF THE SCHOOL POPULATION

One school may have a higher tolerance of individual behaviour than another, e.g. a macho/sporting culture may have a higher tolerance of behaviours which another school might classify as bullying behaviours. Alternatively, another school may have high expectations of working or sitting quietly or sitting still for prolonged periods of silence. A youngster on the attention deficit hyperactivity disorder spectrum may struggle with this.

CASE STUDY 1.5.1 SAM, A PUPIL WITH ADHD

In a small Roman Catholic secondary school, the pupils were expected to sit for an hour and a half for a weekly mass. One boy in Year 7 with mild ADHD found this the most difficult part of the week. His tutor reported, 'Wherever there was low level disruption you would expect to find Sam in the middle of it. It was quite hard to catch him doing anything specific but he was always in the thick of it. For most of the rest of the week teaching him was a delight – a challenge but a delight.'

Interventions may be sought because one or two individuals have highlighted an issue. However, if you intervene at whole-school level, the mental health of everyone improves. The whole population has improved emotional health and increased strategies for dealing with stress. Fewer students present with the same level of emotional distress than previously. However, the greatest gain is for the large group of youngsters with reasonable mental health who now have increased self-knowledge, self-awareness and insight. Future problems in the school community are less likely to escalate.

There may still be a remaining group of pupils, smaller than before, who continue to have a mental health problem. However, their emotional resources will be enhanced in comparison to prior to the intervention. Overall more pupils (and staff) will be helped by a whole-school intervention than by one for a specific individual.

EMOTIONAL INTELLIGENCE OF THE SCHOOL POPULATION

As with good mental health, a high level of emotional intelligence is a desirable outcome of growing older. Interventions encouraging emotional intelligence will benefit everyone in the school.

Emotional intelligence is concerned with:

- self-awareness – knowing one's internal states, preferences, resources and intuitions;
- self-regulation – managing ones' internal states, impulses and resources;
- motivation – emotional tendencies that facilitate reaching goals;
- empathy – awareness of other's needs, feelings and concerns;
- social skills – adeptness at inducing desirable responses in others.

In the educational domain it is also referred to as the emotional literacy movement (Goleman, 1998; Greenberg et al., 1995), which recognizes the need for schools to educate young people in the management of emotions, in settling disputes peacefully and in learning to live co-operatively with one another.

These skills overlap with the abilities described as mental health. The emphasis from Goleman (1998) is that raw emotional intelligence can be developed into emotional competence in the same way that raw intelligence quotient (IQ) can be developed into useful qualifications. He argues that in our present age emotional intelligence at work matters twice as much as cognitive abilities such as IQ or technical expertise (Goleman, 1998). As with mental health of the school population, there are positive benefits for all by instituting a whole-school approach to enhance emotional intelligence.

The challenge is how to teach emotional intelligence in our schools. Some core subjects, such as literature can help develop it, as can newer subjects such as citizenship.

A variety of interventions in this book, such as circle time and circle of friends deal with specific areas of emotional intelligence for young people e.g.:

- recognition of their own emotions;
- control of those emotions so that considered judgements can be made;
- development of empathy.

An example of a programme specifically designed to help develop emotional intelligence is the PATHS (Promoting Alternative Thinking Strategies) programme. This is a 60-lesson intervention composed of units on self-control, emotions and problem-solving. Lessons involve didactic instruction, role-play, class discussions, modelling by teachers and peers, social and self-reinforcement and worksheets. A critical aspect of PATHS focuses on the relationship between cognitive-affective understanding and real-life situations (Greenberg et al., 1995). The components of the curriculum include:

1 Self-awareness:

   (a) self-monitoring and recognition of feelings;

   (b) building a vocabulary of feelings;

   (c) making links between thoughts, feelings and behaviour.

2 Personal decision-making:

   (a) self-monitoring of actions and recognition of their consequences;

   (b) distinguishing between thought-led and feeling-led decisions.

3 Managing feelings:

   (a) self-monitoring of 'self talk';

   (b) challenging negative self-messages;

   (c) recognizing triggers for strong feelings;

   (d) finding ways of handling fears, anxieties, anger and sadness.

4 Handling stress:

   (a) self-monitoring for signs of stress;

   (b) recognition of sources of stress;

   (c) learning to use relaxation methods.

5 Empathy:

   (a) understanding others' feelings and concerns;

   (b) recognizing that different people have different perspectives.

6 Personal responsibility:

   (a) taking responsibility for self-management;

(b) recognizing consequences of actions and decisions;

(c) accepting feelings and moods;

(d) persisting to achieve goals and commitments.

7 Conflict resolution:

(a) understanding the difference between need and want;

(b) using a 'win-win' model for negotiating solutions.

Evaluation by Greenberg et al. (1995) showed that PATHS' most influential impact was on the children's fluency in discussing basic feelings as well as their beliefs in their own efficacy about managing and changing feeling. In some instances, there was greater improvement in children whose teachers had rated them as having behavioural difficulties.

This research gives support to the idea that cognitive knowledge about emotion may affect how we respond to others and how we reflect about ourselves. Thinking ahead about one's actions and their effects on others may therefore lead to greater empathy towards others and a more reflective, responsible stance. More advanced knowledge of emotions may also lead to more advanced strategies for regulating emotions, and so to less impulsivity in action. Greenberg et al. (1995) acknowledge that there was a wide variation among the teachers in the extent to which they modelled emotional awareness, shared their own emotions and created an ethos of respect for others in the classroom. In this sense, progress is likely to be slow in the early stages as educators become used to working more directly with emotions in schools. It could be argued, therefore, that the potential for interventions such as PATHS is much greater than the present results indicate. It is also interesting to note that this type of intervention is part of a wider movement on the promotion of emotional literacy in children and young people. This study illustrates that it is possible to teach aspects of emotional fluency and understanding in school settings, in both mainstream and special education, with positive outcomes.

SUMMARY

This chapter argues that by instituting a whole-school approach, all members of the school community will benefit in terms of mental and emotional well-being.

RESOURCES

Goleman, D. (1998) *Working with Emotional Intelligence*. London: Bloomsbury.
Emotional Intelligence Services, 142 North Road, Sudbury, MA 01776, USA. Tel: 001 (978) 371–5922.
Email: EISGlobal@AOL.com Website: www.EISGlobal.com
Consortium for Research on Emotional Intelligence in Organisations, available at http://www.eisconsortium.org

Where to Start in Matching an Intervention to Your School

> *If certain questions are not asked at the outset or plans not devised to take account of responses then the impact of any attempt to introduce new policy and practice may well be limited and an ineffective use of time for all concerned. (Roffey, 2000, p. 16)*

There is a clear challenge for society in meeting the needs of young people experiencing mental health difficulties and finding a role for schools to play in alleviating the problem. But as we have seen, the underlying causes are many and complex, and, while some have common solutions, others are closely linked to specific environmental or community conditions. There are inevitably many strands to the solution and different levels of analysis of the problem. One strategic response on the part of schools is to carry out a *needs analysis* – a structured and reasonably objective approach to identifying the needs of a particular group, assessing the resources available to meet those needs, planning an appropriate set of interventions and evaluating their effectiveness.

Interventions are more likely to work if based on a full understanding of the problem, of the resources available and of the possible difficulties that will arise in the course of implementing them. A needs analysis provides a structured way of gathering this information and then making plans based on the findings. It also begins the process of involving other relevant people or agencies in the process of addressing the problem, a key step towards effective implementation. Needs analysis has the potential to demonstrate the school's willingness to work in partnership with a range of participants and to deal with the issues that arise in the course of such co-operation. Figure 1.6.1 shows a flow chart for schools to adopt when initiating a needs analysis for their own particular issues. Prior to carrying out the needs analysis, establish a working group to manage the process of addressing the problem, to include young people, for example School Council representatives, staff, parents, governors

and the wider community. The process is ongoing, and the compl
needs analysis cycle is the impetus to modify and continue with the p------

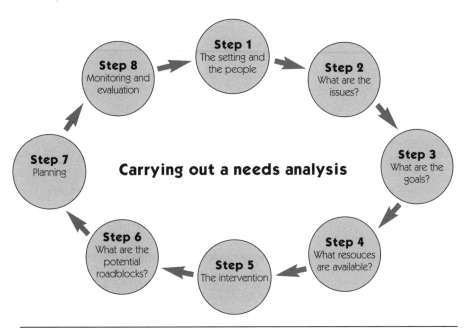

FIGURE 1.6.1 NEEDS ANALYSIS FLOW CHART

STEP 1: THE SETTING AND THE PEOPLE

The first step involves collecting information on the nature of the school context, to include information on the school ethos, the initiatives and policies on
mental health that already exist in the school and the community that the
school serves. Questions to consider include:

- What is the vision of the headteacher?
- What is the culture of the school?
- What is the ethos/philosophy of the school?
- How well does practice match philosophy in the school?
- How are decisions made in the school and by whom?

It is also important to have accurate information about the people who are
likely to be involved, the parents, teachers, governors and the young people
themselves:

- Who are the people likely to be involved?
- What are their demographics – age, abilities, ethnicities,
  genders?

- Are there any demographic differences within the community?

- What is the existing parental involvement in the school?

STEP 2: IDENTIFYING THE ISSUES

The next step is to discover the nature of the mental health problems being experienced by young people in the school and whether they might find certain interventions helpful; and to identify the gaps in positive mental health policies and practices in the school. Initial consultation to discover the issues pertinent to your school may be carried out with staff, parents and young people, and other agencies such as Child and Adolescent Mental Health Services (CAMHS) or the Schools Psychological Services, through focus groups or anonymous questionnaires.

Opportunities should be given to young people to express their views and opinions in a variety of ways including face-to-face interviews, evaluation checklists, focus groups and class discussions.

Other methods that enable young people to take a more active role in the consultation process include drawings, mapping, flow diagrams, jigsaws, drama, storytelling, songs and exercises (for example, Masheder, 1997; Pretty et al., 1995; Steiner, 1993). These approaches promote methods of communication that young people find more meaningful, such that participants are enabled to take the lead in discussion. In addition, they also provide a wide range of opportunities for young people to express their views such that everyone, regardless of age, ethnicity, literacy or disability level, can make a valid contribution.

It is likely to be too difficult for some vulnerable young people, for example the disaffected or those who are depressed or withdrawn, to express their views in front of teachers and adults, so sensitive ways of finding out about their experience and how they might be helped is essential. One way of overcoming this potential problem is to engage the young people themselves in the consultation process as peer researchers. Box 1.6.1 highlights some of the methods of peer research available. Issues to consider include:

- What are the mental health problems experienced by young people in your school?

- How do you know that these are problems faced by young people in your school?

- What problems do you intend to address?

- Why have you selected these specific problems to address?

- What positive mental health policies and practices are

currently in place in your school? (See Box 1.6.2 for reviewing school policies.)

■ Where does further action need to be taken?

An example of a standardized questionnaire for use with young people is the 'My Life in School Checklist' (Arora and Thompson, 1987, cited in Sharp, 1999) (see Appendix at the end of this chapter) which can be used to gauge the extent of behaviour in school at any given time, including bullying, aggression and friendly behaviours. Not only can this highlight specific issues at this stage of the needs analysis, it can also be used as a tool for evaluation and review purposes at a later stage.

It is also worth looking at research findings on the topic for a wider understanding of such phenomena as incidence, risk factors, protective factors and the effectiveness of interventions in other schools.

BOX 1.6.1 INVOLVING YOUNG PEOPLE AS PEER RESEARCHERS

- Engage and train a group of young people as peer researchers who can stay with the consultation from beginning to end, for example, this might be School Council representatives.
- Give young people the opportunity to be involved in the key initial consultation decisions.
- Involve young people in setting the aims and objectives of the initial consultation.
- Take account of young people's views in designing appropriate research tools and conducting the initial consultation, for example, in designing and administering questionnaires or interviews.
- Give young people the opportunity to be involved in data collection and data analysis.
- Give young people the opportunity to be involved in disseminating the findings of the initial consultation, for example, by distributing reports and making presentations to staff, parents, governors and other young people.

Case study 1.6.1 illustrates a needs analysis in action.

STEP 3: DESIGNING A SET OF SHARED GOALS

The next step is to ensure that all interest groups within the school have a sense of 'ownership' of the proposed interventions and that they are involved at each stage of its development.

A lack of consultation will certainly lead to resistance so it is important to find a balance between consultation and action. At this point in the needs analysis the major initiators will need to develop a shared set of goals. Ideally, these will be agreed by most of those involved, to include the staff, parents, governors, young people and other agencies, and any funding bodies that take part. The point of clearly defining goals before the start of the intervention is to provide a baseline against which to measure progress. This will be invaluable when it comes to monitoring and evaluating the progress of the project.

Questions to consider include:

- What changes do you want to see?
- Are your goals shared with your colleagues, young people and parents?

STEP 4: IDENTIFYING RESOURCES/PEOPLE/EXTERNAL AGENCIES AVAILABLE TO THE SCHOOL

It is important to be clear about the costs that will be incurred by developing, implementing and maintaining an intervention, both in terms of time and money. The issue of resources should also be shared with the other interest groups, not least because they may have ideas on how to raise money or how to access services through voluntary agencies, through government funding or through charities.

Questions to consider include:

- What are the financial resources available?
- What are the material resources available?
- What are the human resources available?
- What are the particular strengths of your school, colleagues and young people in relation to the changes you plan to make?
- Can you do anything to increase or make better use of these resources?

Whether the school is in a multi-ethnic or a homogeneous demographic area, further key questions to ask include:

- How does the school best access the resources of these different groups?
- Are there any divisions (for example, racial tensions) that may exist between these groups?
- What are the positive things that these groups can offer?

BOX 1.6.2 PROCESS FOR REVIEWING SCHOOL POLICIES

Appropriate school policies can promote positive mental health in young people. Positive policies include general policies on young people and staff conduct, policies on health and safety, behaviour monitoring and reinforcement, and are linked to information about positive mental health. Effective anti-bullying policies are also a crucial part of this picture. A fundamental step in the development of appropriate policies is to create a dialogue with young people, parents, governors and staff. It is clearly not enough to have the policies in place: they have to be put into practice.

Key processes for reviewing school policies are:

- Assess the school climate through a process of self-audit.
- Review policies and practices (for example, the school's anti-bullying policy and pastoral care system) relevant to the issue of young people's mental health.
- Review behaviour management policies and how they are implemented by all staff.
- Review the extent to which young people are involved in contributing to policies and school rules; consider how Citizenship and PSHE are taught in the school.
- Consider how to promote anti-stigma practices throughout the school and in the curriculum. For example, The Royal College of Psychiatrists has launched a multimedia CD-ROM entitled *Changing Minds* (RCP, 2002) on mental health that aims to raise awareness of psychiatric problems in young people aged between 13 and 17 years. It is designed for teachers to use as part of the PSHE curriculum and includes creative teaching ideas for lessons using the CD-ROM.
- Consider how to promote democratic structures in school.
- Consider staff training needs.

STEP 5: PLANNING THE INTERVENTION

This step requires identifying and assessing possible interventions that might suit the goals and priorities identified in steps 2–4 and in developing an implementation plan. We have highlighted a range of interventions in this book that can either be used in their entirety, adapted to local needs, or simply used as inspiration to design something specific to your situation.

Issues to consider include:

- What are the possible interventions available?

CASE STUDY 1.6.1 NEEDS ANALYSIS IN ACTION

In this case study a school engaged in a rigorous self-audit to evaluate the effectiveness of its policies in promoting a positive school environment conducive to the emotional health and well-being of its young people. The senior management team believed that good behaviour was closely linked to high standards of achievement. They argued that, if the whole-school community was strong and inclusive in its approach, then behaviour and standards would both improve. They were also concerned to reduce inappropriate behaviour, disaffection and truancy. More specifically they identified the following goals:

- To put in place effective policies for the management of positive behaviour.
- To promote pupils' safety and emotional well-being.
- To value individuals by offering support, respect and recognition.
- To promote positive parental/carer involvement.

With the aid of The Essex Schools Award Scheme (2000), the school was able to carry out a rigorous self-assessment of its current situation by measuring how well developed its behaviour policies and procedures were and to assess whether these were reflected in practice across the whole-school community. Self-monitoring indicated the following outcomes:

- Preparation for the award provided a framework within which self-evaluation of current systems and processes could take place.
- The award assessment identified key areas for future development which enabled the school to continue to make further improvements.
- The award assessment was used as an integral document in the School Development Plan and for planning of future initiatives.
- The school was able to use the award assessment to monitor and maintain the standards achieved.

Developed by the Essex County Council Special Educational Needs and Psychology Service, The Essex Schools Award Scheme is aimed at promoting positive behaviour, thus reinforcing the concept of the healthy school as an organization. The scheme offers resources and guidance to help schools assess their current situation, including questionnaires, surveys and interviews, action planning materials, observation checklists, planning development work and evidence recording.

Other needs analysis resources currently available include *Checkpoints For Schools* (Varnava, 2000), *Checkpoints For Young People* (Varnava, 2002a) and the Wirral Health Promoting Schools Scheme.

- Have these interventions been evaluated? If so, what are the advantages and disadvantages of each?

- Is a particular intervention suitable for the goals and issues outlined in step 3?

- Does the intervention need tailoring to suit the needs analysis?

STEP 6: POTENTIAL ROADBLOCKS TO SUCCESS

It is important to identify the problems that might undermine the process of planning and implementing an intervention and think of ways of preventing these potential roadblocks.

Questions to consider include:

- What might get in the way of achieving your goals?

- What can you do from the outset to prevent these potential roadblocks from becoming actual roadblocks?

- Can you change these roadblocks into change facilitators?

CASE STUDY 1.6.2 ROADBLOCKS

The consultation process may help the school to understand the roadblocks that can occur to undermine plans. Once the school has identified such a problem, it is easier to circumvent it at an early stage in the project. It is worth considering that the person who blocks the proposed plans for intervention most actively may have the potential to be the project's most ardent supporter. For example, in one school a teacher considered that the proposed Circle of Friends intervention would undermine classroom discipline by appearing to tolerate aggressive young people's disruptive behaviour. Initially it appeared to be impossible for the headteacher to reconcile the tensions between this colleague's concept of discipline and understanding of the particular needs of a pupil who had been diagnosed by the Child and Adolescent Mental Health team as having attention deficit disorder. By helping this teacher feel less threatened by the proposed intervention and by involving him in the training to facilitate a Circle, the headteacher succeeded in engaging his involvement. In the end, this teacher became one of the most enthusiastic facilitators in the school. This example illustrates the importance of taking account of the varied qualities that colleagues and young people themselves bring to an issue. The headteacher in this case was able to keep a balance between her awareness of potential blocks to success and a belief in the commitment and ability of her staff.

STEP 7: IMPLEMENTING THE INTERVENTION

Reflecting on your analysis of the previous stages, it may be necessary to design awareness-raising events in which all groups can participate before moving on to the intervention itself. Varnava (2002b) has identified six processes for initiating and promoting an intervention:

- Decide on a launch date.
- Devise publicity materials, for example, posters, badges, leaflets, noticeboards.
- Use the materials to publicize the intervention as widely as possible, both within school and outside school.
- Invite a known local personality or celebrity to be a 'moral sponsor' or patron for the intervention.
- Invite representatives from local shops, businesses and newspapers to a presentation of the intervention in order to gather both general and possibly financial support.
- Nominate young people to be ambassadors for the intervention.

STEP 8: MONITORING AND EVALUATION

It is an essential part of the needs analysis to build in some form of monitoring and evaluation so that there is evidence to indicate whether the school has achieved all or some of its goals and information on where changes need to be made. The monitoring need not be statistical or excessively time-consuming but it should be systematic and integrated into the project from the beginning. Some issues to consider include:

- Do you have ways to evaluate whether or not you are achieving your goals?
- Do you have ways of measuring unexpected changes/developments?
- What will you do if your evaluation does not produce the results you had hoped for?

The evidence should include some outcome measures, such as:

- attendance rates;
- percentage of young people achieving five GCSE passes at grades A to C;
- exclusion rates;

- numbers of referrals to Behaviour Support Service;
- results of a standardized questionnaire such as the 'My Life In School Checklist' (Arora and Thompson, 1987, cited in Sharp, 1999). (See pp. 51–2)

It is also important to define your own measurement criteria relevant to your school's circumstances. For example, one school, under threat of closure, was able to measure improvement in overall performance, which impacted on the major problem of bullying, by the reduction of the glazing bill, which was down 51 per cent from the previous year (Varnava, 2002b).

CASE STUDY 1.6.3 A BENEFIT OF MONITORING

One school investigated the impact on attendance rates of introducing a peer support system to tackle the problem of bullying by older young people of new Year 7 young people. The staff involved also gathered qualitative perspectives from users, participants and observers as appropriate, including interviews with all Year 7 young people at the beginning and the end of term to elicit their perspectives on the effectiveness of the peer support system. The co-ordinators of the peer support system were pleased to find out that, not only did attendance rates improve, but overall the scheme was perceived positively by the actual users and non-users alike. They also discovered some areas where the service was being underused and were motivated to develop more proactive outreach work in tutor groups. Without the monitoring, they would not have had the necessary evidence to justify their innovative work.

Monitoring and evaluation are important to:

- ensure that the intervention is not doing harm to vulnerable young people;
- indicate where the intervention is working, where it is not working and where changes and adjustments are required;
- provide information about the intervention in a school's particular context;
- provide evidence to governors or potential funding bodies.

SUMMARY

Interventions are most likely to succeed when they address the needs of the young people concerned, take into account the resources available and the potential roadblocks, and incorporate a planned and methodical review and evaluation process. A needs analysis provides a structured means of achieving this. This chapter has highlighted that instituting change is rarely a 'one-off' procedure rather an ongoing and challenging process.

RESOURCES

Arora and Thompson (1987) 'My Life In School Checklist', cited in S. Sharp, (1999) *Bullying Behaviour in Schools*. Windsor: NFER-Nelson.

The Essex Schools Award Scheme (2000) Essex County Council Learning Services, Information and Publications, PO Box 47, Chelmsford, CM2 6WN. Chelmsford: Essex County Council Learning Services.

Masheder, M. (1997) *Let's Co-operate*. London: Green Print.

Pretty, J.N., Guijt, I., Thompson, J. and Scoones, I. (1995) *Participatory Learning and Action: A Trainer's Guide*. IIED Participatory Methodology Series. London: IIED, 3 Endsleigh Street, London, WC1H 0DD. Tel: 020 7388 2117.

The Royal College of Psychiatrists (2000). *Changing Minds* Book Sales, The Royal College of Psychiatrists, 17 Belgrave Square, London, SW1X 8PG. Tel: 020 7235 2351, ext. 146. Also at www.rcpsych.ac.uk

Steiner, M. (1993) *Learning From Experience: Cooperative Learning and Global Education*. Stoke-on-Trent: Trentham Books.

Varnava, G. (2000) *Towards a Non-violent Society: Checkpoints For Schools*. London: NCB.

Varnava, G. (2002a) *Towards a Non-violent Society: Checkpoints For Young People*. London: NCB.

Wirral Health Promoting Schools Scheme, Health Links, 49 Hamilton Square, Birkenhead, CH41 5AR.

APPENDIX: MY LIFE IN SCHOOL CHECKLIST (SECONDARY SCHOOL VERSION)

Male/Female (please circle)

Age ………………………………….. Form ……………………….

School ……………………………………………………………………….

During this week another pupil:	Not at all	Only once	More than once
1 Helped me with my homework	1	2	3
2 Called me names	1	2	3
3 Said something nice to me	1	2	3
4 Teased me about my family	1	2	3
5 Tried to kick me	1	2	3
6 Was very nice to me	1	2	3
7 Teased me because I am different	1	2	3
8 Gave me a present	1	2	3
9 Threatened to hurt me	1	2	3
10 Gave me some money	1	2	3
11 Demanded money from me	1	2	3
12 Tried to frighten me	1	2	3
13 Asked me a stupid question	1	2	3
14 Lent me something	1	2	3
15 Told me off	1	2	3
16 Teased me	1	2	3
17 Talked about clothes with me	1	2	3
18 Told me a joke	1	2	3
19 Told me a lie	1	2	3

During this week another pupil:	Not at all	Only once	More than once
20 Ganged up on me	1	2	3
21 Tried to make me hurt other people	1	2	3
22 Smiled at me	1	2	3
23 Tried to get me into trouble	1	2	3
24 Helped me carry something	1	2	3
25 Tried to hurt me	1	2	3
26 Helped me with my homework	1	2	3
27 Made me do something I didn't want to do	1	2	3
28 Talked about TV with me	1	2	3
29 Took something off me	1	2	3
30 Shared something with me	1	2	3
31 Was rude about the colour of my skin	1	2	3
32 Shouted at me	1	2	3
33 Played a game with me	1	2	3
34 Tried to trip me up	1	2	3
35 Talked about interests with me	1	2	3
36 Laughed at me	1	2	3
37 Threatened to tell on me	1	2	3
38 Tried to break something of mine	1	2	3
39 Told a lie about me	1	2	3
40 Tried to hit me	1	2	3

Thank you very much for your help

©Arora and Thompson (1987) (cited in Sharp, 1999)

SECTION 2

Creating a School Community

The school setting is then essentially holistic or, as some now label it, 'eco-holistic' to reflect the interrelated nature of the parts and the whole. (Weare, 2000, p. 21)

INTRODUCTION

This chapter looks at organizational practices which do not address specific behaviours but rather aim to develop a positive ethos in the school, making it a place where staff want to work, and pupils want to learn. It covers a range of possible ideas that may improve staff morale, pupil and teacher satisfaction and the sense of community within the school.

THE ENVIRONMENT

The physical and psychosocial environment in and around school plays a crucial role in creating a positive ethos. There is often a well-developed environment at the reception area including frequently changed displays of students' work, photographs of school activities, newspaper reports or certificates for school achievements. It is easy to overlook other areas in school, yet the same attention can be beneficial.

The environment is not only visual. Care also needs to be given to auditory, olfactory and kinetic (see Box 2.1.2) stimulae. Many of these things, such as noisy main roads or smells from nearby manufacturing industry, will not be easy to change. Where they can be considered, i.e. the placing of smelly bins during the summer, taking action will help. Small things can make a difference in combination.

Most young people are very image-conscious and will be aware of fashionable textiles and furnishings. The revolution in lighting in the 1990s has generally passed education by. If you are fortunate enough to be involved in the planning of a new school please consider lighting. Dark areas may become trouble spots. However, bland strip lighting is not the only option for corridors. Windows let in natural light but can be a distraction for those sitting alongside them.

School is a place where we traditionally think of using the dominant side of our brains for academic learning. By stimulating the non-dominant side through visual, auditory and kinetic stimulate, information is allowed to transverse between both sides of the brain allowing for a much more creative process. The effect of this is that individuals have an increased potential to recall information and adapt it in new situations.

It is important to keep a balance, and remember that the overwhelming need is for the environment to be practical for all its users. (See Box 2.1.1.)

BOX 2.1.1 SANDFORD MIDDLE SCHOOL

In Sandford Middle School there were ongoing issues over the telephone lines because there was a high demand at certain times of day. This led to increasing frustration at the difficulty of liaising outside school, including receiving returned calls. The staff proposed a number of creative solutions using the De Bono hats technique (see later) which improved morale considerably among them.

Some schools are looking at pupil-centred ways of improving their environment for example, the children 'owning' their classroom and the staff moving between classrooms or every child having an electronic notepad.

This subject is also discussed in Chapter 2.11.

TOILETS AND LOCKERS

In the same way that every garden has a place which is dry and shady, where plants find it difficult to grow, most schools have problem areas, for example toilets and locker areas. Part of creating a positive ethos in the school is to recognize these areas, not to ignore them. They are often hard to change.

How many children avoid visiting the toilets for the whole day? Probably far more than we realize. These areas are often unsupervised and a poorly resourced part of the school building. They may be physically unpleasant and are also places where vulnerable children can be picked on.

Lockers can be another area which children want to avoid. There may be an assertion of peer hierarchy, leading to shoving, pushing and verbal abuse. Even teachers can subconsciously avoid these areas.

CASE STUDY 2.1.1   DAVID AND THE LOCKERS

David, a quiet and somewhat shy boy, found the transfer to senior school diffi-cult. Most of his friends had gone to the other senior school in town. He found making new friends hard. By the end of Year 7 he was being regularly bullied by a group of boys. The bullying was both verbal and physical. David did not tell his parents or anyone at school what was happening until a particularly unpleas-ant and violent incident at the lockers. He was thrown against the lockers and sustained nasty bruises and cuts which both his teachers and parents noticed. Following this, he told them about the bullying. The school dealt with it swiftly and appropriately, and David was able to return to school confident that the staff would deal with any more bullying should it occur.

COMPUTER SYSTEMS

Computer technology is an important aspect that can contribute to a school's ethos. Computer systems can be a great asset to staff for gathering information about students' behaviour. For example, the School Software Company provides software which can produce reports showing the breakdown of incidents by year group, action taken, student involvement by tutor group, by day of the week, by period (there is often an increasing incidence after breaks), by type of behaviours, by subject and by location (which can help with identification of trouble blackspots). The information gathered this way may suggest patterns which are worth investigating. It does not provide causal evidence. For example, if a school has a number of pupils diagnosed with attention deficit disorder there may be increased reporting of incidents prior to lunch break. This could be a medication effect as some children will experience a rebound effect as their methyl phenidate wears off. Alternatively a number of young people may have skipped breakfast and find that their concentration is less in the lesson before lunch. Timetabling issues may compound the problem. The computer system will only suggest an area which is worth investigating.

Other schools develop their own software packages which enable their own monitoring of pupils and the chance to pick up issues early. One example of this is the system which has been developed at Southwell Primary School. It could be easily adapted for secondary school level. The criteria from 'Supporting School Improvement Emotional and Behavioural Development, QCA 2001' have been tabulated so that each child can be rated on learning behaviours, conduct behaviours and emotional behaviours (see the Appendix at the end of this chapter). The system can be set so that children who score poorly in all three areas, or particularly in one area, can be highlighted.

The teachers complete a form on each child once a year. The information gained is used to assist members of the senior management team and special needs co-ordinator to gain an overall picture of the current state of the emotional well-being of the pupils of the school. It is largely seen as a questioning exercise, particularly in relation to assessing future resources that may need to be targeted, e.g. educational psychologist, Behavioural Management Support or Education Welfare. It is proactive rather than reactive, and enables the headteacher or pastoral team to take a non-academic overview of their pupils. The main difficulty in getting a system, such as this one, to work at secondary school level is deciding who would be best to fill in the forms, who would input them on the system, and who would have access to the reports.

Many schools have computer systems to monitor academic progress and attainment. Reports can be designed to pick up those pupils whose academic work has unexpectedly dropped off. This allows early intervention particularly for the quiet child who has recently started being bullied but has not told anyone, or whose parents are separating. Similarly, electronic registration systems allow the early identification of pupils who are absenting themselves from lessons and school.

LUNCHTIMES

Break times are vulnerable times for young people. Troubles from outside the school may well be brought into the playground. By secondary age, youngsters with difficulties have often learnt to find safe places during break times. This may be the head of year office or the library. Clubs can provide safe places for practising social skills that the free-for-all in the playground cannot provide.

Lunchtime supervision is a skilled job. When to intervene? When not to? How to give the youngsters respect? How to be respected? Do supervisors visit the blackspots in the school playground? Do they leave the pupils to burn off energy which is being repressed for the rest of the day? The lunchtime staff have a difficult job, and it is important to try to engage them in whole-school interventions.

REWARD SCHEMES

The concept is easy, but it is more difficult to get right. The basic principle is to reward behaviours which you want to encourage, and to ignore those that you wish discontinued.

Important things to consider:

- The rewards have to be intrinsically motivating to the young people. Schools use different ideas including tea with the headteacher, visits to other schools, praise postcards, letters home, chocolate, Marks & Spencer tokens, prizes donated by local businesses e.g. McDonald's and, in some schools, money.

■ The rewards have to work at peer group level. The reward is much more reinforcing if most of the youngsters think that it is attractive.

■ The rewards have to be seen to be fair and consistent.

■ It is important to decide what you are rewarding and that the pupils know clearly what they have to do (or not do) to get a merit point/reward.

■ There are already substantial rewards for those who achieve academically. Most merit schemes reward effort. However, the young people may perceive that the rewards are usually given to those who present very neat work and therefore also achieve academically, or to those with significant difficulties who are rewarded for effort. It is important not to exclude the 'average ' pupils and to ensure that they are rewarded for success in some area, for example, creative work, sport, music or drama performance, or social skills.

■ Rewards are sometimes given for following instructions. In one school students were encouraged to read the end of the page before starting an examination by having the bottom line of an instruction sheet state, 'Do not complete sheet but come to see me for a Mars bar'. The reward is lost if the sheet is completed.

■ Most schemes work by giving small rewards which accumulate. Small rewards may be intangible things such as merits, or tokens, or school 'lottery tickets'. These can be added up at the end of term or at another set time. It is important to acknowledge any small rewards which have accumulated even if a pupil has not reached the number required for a larger reward. Schemes which work best have reward staging. An alternative system to consider is to provide a larger reward when a certain number of 'tokens' have been achieved.

■ If the reward is right most pupils will try hard initially in the first term. In the second term those who achieved a big reward (and particularly those who were close) will continue. The majority will be less committed. If you put a lot of effort into trying to achieve an award but fail, there is a tendency to devalue it. Adolescents may view working for a reward as childish.

- Merit schemes need to be constantly proactive rather than reactive, both by regularly reviewing the rewards but, more importantly, also by moving the rules slightly so that others become involved, not so often that it is confusing, but to keep as many young people as possible engaged.

DEVELOPING OTHER SKILLS

COUNSELLING AND LISTENING SKILLS

Many schools now employ a school counsellor, either on their own or as part of a pyramid of schools. These counsellors come from a variety of backgrounds. They may often be teachers who have wished to develop their pastoral role and gone on to do further training in this area. Their roles are dependent on the personalities involved, and have developed in an entrepreneurial fashion over the past decade. This means that the service they provide varies greatly from area to area. It can be an excellent resource for both the staff, who can see a problem reframed, and for the young person who has someone he or she perceives as supportive within the school environment.

Occasionally some schools help all their staff develop counselling skills.

CASE STUDY 2.1.2 KING FURLONG SCHOOL

Basingstoke's King Furlong School introduced a rolling training programme in basic counselling for all staff, including teaching assistants. Ms Freshwater, the head-teacher, comments that teachers cannot ignore the realities where families are beset with problems and the children come into school with emotional baggage and unable to learn. The counselling programme enables staff to be more aware of their pupils' concerns and also encourages active listening and using a non judg-mental approach towards others. Ms Freshwater comments that they became a stronger and shrewder staff.

Source: Times Educational Supplement, 26 April 2002. Phil Revel, *Talking Back to Happiness.*

COGNITIVE SKILLS

'If intelligence is the horse power of the car then thinking is the skill with which the car is driven' (de Bono, 1992, p. 74). Thinking skills usually refer to higher-order thinking, i.e. not the skill required to learn particular spellings but the development of your own mnemonic to help. Thinking strategies can play a role in providing a structure for assessing an issue, particularly if there is considerable divergence of views. For example, Edward de Bono's thinking hats is a way of reviewing issues thoroughly and moving towards change. The premise is that the group wear a different 'hat', i.e. consider a subject from differing perspectives, as the meeting progresses. The 'hats' are:

- fact gathering – white;
- gut reactions and feelings – red;
- negative points – black;
- positive points – yellow;
- creativity and new ideas – green;
- organizing the thinking – blue.

This type of perspective-taking can be very helpful in staff meetings as it enables both negative and positive things to be said, but not in a critical manner. Some schools encourage their pupils to use the thinking hats. Again this allows them to assess their work in a non-threatening manner. It is also useful as an examination technique and as a way of structuring essays.

Mind mapping (also known as concept mapping or model mapping) provides a visual way of understanding a thinking process. The brain's natural way of thinking is to make links and associations in all directions. List making restricts the creative process. Tony Buzan (2001) developed a creative thinking tool called a mind map. It has a basic image at its centre from which radiates main branches of thought associated with this central image. Each of these branches can then have smaller branches of connected ideas. It can be a helpful way of setting down complex information, or presenting it to others. It can also be a useful tool for brainstorming during the early stages of a needs analysis (Chapter 1.6).

RELAXATION AND FOCUS

An alternative approach to creating a positive ethos involves the consideration of complementary therapies. More than 80 per cent of teachers are using complementary therapies such as massage to cope with the growing stress of their jobs according to an informal survey by the School of Emotional Literacy (*Times Educational Supplement*, 26 April 2002). An increasing number of schools are bringing these interventions into the classroom by accessing voluntary skills of parents or or paid skills of practitioners to teach, for example, yoga, the Alexander technique, head massage and hypnosis, particularly around examination time. At the Maharishi school (a small private school with motivated parents which has good academic results) each class has a ten-minute 'meditation' after registration every single day (*Times Educational Supplement*, 31 January 2003).

BOX 2.1.2

Penwith Network consists of six secondary schools, 13 primaries, one tertiary college and one out-of-hours learning zone. They have decided to introduce more massage/gymnastics/other kinetic experiences into the classroom and have had encouraging results. Much of what happens in school is predominantly visual or auditory but boys in particular, like to be involved with movement. Some classes start with self-massage, others with stretches.

Source: Times Educational Supplement, 14 March 2003.

Secondary schools, out of necessity, are driven by deadlines and the timetable. This can create a constant low level of hassle – the need to respond to outside demands. These stresses continue into adult life. Encouraging young people to learn to pace themselves and relax successfully are useful goals. Techniques include yoga, the Alexander technique and hypnosis.

- *Yoga* can be employed by schools to provide a short period of non-competitive time within the week to search for stillness and focus, in a structured way.

- *The Alexander technique* has been used in dramatic and musical circles for many years. It helps with balance and confidence, and in putting the 'thought' before the action.

- *Hypnosis* has recently been employed in schools to counteract anxiety prior to exams. It is of particular importance that a reputable practitioner is involved.

When considering employing or using one of these practitioners it is important to ask:

- Is the practitioner appropriately qualified?
- What are the goals of the intervention?
- For whom is it available?
- How should it be advertised?
- How will we know if it has achieved what we wanted? (See Chapter 1.6.)

In the following chapters we look at a variety of behaviours and suggest whole-school interventions which aim to improve school life for everyone. A number of themes recur throughout the chapters. These include:

BOX 2.1.3 RALPH ALLEN SCHOOL

In Ralph Allen School, Libby Lee proposed a staff health week soon after she had become head. It was about positive living and stress management. The sixth form were also included in some of the sessions. The week included yoga, and Indian head massage. The Year 11s learned about stress management with the school nurse. The whole school had themed menus during the week, two chip-free days, and a great variety of different foods which was very popular. One of the things that came out of the 'stress week' was that the number of meetings for staff was reduced. The walls in the staffroom were painted and the notice-boards were moved so that the environment was more relaxing for the staff. The staff made the room next door into a working room, to give them a social room and a working room.

- treating youngsters as individuals (can be difficult in a school setting);
- developing pupils' self-esteem;
- giving the youngsters a voice;
- giving the staff a voice;
- networking with other schools. This allows resources to be pooled, knowledge to be shared, buying power to be increased;
- liaison with the outside communities;
- liaison with external help – key workers within school, who develop particular knowledge of local facilities, help this process;
- the emotional health of staff which is crucial to developing ideas;
- uniting vision;
- channelling the strengths of staff/parents;
- resourcing ideas with time, even if financially it is difficult;
- acknowledging the work done by individual staff and pupils;
- reviewing new ideas, in a planned way to assess both strengths and weaknesses, rather than 'fire-fighting';
- recognizing when intervention has served its time.

TABLE 2.1.1 SUMMARY OF INTERVENTIONS

Chapter	Behaviour	Main intervention	Other interventions/strategies discussed
2.2	Disaffected	Circle Time	Post-14 vocational training Thematic learning Learning support units Behaviour management consultancies Home–school support workers Behaviour and education support teams
2.3	Violence	*Leap*	Checkpoints CRISP ChildLine in partnership with schools
2.4	Bullying behaviours	Peer support	Whole-School policy Teaching co-operative values Method of Shared Concern The No Blame Approach Assertiveness training Working with provocative victims Working with persistent bullies
2.5	Sexual health	Teens and Toddlers	School policy Sexual and relationship education provision A PAUSE
2.6	Alcohol, drug and substance	The Big Fish Theatre Company	School policy Whole-school approach to drug and alcohol education BNTL Freeway Drug and Alcohol Service for London
2.7	Socially isolated	Circle of Friends	Organizational strategies Social skills groups Social stories Comic strip cartoons
2.8	Dealing with loss	Winston's Wish	Models of intervention
2.9	Eating problems	Education programme	Raising self-esteem strategies Learning to use cognitive behavioural techniques
2.10	Deliberate self-harm	Guidelines for staff	Education programmes Consider bullying and self-esteem raising strategies
2.11	Attention deficit disorder	Creating a calm environment	Practical classroom strategies

Table 2.1.1 summarizes the interventions to be found in the following chapters.

SUMMARY

Creating an emotionally healthy school community is a complicated, multi-faceted process. It requires clear leadership, vision, liaison with the local community and an appreciation of individual skills in both the student and staff population. Environmental factors play a part so consider whether there is a good use of the physical resource. Computer systems can be used to identify possible problems early. All schools will have problem areas, which though difficult to change are best not ignored. The benefits of a whole-school approach are huge, and will create a stable and developing staff population, and pupils who are achieving their potential. Consideration of environmental factors plays a part in this holistic approach.

RESOURCES

Brennan, R. (1992) *The Alexander Technique Workbook.* Dorset: Element.

British Association of Counselling and Psychotherapy 0870 4435 252, also at www.bac.co.uk

Bono, E. de (1992) *Teach Your Child How to Think.* London: Viking.

Edward de Bono website www.edwdebono.com, details his vast range of books, games and resource packs, some of which are targeted towards schools.

www.mind-map.com features more details of books, and courses on mind mapping developed by Tony Buzan.

www.braingym.org is a website devoted to the use of physical exercise to promote learning.

Mehta, S., Mehta, M. and Mehta, S. (1990) *Yoga: The Iyengar Way.* London: Dorling Kindersley.

Southwell Primary School
Assessment of Pupils'
Emotional & Behavioural Development

Learning Behaviour	Not at All (1)	Rarely (2)	Sometimes (3)	Fairly Often (4)	Often (5)	Always (6)
L1. Is attentive and has an interest in schoolwork, e.g. is not easily distracted, completes work, keeps on task & concentrates, has good motivation, shows interest, enjoys schoolwork.						
L2. Good learning or organisation, e.g. works systematically, at a reasonable pace, knows when to move on to next activity, can make choices, is organised.						
L3. Is an effective communicator, e.g. speech is coherent, thinks before answering.						
L4. Works efficiently in a group, takes part in discussions, contributes readily to group tasks, listens well in groups, works collaboratively.						
L5. Seeks help where necessary, e.g. can work independently until there is a problem that cannot be solved without teacher's intervention.						

Conduct Behaviour	Not at All (1)	Rarely (2)	Sometimes (3)	Fairly Often (4)	Often (5)	Always (6)
C1. Behaves respectfully to staff, polite, does not interrupt or deliberately annoy, does not show verbal aggression.						
C2. Shows respect to other pupils, e.g. does not tease, call names, swear, use psychological intimidation.						
C3. Only interrupts & seeks attention appropriately, e.g. does not talk when others are talking, does not seek unwarranted attention.						
C4. Is physically peaceable, avoids fights, is not cruel, does not strike out in temper.						
C5. Respects property, e.g. does not damage or steal property.						
Emotional Behaviour	Not at All (1)	Rarely (2)	Sometimes (3)	Fairly Often (4)	Often (5)	Always (6)
E1. Has empathy, shows tolerance & understanding, is considerate.						
E2. Is socially aware, e.g. interacts appropriately, is not a loner or isolated.						
E3. Is happy, e.g. has fun when appropriate, smiles, laughs, is cheerful, is not tearful or depressed.						
E4. Is confident, e.g. is not anxious, has high self-esteem, is relaxed, does not fear failure, is not shy, is robust, is not afraid of new things.						
E5. Is emotionally stable, & shows self control, e.g. moods remain relatively stable, does not have frequent mood swings, is patient, is not easily flustered, is not touchy.						

Disaffected Young People

'We learnt that it was all right to do the bare minimum, to keep the teachers off your back. But any more made you toadying, self-important and boring. Praise stopped being something to be proud of and started being embarrassing' (David). (Times Educational Supplement, 4 December 2001).

WHAT BEHAVIOURS ARE WE TALKING ABOUT?

Part of growing up is about learning to think for oneself, to decide what beliefs and attitudes of the adult world will be internalized. Therefore, from the adult perspective, young people frequently challenge, provoke and dispute ideas for their present time management. Are they disaffected? Where does this term start and end? Disaffected is a social term suggesting someone who is rebellious, disgruntled, dissatisfied, mutinous or antagonistic. It contains an element of poor motivation for change. There is a sense that the young person has been so failed by his or her world that they wish to have nothing to do with it. It can lead to delinquency, truancy, theft, violence, vandalism and lying.

Disaffected children can be given different labels depending on their social environment. In school the disaffected child is often referred to as 'outside inclusion'. In health settings, a young person presenting with these issues may be diagnosed as having a conduct disorder (socialized or unsocialized) or as having oppositional defiant disorder. Whatever label is chosen, it includes the idea of a young person who reacts negatively to another's perspective. It can generate feelings of anger, despair and vulnerability, and the feeling of impotence in those they challenge.

Young people can be disaffected from either the adults in their world, their peers or both. Is there a cut-off point where a young person is perceived as disaffected? There are youngsters who present as disaffected in every social situation; others will be less consistent. This suggests that there are 'degrees of disaffection'. The young person who is disaffected from all his or her social contacts is the most seriously damaged and the most challenging.

Rutter et al. (1998) suggest that there are four causal routes to youngsters developing antisocial behaviour:

- impaired social development leading to poor relationships and poor social problem-solving;
- learning that aggressive behaviour pays off;
- relative failure to develop social bonds;
- poor supervision leading to the development of delinquent groups.

By the time the most severely affected youngsters present in secondary schools, they have a long-standing sceptical view of how adults perceive them. Staff may have a similarly sceptical view of particular youngsters. A young person who consistently challenges throughout the course of a year, particularly early on in a teaching career, will leave a lasting shadow. Jonathan Smith in *The Learning Game* talks about a child whom he remembers well: 'It was the only thing in that excellent year in Australia which made me feel sick deep in the pit in my stomach … ' 'The absolutely worst pupil I've ever taught, though taught isn't the word, sat smack bang in the middle row, as central to my line of vision as it was possible to be' (Jonathan Smith, p. 53).

On a milder level, there are youngsters, in about Year 9, who decide that the challenge of academic work is too great. Without overtly acknowledging the fact, they realize that they are struggling to achieve what is being expected of them. Looking round at their peers, they may choose alternative role models, such as those whom they perceive as courageously standing up to authority. Poor school attainment is a risk factor for delinquency though it is not clear whether this stems from low ability or scholastic failure (Rutter et al., 1998).

WHAT BENEFITS ARE TO BE GAINED BY TACKLING DISAFFECTION?

- There will be exceptional youngsters who, because of their own personal characteristics and previous poor experiences, will have continuing difficulties with their social environment. However, the majority of youngsters, who develop some value within the school community, can respond well to positive labels. Tackling the disaffected youngsters within the school community can lead to increasing self-esteem and self-value for the individuals involved. This may spin off into areas where they were not primarily presenting a problem.

- The peer group benefits, as there is less negative peer pressure and less disruption in class. This allows the attention of members of staff to be more equally distributed and focused on the task of teaching.

- There are very positive benefits to staff well-being. It helps to give back feelings of personal control over the environment. No one likes regularly to deal with confrontation. It is wearing, demoralizing and deskilling. There are parts of the timetable and particular subjects which can be more vulnerable to the challenge of disaffected youngsters; note Friday afternoon and particular subjects.

WHAT ARE THE POSSIBLE INTERVENTIONS TO TACKLE DISAFFECTION?

Approaches that have successfully addressed the needs of disaffected young people include: vocational training, co-operative group work, on-site learning support, behaviour management consultancy, home–school support work, behaviour and education support teams and Circle Time. Circle Time is looked at in more detail at the end of this chapter.

POST-14 VOCATIONAL TRAINING

In *14–19 Opportunity and Excellence* (DfES, 2002) the government has been addressing the issue of post-14 vocational training. This represents a new direction with significance for the future provision of education and training. It aims to give all young people an opportunity to combine their general education with a choice of university-driven and industry-driven specialist subjects. It is beginning to rise to the challenge of providing accumulating career and training opportunities that open up in front of young people rather than close off behind them.

The Vocational Education and Training in Schools Programme (VETS) in Australia has had more than 200,000 pupils doing vocational courses as part of their secondary studies. The number has been rapidly rising for the last seven years and has been eagerly adopted by teachers in the 2000 secondaries in every state, though in a variety of ways, e.g. in some areas some of the cost is borne by the students. (Australian Education Union Report, 2003.)

BOX 2.2.1 KNOWSLEY COLLEGE

Knowsley College in Merseyside acts as a single institution for 14–16-year-olds. It has a strong reliance on local manufacturing industry links. Hairdressing and construction are examples of some of the courses it provides. However, Sir George Sweeney, Principal, believes strongly that the generic skills which are acquired on the variety of courses, make young people more employable. They also help to engage them in learning, which, in many cases schools have failed to do. He says, 'It is not about just dumping people on colleges. I don't have that kind of cynicism'.

Source: *Times Educational Supplement,* 24 January 2003. Steve Hook, Closer Links Bind Colleges to Schools.

Germany, Austria, Switzerland and the Netherlands have been building links with industry over the decades. As a result, the proportion of school leavers taking apprenticeships in these countries ranges from 55 to 75 per cent. Because of the length of university education in German-speaking countries, apprenticeships are popular even among able pupils. Therefore companies want, and get, high-calibre trainees. As increasing vocational links are developed in this country the challenge is how to access these new educational approaches. When choices have to be made at 14 years or earlier the risk is that those from backgrounds with low expectations will wrongly opt for technical school and not fulfil their potential. To avert this, says Dr Emer Smyth from Dublin's Economic and Social Research Institute, 'Routes need to be kept open between academic and vocational systems as long as possible, so that early decisions can be reversed'. (*Source: Times Educational Supplement* 2 February 2003, p.12)

In summary the trend in education to offer a wider range of both academic and vocational training should positively affect the numbers of youngsters presenting with disaffected problems, by allowing attributes and interests of the child to be developed and appreciated.

■ THEMATIC LEARNING/OPENING MINDS PROJECT

This is a type of co-operative group learning. Johnson and Johnson (1992) looked at 520 studies and concluded that co-operative group learning raised achievement in subject matter and encouraged positive social relationships, especially if the teaching was well planned and instituted. One example of a co-operative group learning approach is a Royal Society of Arts pilot, the Opening Mind Project, (www.rsa.org.uk/newcurriculum) which has supported a small number of schools to develop the curriculum radically to suit their school community. There is a willingness to be creative and inventive with the curriculum and an emphasis on five competencies:

- learning to learn;
- citizenship;
- relating to people;
- managing information;
- managing situations.

At the St. John's School Community College, Marlborough, Wiltshire, staff initially wrote and taught a thematically based curriculum to one-third of their Year 7s. The rest followed the National Curriculum. Staff used six modules to span the year which were taught by a group of six to eight teachers. The teacher's role was as a guide and mentor rather than the knowledge giver. The children often worked in pairs or small groups. They would organize their own questions to answer, and then explore ways of doing so. After the first year at St John's the alternative curriculum group scored 12 per cent higher than the other part of the year, in the optional Qualifications and Curriculum Authority tests. Even more striking was that they were hardly ever off sick and they accounted for only 4 per cent of detentions. The youngsters were absorbed, enthused, focused and switched on to learning. Relationships overall were good including with staff and they developed good negotiating skills. They knew how to support and help each other.

ON-SITE LEARNING SUPPORT UNITS/BEHAVIOUR SUPPORT UNITS/LEARNING INTERVENTION CENTRES

These are small separate units taking six to ten children, mostly from schools in which they are based, where there is a high staff–student ratio. They aim to keep pupils at schools who are at risk of exclusion, providing short-term teaching and support programmes to tackle poor behaviour, with the aim of reintegration into mainstream school as quickly as possible. (See Boxes 2.2.2, 2.2.3)

> *Essentially, we teach sociable and emotional literacy in do-able, manageable steps.* (Moira Healey, head of a Learning Support Unit, (LSU) in Birmingham, in 'The Issue'. Times Educational Supplement, *6 December 2002. p. 17. Elaine Williams,* Behaviour: Part 3.)

BEHAVIOUR MANAGEMENT CONSULTANCIES

These consultancies may provide support and advice for the school. They can offer an outside view on the problems a school may be experiencing. They may challenge teachers to examine their day-to-day routine and question basic reflex responses. Acknowledging that a school may have limited power to cover the child's broader excesses of behaviour, some experts choose to complement school sessions with seminars for parents, offering guidelines on establishing clear unequivocal boundaries for unruly adolescents. It is about creating a broad positive ethos that is sustained over time. Inevitably, different organizations vary in their approach. (See Box 2.2.4)

BOX 2.2.2 THE PHOENIX

The Phoenix at St Matthew's in Manchester caters for no more than ten pupils from Years 7 to 11, some full time, some mornings only, some coming in simply to register. No pupil stays longer than two terms. Although the Phoenix focuses on developing social skills, relationships and pupils managing their own behaviours, it is staffed by mainstream teachers across the curriculum and is integral to the whole-school provision. There's a clear admissions policy, as well as step-by-step reintegration into mainstream. Classroom teachers who make referrals are involved in the whole process.

Source: 'The Issue', *Times Educational Supplement*, 6 December 2002. p. 17. Elaine Williams, Behaviour: Part 3.

BOX 2.2.3 JOHN MASEFIELD HIGH SCHOOL

John Masefield High School includes a behavioural support unit which is called a learning intervention centre. It aims to support students who are struggling to cope with mainstream classes or who need intensive short-term emotional and behavioural support. It is also a staging-post for those returning to school following long-term illness, temporary exclusion or school refusal phobia. A small number of disaffected students who consistently disrupted classes were also helped with their education. However, it aims to enable all students to get back into full-time classes as quickly and successfully as possible. In the first year the Learning Intervention Centre (LIC) provided superb support for a group of very bright examination students who found the pressure and stress of mainstream too much. These youngsters use the centre's space to enable them to cope without resorting to truancy. In its second year the behaviour of the small group of disaffected boys visibly started to improve. They still demonstrated disruptive behaviour but had not been excluded.

Source: 'The Issue', *Times Educational Supplement*, 6 December 2002 p. 18.

BOX 2.2.4 EDUCATION WORKS

Education Works, a behavioural consultancy in Totnes works on a whole school level. Rob Long who runs the organization says 'if we are looking at why a particular type of behaviour is happening, it helps if everyone is trying to work collaboratively.' A school can invite Mr Long to run a training day. He will work together with a school to develop an Active Research Project and set up a review structure. He can provide In-Service Training, Staff Development, Project Work and Group Work on a range of topics. He has an excellent resource list.

Source: Times Educational Supplement, 7 February 2003.

■ HOME–SCHOOL SUPPORT WORKERS

Home–school workers provide support for some of the most challenging young people. They were piloted in a three-year project in Yorkshire comprehensives. By doing this, both exclusions and truancy rates were reduced and it was highly cost-effective. Five support staff – all trained social workers – were placed in seven relatively disadvantaged schools in North Yorkshire and the City of York. Each was given a caseload of up to ten pupils at a time, selected by the senior management mostly because of their behaviour. Three-quarters of the pupils had severe problems and half had offended. The support workers befriended the pupils, taught them to manage their anger and tried to improve their self-esteem and relationship with others. They also supported their families and stepped in immediately to help with crises in school that could lead to exclusion. Over three years, they helped 208 challenging pupils, nearly two-thirds of whom were boys. Half were in Years 9 and 10. Senior managers at school estimated that they had reduced the exclusion rates by 25 per cent over the three-year period. The intervention of support staff led to a sharp reduction in the number of fixed-term exclusion for some pupils. However, the number of exclusions rose in the case of others who were coaxed back after long-term truancy and found it hard to readjust (Vulliamy and Webb, 2003).

■ BEHAVIOUR AND EDUCATION SUPPORT TEAMS

Behaviour and education support teams (BESTS) are teams that include education, social work and health professionals. They are part of the Behaviour Improvement Programme (BIP) announced by the government. Schools with a high proportion of pupils at risk of developing behaviour problems and dissatisfaction can access the services. Their purpose is to provide early intervention, therapeutic inputs and ongoing support for individual children and families, as well as supporting schools and pupil referral units in developing whole-school approaches for behaviour strategies and training staff in promoting emotional well-being.

CIRCLE TIME

WHAT IS CIRCLE TIME?

Circle Time is a time set aside each week in which teachers and young people sit in a circle and take part in activities, games and discussion. It usually lasts for about 20–30 minutes, and provides a useful forum for the discussion of important issues including peer relationships, democratic principles, friendships, justice and individual freedom. The positive atmosphere that is generated in a well-managed Circle usually spreads into other areas of curriculum activity. Circle Time gives young people the opportunity to discuss matters of personal concern, to explore relationships with adults and peers, to develop a sense of being members of a community and to learn about the experience of reflection and silence. The method is highly relevant to the prevention of mental health difficulties. For example, where the focus of discussion concerns bullying, the ground rule would be that the Circle addresses the item of behaviour and not the participants themselves. Circle Time encourages group members to listen to one another, to learn to take turns, to give and receive affirmation, to discuss difficult issues from a problem-solving stance and to keep to the rules – rules that *they* have played a part in forming.

Circle Time is often highly structured with each pupil being invited to speak without interruption on a particular topic, sometimes with the help of an object that is passed around. Those who do not want to contribute simply say 'pass'. Such a structure encourages vocal pupils to wait their turn and to stick to the theme, rather than react impulsively to the previous statement, while providing quieter pupils with a safe and productive environment in which to speak.

Although Circle Time was originally developed in primary schools, Mosley (1988) and Tew (1998) report very positive feedback from young people and staff about the effectiveness of Quality Circle Time in the secondary school context. Outcomes include the following:

- enhanced communication among members of a class group;
- affirmation of the strengths of each member of the group;
- creation of a safe space in which to explore personal issues of difficulty experienced by members of that group.

The following case study is an example of how one secondary school used Circle Time alongside its existing practices to develop a new intervention in collaboration with an outside agency for enhancing pro-social behaviour among pupils.

CASE STUDY 2.2.1 RALPH ALLEN SECONDARY SCHOOL

Ralph Allen Secondary School started a programme to introduce Quality Circle Time into the school. There was a concern in the school to build on their successful systems by introducing interactive work in the classroom specifically designed to develop pupils' capacity to reflect on their own behaviour, to learn to regulate their own behaviour, to become tolerant of one anothers' behaviour and to gain the experience of discussing interpersonal issues in a supportive group. Jenny Mosley Consultancy ran the initial training in Quality Circle Time with Year 7 tutors:

> *The training was organized and I think it was good training. We had a whole morning of something here and I wouldn't have liked to have done it without the training, I wouldn't like to have done it without seeing someone who was versed in it do it first. (Teacher)*

As the following extracts from parents and teachers indicate, there was evidence that Quality Circle Time was encouraging a significant number of young people to speak openly and confidently about interpersonal issues. None sat nervously with eyes averted. Conversation felt easy and enjoyable. Some young people who were uncooperative in lessons appeared to be cheerful in Quality Circle Time and showed the capacity to give accurate self-appraisals. The Circle also provided a safe arena for the fuller discussion of PSHE topics.

> *'It has been a brilliant classroom management strategy, particularly for a very difficult couple of members of my tutor group.' (Teacher)*

> *'It teaches children to listen to each other and to have patience and compassion.' (Teacher)*

> *'My son gained a lot from this in being able to discuss issues with other adults and his peers.' (Parent)*

> *'It builds understanding and awareness of what could be awkward or uncomfortable subjects.' (Parent)*

Quality Circle Time in this school appeared to provide a useful structure for enabling some children who otherwise might contribute little to school to have a voice and, therefore, to be less likely to become disaffected.

> *I can think of one child in my group that circle time has given him more confidence. He was really very, very weak and he has really shone. He has gained confidence in his tutor group and has since become less disaffected. (Teacher)*

Teachers were confident that, as more of the school became involved in Quality Circle Time, there would be an increased sense of community and some were planning ahead to use Quality Circle Time with young people whose behaviour was disruptive.

> *There is a child who has not spoken all year but has spoken in circle time. (Healthy School Co-ordinator)*

WHO NEEDS TO BE INVOLVED?

Circle Time requires full backing of the senior management team, and an enthusiastic senior teacher to co-ordinate the scheme. The school needs to have a discipline structure already in place. Circle Time can become widely used in school by both pupils and teachers, but it may need to be introduced gradually, starting with the youngest pupils who may well have experienced it in their first schools.

It may be necessary to provide additional support to particular teachers who find the skills of facilitation and handling of group dynamics different from the usual skills required in a classroom. The charismatic teachers who naturally find class discipline easy may be more prepared to make the shift into the different dynamics of Circle Time.

It is important that the staff who feel vulnerable and challenged by the differing class format are given a regular place to air their concerns, probably on a monthly basis. There is good backup literature supplied by Jenny Mosley Consultancies (Mosley, 1998), White (1992; 1999) and Bliss, Robinson and Maine (1996). Jenny Mosley (1996) has written extensively about Circle Time and developed 'Quality Circle Time'.

HOW LONG SHOULD CIRCLE TIME LAST?

This particular intervention is not short-term, but aims to become integral to whole-school functioning. As with most interventions in school, it is important that a review date is set into the initial planning of the intervention.

BENEFITS OF CIRCLE TIME

There are major gains to be had from introducing Circle Time into a secondary school. By increasing the sense of belonging and community throughout a school the method can make the school's aims – academic, emotional and social – much more achievable. Our own evaluation of Quality Circle Time indicated largely positive outcomes:

- young people became better listeners;
- quieter pupils were more able to develop and air their views in the group;
- the Circle was a good arena for addressing interpersonal issues among young people;
- the Circle provided a helpful forum for pupils who might otherwise externalise their personal issues through disruptive behaviour.

If the circle works well and the group dynamics are positive the benefits can be great including positive peer pressure, improved discipline within the group, increased sense of community and possibly therefore improved performance in class. As more of the school becomes involved in circle time the increased sense of community enables the aims of the school to be more readily achieved.

■ POTENTIAL PROBLEMS

Circle Time initially requires high-quality training and support. It is essential for the facilitators to be skilled and confident in their understanding of group dynamics since the quality of the group experience is strongly influenced by the nature of the interaction between facilitator and pupils.

Discipline is an issue and Circles will work best where the school ethos and atmosphere encourages respect and value for each individual. Low-level disruption is probably the biggest challenge.

Backup support is viewed as expensive and time-consuming and, therefore, is not regularly arranged. However, it could turn a mediocre circle which is a struggle into a positive experience

A key issue concerns how the facilitator deals with sensitive disclosures on the part of the members. Talk time (developed by Jenny Mosley Consultancies) can be established as a type of follow-up arrangement for issues raised in Circle Time. If the young people are encouraged to contribute, they need to be certain that there is a safety net so that disclosures by an individual can be picked up and supported.

There can be practical issues of how to arrange the chairs in a circle in some classrooms.

■ COST

There is an initial training cost. Jenny Mosley Consultancies, for example, charge £600–£1,000 for a day. It will take one school training day for the set up which has an obvious cost not only in time, but in that there are always significant competing demands for this time. There are ongoing time implications in adapting the PSHE material for use, and in providing support for the facilitators. Jenny Mosley Consultancies is available for further refresher courses or advice. There is a cost for this (See Box 2.2.5).

SUMMARY

Young people, who feel isolated by society and angry towards authority, present considerable difficulties within the school community. There are a number of strategies which schools can employ to engage these students. Circle Time requires a good discipline structure but can encourage each member of the school community to have a voice.

RESOURCES

Ballard, J. (1982) *Circlebook.* New York: Irvington Inc.

Bliss, T., Robinson, G. and Maines, B. (1996) *Developing Circle Time.* Bristol: Lucky Duck Publishing.

Education Works, Rob Long, tel: 01803 866745.

Jenny Mosley Consultancies, 8 Westbourne Road, Trowbridge, Wiltshire BA14 0AJ.

Lucky Duck Publishing Ltd, 3 Thorndale Mews, Clifton, Bristol BS8 2HX.

Mosley, J. (1996) *Quality Circle Time.* Cambridge: LDA.

www.rsa.org.uk/newcurriculum is a website citing co-operative group learning, a Royal Society of the Arts pilot project.

White, M. (1992) *Self-esteem, its Meaning and Value in Schools.* Bristol: Daniels Publishing.

White, M. (1999) *Magic Circles.* Bristol: Lucky Duck Publishing.

BOX 2.2.5 HOW TO DO CIRCLE TIME

Preparation

- Research Circle Time resources, e.g. Quality Circle Time from Jenny Mosley Consultancies.
- The discipline structure in the school needs to be good.
- A key person with support from the senior management team needs to be involved.
- The introduction of Circle Time needs to be well thought out and planned.
- Resource materials need to be adapted appropriately.

Training

- Various consultancies offer in-house training and support (see resources list).
- All staff need to be involved in initial training.
- Backup and a review need to be set up prior to the introduction of the intervention.

Implementation

- The Circle would run each week for 20–30 minutes.
- Techniques could include passing round an object.
- Everyone sits in a circle.
- Staff are facilitators in this situation rather than 'teachers'.
- Clear boundaries of trust need to be built so that the personal things said in the circle do not become playground gossip.

Cost

- Preparation time for the key worker.
- Cost for the consultancy training.
- INSET training-day time.
- Cost for the time for ongoing supervision.

CHAPTER 2.3

Violent Behaviours

Children have the right to be educated in a safe environment and every member of the school community is equally entitled to that right. (Varnava, 2002, p. 3)

WHAT BEHAVIOURS ARE WE TALKING ABOUT IN THIS CHAPTER?

Despite anecdotal evidence, for example, in the media and on telephone helplines such as ChildLine, the subject of violence in schools has received little academic research interest to date. However, in extreme circumstances, for example, the killing of Philip Laurence and the Dunblane massacre, violence in schools receives a high media profile. With the exception of one or two studies, school bullying, a subset of violent behaviour, has tended to dominate research on violence in schools (for an overview see Cowie and Smith, 2001). Indeed, a report by Cowie, Jennifer and Sharp (2002), concludes that, at the present time, there is little in the way of agreed definitions or descriptions of school violence in the UK, no systematic collection of school violence statistics and little research into the nature and prevalence of violence.

An extensive literature search yields little in the way of definitions or descriptions of violence in either statistics or school regulations. However, definitions and descriptions from other sources include the following:

> *where the actor or perpetrator uses his or her own body or an object (including a weapon) to inflict (relatively serious) injury or discomfort upon another individual.* (Olweus, 1999, p. 12)

> *Violence may be expressed in the form of physical, psychological or structural abuses of power, the perpetrators may be individuals or organisations, the victims may be*

individuals, objects or organisations, the nature of the damage may be material, physical or psychological, the consequences may be or may not be premeditated, the context may or may not be legitimate ... (Vettenburg, 1999, p. 29).

Youth violence is defined as behaviour that is intended to cause, and that actually causes, physical or psychological injury, and that is committed by persons aged roughly between ages 10 and 21. (Farrington, 2002, p. 13)

According to Vettenburg (1999), the diversity of definitions suggests that violence does not fall into a discrete category, rather it is a matter of social construction, with meaning varying according to the individuals, culture and environment concerned. The term 'bullying' is usually defined as a subset of aggressive behaviour, which includes verbal aggression and relational/indirect aggression, characterized by repetition over time and an imbalance of power (Olweus, 1999) (see Chapter 2.4).

Large-scale studies show that:

- being physically hurt is experienced by over one-quarter of pupils (Whitney and Smith, 1993);

- around 20 per cent of girls, aged 13–18 years, have been violently attacked (Katz et al., 2001);

- 67 per cent of pupils engage in pushing and 38 per cent engage in punching (Glover et al., 2000);

- 83 per cent of teachers thought that violence was a serious threat to staff morale (Gill and Hearnshaw, 1997);

- 40 per cent considered that schools were no longer safe places in which to work (Gill and Hearnshaw, 1997);

- 16 per cent of schools reported pupils assaulting staff in terms of spitting, pushing and unwanted touching (Gill and Hearnshaw, 1997);

- 19 per cent of schools reported pupils assaulting staff in terms of hitting, punching or kicking (Gill and Hearnshaw, 1997).

In response to recent concern about disruption in schools, the National Union of Teachers (NUT) commissioned a survey of its members in England and Wales entitled *Unacceptable Pupil Behaviour* (Neill, 2001). A total of 2,575 questionnaires, representing the composition of the teaching force in general, were returned. The most frequent of the serious problems witnessed by teachers were threats of pupil–pupil violence, with 83 per cent of teachers reporting this at least once a year and 43 per cent on a weekly basis. Regarding threats of physical violence to themselves, 34 per cent of teachers personally experienced this from a pupil at least once a year and 5 per cent from parents. Pushing, touching or other unwanted physical contact was personally experienced by 37 per cent of teachers at least once a year and by 9 per cent of teachers weekly; this was greater in secondary schools.

The World Health Organization (WHO) (1999) suggests that factors that contribute to violent behaviour include individual characteristics, family characteristics and economic and societal characteristics. This framework is supported by research conducted into school bullying and violence and one or two studies on violence in schools (for example, Farrington, 2002; Smith and Sharp, 1994). Farrington proposes a risk and protective factors framework related to youth violence. Risk factors are variables that predict a high rate of youth violence. While they do not cause violence, the presence of a higher number of risk factors increases the potential for violence. Protective factors act to protect an individual from offending (Farrington, 2002). The major long-term risk factors are:

- psychological (high impulsiveness and low intelligence);
- family (poor supervision, harsh discipline, child physical abuse, a violent parent, large family size, a broken family);
- peer delinquency;
- low socio-economic status;
- urban residence;
- residing in a high crime neighbourhood (Farrington, 2002).

Short-term risk factors include alcohol consumption and actions leading to violent events, for example, the escalation of a trivial altercation (Farrington, 2002).

WHAT BENEFITS ARE THERE TO BE GAINED BY ADDRESSING VIOLENT BEHAVIOURS?

The World Health Organization (WHO, 1999) suggests that 'Violence affects everyone'. Not only does it undermine the health, learning potential and economic well-being of young people, staff and community members, but 'reducing and preventing violence is necessary to help schools achieve their full potential' (WHO, 1999, p. 3).

More specifically, from the perspective of the staff and organization as a whole, reducing violent behaviour in turn reduces disruption, creates a safe school environment and supports the authority of the school staff (Hayden and Blaya, 2001). A safe learning environment supports pupil participation and interaction with teachers. It can also decrease tension between staff, decrease workloads, improve the utilization of resources and decrease disruption to the teaching and learning process (Glover et al., 2000; Hayden and Blaya, 2001; Neill, 2001). It may also prevent teachers from leaving the profession altogether (Neill, 2001).

From the pupil's perspective, research suggests that a safe learning environment supports pupil participation and interaction with teachers (Turunen et al., 1999). In turn, positive peer relations in school, operationalized in the school playground, are linked with adjustment to school life generally and with academic success (Coie and Dodge, 1998; Pellegrini and Blatchford, 2002). However, academic achievement and positive peer relations are not the only factors to be considered; if violence prevention enables children and young people to function more effectively and develop within the school context, then not only do they benefit individually, but the school and the community must surely also benefit (Watt and Higgins, 1999).

WHAT ARE THE POSSIBLE INTERVENTIONS?

Interventions currently in place around the country, specifically relevant to the promotion of non-violence in schools, include a wide range of approaches, such as conflict resolution and peer mediation, school award schemes, health-promoting school schemes, anger management programmes and self-auditing tools.

'Checkpoints' is a series of publications aimed to facilitate the promotion of non-violence in schools. They include *Towards a Non-Violent Society: Checkpoints For Schools* (Varnava, 2000) and *Towards a Non-Violent Society: Checkpoints For Young People* (Varnava, 2002), and can be accessed on Sage Publications' website www.sagepub.co.uk. 'Checkpoints' is a self-help tool with three main functions: to raise awareness, to facilitate institutional self-audit and to offer guidance. The use of 'Checkpoints' leads to the formulation of assessment criteria by which the school's progress in behaviour management can be measured. This is achieved through the use of a framework representing the main aspects of school life: home/school/community; values; organization; environment; curriculum; and training. It includes a web diagram which, when completed, illustrates a school's strengths in violence prevention and highlights areas where further action may be taken. Case study 2.3.1 describes how one school addressed the issues of bullying and violent behaviour using this approach.

Working in partnership with schools, the *Conflict Resolution in Schools Programme* (CRISP) currently operates across Leicestershire offering a peer mediation package which empowers young people with the skills to effectively manage human conflict, and provide a safer supportive learning environment. CRISP can deliver both staff in-service (INSET) training and PSHE training for young people, and recruit and train peer mediators. Results suggests that, in

CASE STUDY 2.3.1 CHECKPOINTS FOR SCHOOLS

This large, inner-city secondary school held its annual one-day Student Council Conference on the topic of 'Taking practical steps to make the school a safer, happier place with improved facilities'. The conference included an introduction to *'Checkpoints For Schools'* followed by group discussions, comprising a mix of young people across all year groups, using Checkpoints. A post-16 student facilitated each group. Each discussion group was invited to make three recommendations for an overhead projector (OHP) presentation on the practical steps to make the school a happier, safer place. These were debated and key recommendations put to the Principal for further consideration and action. Key recommendations included:

- improvement in communication channels among young people, staff, parents and local community;
- provision of staff training to deal with bullying and violent behaviours;
- regular profiling of Anti-Bullying Policy and Code of Conduct to all members of the school community, including parents and application of sanctions when necessary;
- provision of alternative areas on the school site for recreation – more available space would ultimately lead to reduced tension and aggression;
- installation of closed-circuit television (CCTV) systems in 'hot spots' such as locker areas and the library;
- refurbishment of school buildings.

The conference provided an ideal opportunity to engage young people in the first stages of the school's strategy to address bullying and violent behaviour. Student involvement and commitment greatly increase the chances of success.

Source: Varnava, 2002b.

schools where peer mediation is allowed to flourish, as well as providing an effective arena to resolve conflicts, it contributes to increased student responsibility, increased emotional literacy and ability to maintain stable relationships (Bitel, 2000). Cunningham et al. (1998) conclude that as a relatively low-cost intervention, it merits wider use as part of an anti-violence school programme.

ChildLine in Partnership with Schools (CHIPS) was introduced into secondary schools in England, Scotland and Wales in October 1997 and, to date, in excess of 1,000 schools are involved. CHIPS is a partnership between ChildLine, young people and schools, the aim of which is to raise awareness about ChildLine and to encourage schools to support their pupils in setting up projects run by and for pupils in tackling issues that affect their lives, such as bullying and violence. CHIPS endorses the view that young people can help one another, that they have a right to be heard, especially with regard to key issues in their lives, and that they can play an important part in making changes to improve the quality of their own lives. CHIPS initiatives include national conferences, awareness days and resources for PSHE and Citizenship lessons. Many schools request training from CHIPS on how to set up peer support systems to strengthen their anti-bullying policies (ChildLine, 2000). Case study 2.3.2 illustrates how one school set up a peer support system.

CASE STUDY 2.3.2 CHIPS

Golborne High School was experiencing incidents of bullying which resulted in a group of staff, young people and a governor attending a ChildLine conference where they learnt more about peer support schemes. A decision was made to start their own peer support scheme using the ChildLine publication *Setting Up a Peer Support Scheme* (2002). The school started by working with groups of young people and staff to identify a suitable scheme and draw up an action plan. A 'Buddies Scheme' was decided upon and marketed through displays and presentations at assemblies and in classrooms to attract potential buddies. Buddies were recruited through a selection process and successful applicants and their parents were notified. Buddies, trained by ChildLine, were introduced to the rest of the school at assemblies and through a noticeboard of photographs so that they could be easily identified in school. An ongoing monitoring, review and evaluation of the scheme was put in place and the scheme has developed as a rolling programme; each year new buddies are trained. The school has since received a Healthy Schools Award for emotional well-being.

LEAP CONFRONTING CONFLICT

Leap Confronting Conflict was founded by The Leaveners (a Quaker community arts charity) in 1987, to explore, through the use of drama and group work, the causes and consequences of conflict and violence in young people's lives. Through interactive group work and active participation, *Leap* trained facilitators use a range of contemporary art forms that is both challenging and well supported. One of *Leap*'s aims is to ensure that the active processes of conflict resolution and mediation lie at the heart of all personal and social education for young people. To this end, *Leap* have developed the Confronting Conflict in Schools training programme, which provides young people with a range of opportunities for addressing the conflicts that arise in their own school. The following describes how one school addressed extreme racial tension and conflict that was undermining the emotional well-being of the whole-school community and causing widespread fear, anxiety and stress among staff, pupils and parents.

In the early 1990s Morpeth School, situated in the London Borough of Tower Hamlets in the heart of London's East End, went through a period where violence and conflict, heightened by racial tension, were creating a climate of fear and anxiety among staff and pupils, and preventing young people from achieving their potential. Examination results were among the poorest in the borough, much staff time and energy were required to maintain order and morale was falling. A white boy had been stabbed in school by two Bengali boys. Young people were afraid as they moved from lesson to lesson. Finally, a mini-riot in a local shopping centre, involving pupils, prompted the senior management team, for the sake of the mental health of the whole-school community, to move from a reactive position as far as behaviour management was concerned to a more proactive stance. Their aims were to:

- reduce racial tension in the school;
- ensure that young people and staff became more aware of conflict issues and acquired a range of skills for dealing with them;
- create a more positive school ethos that enhanced the emotional health and well-being of young people and staff.

To this end, they called in the help of *Leap* Confronting Conflict.

WHO NEEDS TO BE INVOLVED IN *LEAP*?

The programme aims to ensure that young people and staff become more aware of conflict issues and acquire the skills for dealing with them through an understanding of the causes of conflict, working with diversity, working in teams, and learning communication and negotiation skills.

The principles underpinning the *Leap* Confronting Conflict programme are based on a desire to include as many young people and staff as possible in a clearly structured programme. In this way the programme aims to ensure that young people and staff become more aware of conflict issues and acquire the skills for dealing with them through an understanding of the causes of conflict, working with diversity, working in teams, and learning communication and negotiation skills. Participation in the programme changes the ethos of the school through:

- older young people being given valued training and meaningful responsibilities;
- older young people becoming respected role models to younger young people;
- the build-up of self-esteem and self-confidence among young people;
- an impact on staff understanding of conflict issues and the use of new skills;
- enhancing the learning potential of the school as a healthy community;

■ clearly embedding the values of the school in the training process.

COSTS – OVERT AND HIDDEN

Autumn term	Residential weekend and administration	£6,600
Spring term	Leadership workshops	£11,000
Summer term	Workshops and administration	£10,000

In addition to these overt costs, there were other costs in terms of taking young people and staff off timetable to allow them to participate in training, staff time in terms of organization and administration of the intervention, and student time in terms of participating in training outside of school hours at residential weekends.

HOW LONG SHOULD *LEAP* LAST?

After an initial conflict, audit carried out by *Leap* staff, a three-year programme ran from 1994 to 1997. A further programme ran from 1998 to 1999. Since then the project has continued to evolve year by year. Currently, the programme includes the following strands:

- In the summer term, all tutor groups in Year 9, and their tutors, receive one-day training from *Leap*.
- Following the training, Year 9 young people are invited to volunteer for further training to become peer trainers in Year 10.
- A group of 20 Year 10 young people are selected by the senior management team to attend an intensive weekend residential training that is also attended by staff volunteers. The training includes further conflict resolution skills and facilitation skills.
- The trained Year 10 group delivers training workshops to Year 7 young people, supported by members of staff and *Leap* facilitators.
- Year 10 young people have an opportunity to attend a second residential weekend in Leadership Skills, that includes training in conflict resolution and peer mediation.

BENEFITS OF *LEAP*

An evaluation of the *Leap* Confronting Conflict programme at Morpeth School has recently been conducted as part of a wider report on the 'Evaluation of Tower Hamlets Conflict Resolution Project' (Inman and Turner, 2001). This included a review of school documentation, semi-structured interviews with staff and young people and

Leap facilitators, and observations. Our own interviews with staff, *Leap* facilitators and pupils came to similar conclusions. Benefits included:

- a positive change in school culture and ethos;
- a significant reduction of high-level conflict previously experienced by both young people and staff, with bullying less likely to escalate into physical violence;
- staff feeling less threatened by conflicts when they do occur and more confident in dealing with them;
- greater self-confidence among young people to take responsibility for their behaviour and achievement;
- an increase in annual attendance rates year on year since 1995;
- a fall in the number of permanent exclusions since 1995/96;
- general improvement in GCSE examination results year on year since 1996.

Those interviewed, who knew about the programme, generally agreed that it worked. The Headteacher had no doubt that the programme contributed to the positive ethos of the school. Others saw an increase in student self-esteem, self-confidence and responsibility: 'It makes us kind of responsible and trustworthy because they [other young people] can come up to us and tell us their problems' (ex-Year 11 seniors); 'it is a way of getting pupils who may have had a bad press, behaviour issues … it is a way of involving everyone' (Deputy Headteacher).

POSSIBLE PROBLEMS

- Racial tension was at a high level both within the school and outside in the community; this was a very challenging issue to confront. The particular approach of *Leap* was felt to be especially appropriate since, before any intervention begins, *Leap* carries out a full process of consultation within the school. Based on their initial conflict audit, the *Leap* team designs a purpose-built peer education/mediation approach.
- To ensure success, the *Leap* Confronting Conflict programme must become an integral part of the whole school development process rather than an 'add on'.
- The financial cost of the intervention was high. However, the senior management team decided that, in the light of the seriousness of the issue, they would make that financial investment. The long-term nature of the intervention requires funds to be available on an ongoing basis.

- The long-term nature of the intervention involves a need to keep the initial momentum going in terms of public relations (PR) and marketing. For example, several interviewees commented on the lack of involvement in the scheme among some staff and new staff had not been inducted into the programme of training. Surprisingly, neither the Joint Special Educational Needs Co-ordinator, the School Counsellor nor the Lunchtime Supervisor had any knowledge of the intervention, indicating the need to monitor how communication is channelled throughout the school. As we saw in Case study 2.3.1, young people themselves identified communication as a key factor in the promotion of non-violence. In addition, there were some difficulties in establishing a higher profile within the wider community.

- Levels of involvement in the programme result in different levels of understanding of the programme. For example, those members of staff who have attended one-day workshops with their tutor group or volunteered for the intensive weekend have a better understanding of the programme than those staff who have not been involved.

- Staff and young people who had participated in an intensive weekend or those who were involved with the project on a day-to-day basis all mentioned commitment as an issue.

- There were some perceived threats to staff by the presence of external facilitators and to young people by the presence of tutors during training workshops. This suggests a lack of trust and possibly some defensiveness around the sensitive issues of violence and race.

BOX 2.3.1 HOW TO INSTIGATE *LEAP*

- *Start the discussion*: form a working group; identify a project facilitator.
- *Identify where you are now*: carry out a needs analysis as described in Chapter 1.6.
- *Plan of action*: define priorities and targets based on the needs analysis; identify costs and resources required; identify a timescale.
- *Identify and develop an intervention*: identify possible interventions; consult with outside agencies.
- *Review and evaluate*: monitoring and evaluation should be incorporated into the planning process.

SUMMARY

- In this chapter we have been talking about violent behaviour that causes physical or psychological harm.

- Reducing and preventing violent behaviour in school is necessary to enable young people and staff to learn and teach in a safe environment thus allowing schools to achieve their full potential.

- Possible interventions include a wide range of approaches, such as, conflict resolution and peer mediation, school award schemes, health-promoting school schemes, anger management programmes and self-auditing tools.

- *Leap* Confronting Conflict use drama and group work to explore the causes and consequences of conflict and violence in young people's lives. Its aim is to ensure that the active process of conflict resolution and mediation lie at the heart of all personal and social education for young people.

- To ensure success, the *Leap* Confronting Conflict approach must become an integral part of the whole-school development process rather than an 'add on'.

- The benefits of this approach include a significant reduction of high-level conflict and a positive change in school culture and ethos.

RESOURCES

ChildLine (2002) *Setting Up a Peer Support Scheme: Ideas for Teachers and Other Professionals Setting Up and Supporting a Peer Support Scheme.* London: ChildLine, 45 Folgate Street, London, E1 6GL.

CHIPS, ChildLine, 45 Folgate Street, London, E1 6GL. Tel: 020 7650 3231. Also at www.childline.org.uk

CRISP, Leicestershire Mediation Service, 7th Floor, Epic House, Charles Street, Leicester, LE1 3SG. Tel: 0116 253 2900. Also at www.leicestershiremediation.co.uk

Leap Confronting Conflict, The Leap Centre, 8 Lennox Road, London, N4 3NW. Tel: 020 7272 5630. Also at www.leaplinx.com

www.peersupport.co.uk This is the site of the Peer Support Networker, the newsletter of the Peer Support Forum: www.ncb.org.uk.psf/. The site provides a forum for the exchange of ideas on peer support, for the review of interventions to address the problem of bullying whether in schools or the workplace, for making links with other people who have a shared interest in this area, for hearing about training opportunities in peer support and for reading about the latest research updates in the field.

www.ukobservatory.com This site carries information about the work of the UK Observatory for the Promotion of Non-Violence and disseminates information about current research. The UK Observatory offers a unique combination of experts in research, practice and training from a range of disciplines, all committed to addressing the issue of violence in education. The UK Observatory benefits and informs not only teachers and local education authorities but also policy-makers in the UK.

Bullying Behaviours

'I pound the pillow at night because I have no-one to talk to.' (Laura, a 12-year-old bullied pupil)

'Most people don't tell anyone when they are being bullied. They try to keep quiet. It's their reputation'. (James, a 13-year-old bystander)

'They (the bullies) say, "If you tell, you're going to get twice the beating" … ' (Ben, a 13-year-old bullied pupil)

WHAT BEHAVIOURS ARE WE TALKING ABOUT?

A substantial proportion of school pupils are involved in bully–victim relationships; in these, one or more bullies deliberately hurt another peer, the victim, over a period of time, and the victim is not able to defend him- or herself. Olweus (1999, p. 12) views bullying as a subcategory of aggression or aggressive behaviour with 'certain special characteristics such as repetitiveness and an asymmetric power relationship' (meaning that the victim is unable to defend him- or herself). Bullying is particularly unpleasant since it is directed at vulnerable people who are usually unable to defend themselves. Bullied children may be outnumbered, or be younger, weaker or simply less confident. Some bullying is carried out by physical means, for example, hitting, kicking and pushing; but a great deal is expressed without violence, for example, bullying with words and gestures, and through deliberate social exclusion.

The commonest type of bullying (Table 2.4.1) is name-calling, followed by being hit, threatened or having rumours spread about one. Bullying starts young, with around 27 per cent of primary school children and 10 per cent of secondary school pupils reporting that they are being bullied 'sometimes or more frequently' at any given time. So far as reporting taking part in bullying others is concerned, around 12 per cent of primary school pupils and 6 per cent of secondary pupils admit to bullying others 'sometimes or more frequently' (Smith, 1999). Such bullying can have severe consequences for all concerned, including even the onlookers to bullying events.

TABLE 2.4.1 COMMON FORMS OF BULLYING

Physical violence
Threats
Verbal (name-calling, sarcasm, spreading rumours, persistent teasing)
Emotional (excluding from a group, tormenting, ridicule, humiliation)
Racist (taunts, graffiti, gestures)
Sexual (unwanted physical contact, abusive comments)

PARTICIPANT ROLES IN BULLYING

Based on peer nominations (that is, asking young people to nominate peers who are bullies, victims, bystanders and so on), Salmivalli et al., (1996) found that 87 per cent of the pupils participated in some way when a bullying episode occurred (Table 2.4.2). The most common types of participants are 'assistants' who physically help the bully, 'reinforcers' who incite the bully, 'outsiders' who remain inactive and pretend not to see what is happening and 'defenders' who provide help for the victim and confront the bully (see the case of Sonia, Case study 2.4.1). This approach looks beyond the individual aggressive child and his or her behaviour, to the social system within which the aggressive acts take place. From this perspective, bullying is a group phenomenon in which a wide range of pupils is involved whether directly or indirectly. If adults focus only on individual bullies and victims they may find it difficult to effect much change. It is useful for adults to understand the different parts that pupils can play within a bullying situation in order to design effective interventions. Using the Participant Role Scales (for details see Sharp, 1999) Salmivalli (1998) assigned different types of behaviour to each role (Table 2.4.2).

TABLE 2.4.2 SALMIVALLI'S PARTICIPANT ROLES IN BULLYING

Bully: leading and initiating bullying behaviour, actively involved
Assistant: becoming actively involved at the instigation of others, supporting the bully
Reinforcer: providing those directly involved in bullying with positive feedback, for example, acting as an audience or laughing at the victim
Victim: frequent target of bullying behaviour
Defender: providing direct or indirect support to the victimised pupil, trying to stop the bullying
Outsider: withdrawing from bullying situations

Source: adapted from Sharp, 1999, p. 21.

Once these participant roles have been identified, the teacher can map out the bullying relationships within the class and then plan appropriate interventions. For example, if the bullying is confined to a small number of pupils, it may be useful to use the No Blame Approach advocated by Robinson and Maines (1997). If a larger number of pupils are involved, it may be useful to use curriculum-based anti-bullying work in PSHE lessons in order to increase the defending work of pupils who are not directly involved as bullies or as victims. Again, where there is a peer support system in place, it may be helpful to invite peer supporters to work with the class using class discussions or drama workshops, or to use conflict resolution techniques to mediate between bully and victim.

CASE STUDY 2.4.1 SONIA, A DEFENDER

Sonia was a popular and happy girl at primary school. She was successful at her work. Unfortunately, she was the only girl who went from her primary class to her new secondary school. She appeared a little shy at first and was targeted by a group of domineering girls who had all known one another in Year 6. Sonia was a resilient girl who quickly dealt with the problem with the help of peer supporters in the school who encouraged her to join a group of girls where she found that she was valued for her qualities of friendship and loyalty. She soon became a popular member of this group who worked well in class and who met often after school. However, she felt that she would like to repay what she had gained from her experience of being helped. Her empathy for victims was high and she had a strong wish to play an active part in creating a more friendly and co-operative climate in her school. In Year 8 she applied to become a peer supporter and was trained in active listening skills. Her first task was to take part in drama workshops designed to help integrate pupils from primary school as they made the transition to secondary school. She valued the social skills that she learned and discovered that she had a real aptitude for caring. She decided that she would aim for a career in medicine.

VICTIMS

Some victimized children unwittingly contribute to the problem, for example by overreacting in ways that only reinforce the bully's standing in the social group, since some onlookers may enjoy watching another's discomfort and humiliation. Some victimized children are passive and withdrawn and virtually never attack other children, whereas other victimized children are socially active, disruptive and sometimes even highly aggressive. Olweus (1999) labelled children who are high on both aggression and victimization as 'provocative victims' (also called 'bully/victims') and labelled children who are victimized but not aggressive as 'passive victims'.

Salmivalli et al. (1996) focused on victimized pupils' reactions to harassment, using both peer- and self-evaluations as methods of study. One issue was: what behaviour on the part of the victims is likely to (a) make the others start or continue bullying or (b) diminish bullying or put an end to it. Three different subtypes of victims were identified, through peer evaluation (the victims' self-evaluations of their behaviour supported these views): the *counter-aggressive*, the *helpless* and the *nonchalant*. Helplessness and nonchalance were found to be typical responses of the girl victims, while boy victims tended to react to bullying with counter-aggression or nonchalance. Helplessness and counter-aggression in the case of girl victims and counter-aggression in the case of boy victims were perceived as making the bullying start or continue. The absence of helplessness in the case of girl victims, and nonchalance as well as the absence of counter-aggression in the case of boy victims were perceived as making bullying diminish or stop.

CASE STUDY 2.4.2 CLAIRE, A COUNTER-AGGRESSIVE VICTIM

Claire is small in stature and complains frequently that she is being bullied. She finds it hard to think of anything positive to say about her classmates, has no one that she likes to work with and is frequently on her own during break time. Her conversation is dominated by references to quarrels and arguments with peers. She has tantrums regularly both in class when she finds the work too hard and in the playground when she is in conflict with peers. She says nasty things about other girls because, in her view, 'they annoy her first and it is not her fault'. At the same time, she readily admits that she likes to 'wind other people up' and that she often pushes in where she is not wanted. Recently Amira joined the class from another school and found it hard to make friends. Claire took pleasure in putting her down and in making rude comments about Amira's appearance. Classmates do not like Claire much since she is not a co-operative partner in group work and since she has a tendency to say spiteful things about them. She is rarely chosen to be a partner in teams.

▨ BULLIES

Perry et al. (1988) report that bullies are more likely than other peers to derive some sense of satisfaction and pleasure from their attacks on victims. They also tend to interpret ambiguous signals in hostile ways and more easily choose aggressive behaviour to solve social conflicts. As part of a longitudinal study of boys, Farrington (2002) reports inter-generational links. Fathers who were aggressive at school themselves are more likely to have sons who are in turn bullies. Many bullies and bully/victims perceive their families as lacking in warmth and affection, and report that monitoring of their behaviour is poor. Bullies tend to perceive their families in terms of power relationships with siblings and parents. There has been some debate about the social skills of bullies, with some literature suggesting that children who bully tend to be deficient in some aspects. However, Sutton et al. (1999) suggested that many children who bully are skilled manipulators, possessing good theory of mind abilities that enable them to organize a gang efficiently, use peers as lookouts and expertly avoid detection by teachers. The number and physical strength of perpetrators, and their social standing in the group, are factors that play a significant part in the appearance of bullying behaviour and influence the responses of bystanders towards the victim. Pressures from the peer group can also influence the extent to which pupils are able or willing to seek out help when they are being bullied.

The social culture of the school has a strong influence on whether pupils report bullying (O'Connell and Pepler, 1999). One factor may be the power of adults and peers to shift power differentials away from the bullies (Salmivalli et al., 1996). It can be difficult for peers to intervene to model pro-social behaviour on behalf of victims in these circumstances, and the planning of interventions is almost bound to fail if such social factors are not taken into account.

WHAT BENEFITS ARE TO BE GAINED BY TACKLING THE BEHAVIOURS?

One of the greatest benefits gained by tackling the problem is the creation of a school climate where it is acceptable to report bullying and to challenge it. Whitney and Smith (1993) found that around 50 per cent of bullied pupils claimed to have told neither a teacher nor a parent that they were being bullied. Pupils disclose that there are difficulties involved in telling someone that they are being bullied. Interviews with pupils suggest that the barriers to telling include fear of the bully's reaction, fear of peer hostility or indifference and the chosen strategy of 'coping on their own'. Researchers have proposed a number of explanations. Pupils may not always know that they are being bullied, for example, when they are socially excluded. Even when they are aware of being bullied, they may fear further retaliation from their tormentors, they may anticipate ridicule from peers, or they may have no faith in the support systems in their school or at home. Craig and Pepler (1995) identified a discrepancy between young people's stated interest in helping victims and their actual behaviour. In their study, global ratings of peer behaviours indicated that peers were coded as showing more respect for bullies than for victims. O'Connell and Pepler (1999) suggest that the relative lack of intervention on the part of bystanders may reinforce the bullies' behaviour, and it may signal to victims an accurate lack of sympathy for their plight.

Many bullied pupils who tell someone – whether parent, teacher or peer – about the problem report that it helps to share their problem with another person. They also claim that the process of talking gives them the strength to overcome the problem and that they appreciate having someone who cared (Cowie et al., 2002b; Naylor and Cowie, 1999). Naylor and Cowie (1999) investigated a sample of 52 schools with well-established anti-bullying policies and systems of peer support. They found that the pupils perceived these schools as being safer and they valued the fact that the staff cared about them enough to establish and support such systems. Furthermore, in these schools the proportion of victimized children – 14 per cent – who told no one of their plight was substantially lower than in other schools.

WHAT ARE THE POSSIBLE INTERVENTIONS?

THE WHOLE-SCHOOL POLICY

All schools are now required to have a whole-school policy on bullying that aims to create a climate in which pupils can trust adults to respond fairly and consistently to incidents when they occur and where there are clear sanctions against bullying. There are four main stages to establishing a policy (DfES, 2000):

- *Stage 1: awareness raising and consultation with adults and children in the school.* The agreed policy should be succinct and written in a language that all can understand. The anti-bullying policy should be consistent with the school's behaviour policy and there should be clear guidelines on sanctions, when they apply and how they will be implemented.

- *Stage 2: Implementation.* There should be a clear lead from senior managers. A launch involving the whole school is helpful. The policy should be applied with consistency and fairness while retaining a degree of flexibility for unusual circumstances. It should also be promoted regularly, for example in assemblies, tutor groups, projects and at collective worship. Direct action should remind pupils that bullying behaviour is unacceptable. Parents should be involved at an early stage when a bullying episode occurs.

- *Stage 3: Monitoring.* A key member of staff should be responsible for keeping records of bullying, following-up the implementation of the policy and giving it a prominent profile in the school.

- *Stage 4: Evaluation.* Data from monitoring and feedback provided by pupils, parents, teachers, non-teaching staff and governors should be used to review and update the policy at least once a year.

▓ CO-OPERATIVE VALUES

Teachers can promote co-operative values in the classroom that encourage pro-social behaviour and increase co-operative relationships based on trust; teachers should also know their students as individuals. Co-operative group work (CGW) is one method that can promote pro-social values as part of the learning process. It takes a number of forms: working individually but in a group, working individually on 'jigsaw' elements for a joint outcome or working jointly for a shared outcome. In essence teachers who use co-operative methods expect participants to show respect for others, to have empathy for their feelings, to be co-operative and democratic. More recently, the Department for Education and Skills (DfES) has issued guidelines on the teaching of 'Citizenship' to all pupils, with the aim of teaching young people to be active, responsible members of their community and, in the future, better parents.

▓ PEER SUPPORT

Another successful approach has been one that empowers pupils themselves to tackle bullying. Some peer support arises spontaneously, as Salmivalli and her colleagues discovered, where 'defenders' (more often girls) run for help or to comfort the victim, or where girls demonstrate constructive conflict-resolution abilities. In the wider context of the whole school, a critical factor would seem to lie with structures, such as peer support systems, which encourage a pro-social response on the part of onlookers and bystanders when the bullying takes place, often outside the classroom (Cowie and Wallace, 2000; Cowie et al., 2002b).

Peer support is a form of defending. It is a direct anti-bullying intervention where selected pupils are trained by adults to intervene in response to a request for help (Cowie and Wallace, 2000). Peer support systems use a number of approaches:

- befriending schemes – where peer supporters are trained to offer friendship or support informally, in everyday interactions with peers;

- mediation schemes – non-punitive intervention where peer supporters are trained to bring the bully and victim together to resolve a dispute (see Chapter 2.3);

- counselling-based schemes – a more structured system where support takes place in specially designated rooms, usually by appointment, and with regular supervision by adults;

- mentoring schemes – where older pupils are trained to offer encouragement and guidance through a one-to-one relationship with a younger pupil. This method has been adapted from mentoring schemes that involve adults from the community who work with young people to encourage them and offer advice (see also chapter 1.4).

While peer support schemes do not always reduce bullying, they can be an effective preventative measure. Above all, they reduce the negative impact of bullying on victims and make it more acceptable for them to report it. There are a number of reasons for this:

- Peers are able to detect bullying at a much earlier stage than adults could.

- Young people are more likely to confide in contemporaries than adults.

- Victims have someone to turn to and see the school taking action.

- Peer supporters gain confidence and valuable social skills.

- The school enhances its reputation among parents and the community.

Research suggests that, over time, peer support systems improve the social climate of the school so that it becomes a school that cares.

THE METHOD OF SHARED CONCERN

This is a counselling-based approach for resolving bullying that was devised by Anatol Pikas in Sweden (for a detailed description, see Cowie and Sharp, 1994). It focuses on the children doing the bullying as well as those being bullied, and is designed for situations where a group of pupils has been bullying one or more pupils on a regular basis for some time. The method uses a combination of a simple script with specific non-verbal cues. Training is needed to ensure a thorough grasp of the technique. The overall aim of the Method of Shared Concern is to establish ground rules that will enable the pupils to coexist within the same school. It does not aim to create friendship among the pupils, or to uncover the details of the bullying situation. The method starts with a series of brief, individual 'chats' with each pupil involved, in a room that is quiet and where there will be no interruptions. The pupils doing the bullying are seen first. The talks are not confrontational; the premise is that there is a problem since others have witnessed that the bullied pupil is unhappy and has experienced bullying. The teacher follows a structured script with each pupil leading to mutual agreement that the bullied pupil is unhappy, and concludes when each pupil agrees to help improve the situation. Common outcomes are that participants leave the bullied pupil alone or become friendly towards him or her.

This is an effective method against bullying. Teachers recommend:

- following-up the pupils involved to make sure the bullying has stopped;

- monitoring to see whether the bullying starts again or targets another pupil;

- if a pupil is persistently involved in bullying, combining the method with some other intervention, for example parental involvement or a change of class.

When the follow-up talks are particularly successful, teachers can be tempted to miss out on the final group meeting. But it is this final meeting that leads to an agreement about the long-term maintenance of the change in bullying behaviour.

The Method of Shared Concern can be effective as part of the graded disciplinary procedure set out by the school's anti-bullying policy. It is most useful as an interim measure against group bullying. It usually results in an improvement in the bullying situation that can be maintained if additional action is taken to change the ringleader's behaviour.

THE NO BLAME APPROACH

The No Blame Approach (Robinson and Maines, 1997) has been used in primary, secondary and college environments since 1990 (Young, 1998). This method adopts a problem-solving approach by forming a support group for the bullied pupil consisting of those directly involved in the bullying episode and bystanders. The group is given responsibility for solving the problem and for reporting back on progress. The No Blame Approach is similar to the Method of Shared Concern, particularly in its identification of shared concern and its non-punitive stance. The method differs in that (a) the order in which the participants are seen by the adult facilitator; (b) the timing of individual meetings with bullies (Pikas sees them first individually while Maines and Robinson see them as a group); (c) the No Blame Approach places more emphasis on the feelings of the victim; (d) Pikas works on the partnership between adult facilitator and bully while Maines and Robinson make more use of group dynamics; (e) Maines and Robinson do not attach the label 'bully' to any of the participants. The first aim of the No Blame Approach is to arouse in children who bully a sense of empathic concern for those whom they have bullied. The second aim is to elicit responsible action that will assist in the resolution of the problem. The method is based on the assumption that empathic concern can only be achieved in a non-punitive context. It also assumes that bullying is often a group phenomenon that can be resolved by working with the responsible group. It is also important to monitor the development of new patterns of behaviour. There are seven steps in the No Blame Approach:

1 Talk with the victim.

2 Convene a group meeting.

3 Communicate to the group how the victim feels.

4 Share responsibility.

5 Elicit helpful suggestions.

6 Hand over responsibility to the group.

7 Individual meetings with participants.

A key aspect of this approach is that it places responsibility for change on the pupils who have participated in the bullying. The group co-operation involved in the process can have a powerful influence on individual members. Robinson and Maines (1997) have found that in the majority of cases the bullying stopped completely or the victim no longer required support.

ASSERTIVENESS TRAINING GROUPS FOR BULLIED PUPILS

Assertiveness techniques as described here are for use in small group settings; but they can also be used with individual pupils, or introduced to whole classes within the school (Sharp and Smith, 1994). To provide a safe, supportive environment for bullied pupils to talk about their experiences, and to learn and practise effective responsive behaviour. Assertive techniques encourage the use of clear, direct and honest messages and avoid interactions that are deliberately manipulative, threatening, intimidating or dishonest. These techniques employ a standard formula, and provide pupils with a clearly defined structure to use in any situation where they are feeling pressured to do something they do not want to do, or treated in a way they do not like. Pupils are encouraged to respond in a neutral but direct way that de-escalates the situation as follows:

- Make assertive statements.
- Resist manipulation and threats.
- Respond to name-calling.
- Leave a bullying situation.
- Escape safely from physical restraint.
- Enlist support from bystanders.
- Boost their own self-esteem.
- Remain calm in stressful situations.

Within the group the pupils usually develop supportive relationships so teachers need to take care in ending sessions. The last meeting should be carefully managed to emphasize the gains the pupils have made from the group but at the same time to draw the group to an end. Evaluation (Sharp and Smith, 1994) shows that assertiveness training boosts pupil self-esteem and self-confidence. Pupils used the techniques to respond to and avoid bullying situations. They became more assertive and less aggressive or passive in their relationships with other pupils. The gains the pupils made in these kinds of groups lasted longer if they were offered some kind of continuous support, albeit not as intensive as the group. A meeting once a term or a drop-in room for lunchtimes maintained pupils' self-esteem and encouraged them to practise assertiveness techniques.

DEALING WITH PERSISTENT BULLIES

A small but significant proportion of pupils persistently engage in aggressive and bullying behaviour. While personality and temperament may play a part, there is evidence that home circumstances have a strong impact on this. Children who experience ineffective discipline, lack of parental warmth and poor parental monitoring at home, are more likely to behave aggressively with their peers. Persistently bullying pupils are less likely to respond well to Shared Concern or No Blame approaches. They are more likely to interpret their environment as hostile and they prefer an aggressive strategy to deal with conflicts over other problem-solving approaches. These pupils place value on the outcomes of violence, such as enjoyment in the victim's distress, a sense of power, and gaining tangible rewards, such as money or possessions. Interventions that increase empathy for victims (Shared Concern, No Blame) may decrease peer approval of bullying. But by adolescence, persistently bullying pupils will have gravitated to social networks that affirm anti-social behaviour, so it is much more difficult to change their belief, founded in experience, that they can win respect through violent actions. Although adults and some pupils disapprove of their behaviour, these pupils care less about the rejection and seem to consider that the benefits in terms of outcomes outweigh the disadvantages. In Table 2.4.3 we have summarized some strategies.

TABLE 2.4.3 CHANGING THE BEHAVIOUR OF **PERSISTENT BULLIES**

- Approaches to change the behaviour of persistent bullies should attempt to minimize the impact of their anti-social peer group. This is in line with the methods described in this chapter. Pro-social behaviour can be learned in the context of the class or school group, and can be nurtured through encouragement, praise and the acknowledgement of success. If a potential victim has some friends or peer group support, even persistent bullies may be discouraged from targeting them.
- Helping these pupils understand the consequences of their behaviour for themselves, for their peers, their families and the wider community plays an important part in reducing this kind of behaviour.
- Co-operation between schools and the police is important and initiatives like South Wales Schoolwatch have demonstrated the value of this kind of collaboration. These indicate the effectiveness of working co-operatively with other agencies in the community to target young people who are persistently aggressive and violent towards their peers. The responses to anti-social behaviour can be initiated quickly and solutions can then be linked to the local context. For further information about such initiatives, contact your local police Schools Liaison Officer.
- It is important to work on the prevention of bullying rather than to wait until the behaviour has got out of control. Where possible, staff should try to divert or change anti-social behaviour at an early stage.
- Where the behaviour of the persistent bully is particularly difficult to change, additional help from other professionals, for example from an educational psychologist with specialist expertise or the CAMHS team, or work with the pupil in the context of the family, may be necessary.

WORKING WITH PROVOCATIVE/AGGRESSIVE VICTIMS

Without in any way condoning the bullying behaviour, it can be said that the behaviour of the provocative or aggressive victim contributes to their being bullied. These pupils often find it hard to concentrate in class and are hyperactive, and behave in ways that irritate others. They may be easily roused to anger, and fight back when attacked, or even slightly provoked. These children may provoke negative reactions on the part of a large number of classmates and may be actively disliked by adults, including the teacher. They also may themselves bully weaker pupils. In Table 2.4.4 we describe some strategies for intervening to help such pupils.

THE PEER SUPPORT INTERVENTION

HOW THE INTERVENTION WORKS IN LLANTWIT MAJOR

A peer support scheme was launched at Llantwit Major School six years ago following a discussion about bullying in a PSHE lesson. At the same time the school received some literature about ChildLine in Partnership with Schools (CHIPS) who piloted the peer support scheme for Wales. Initially, sixth formers were trained by the CHIPS team over a period of two days. They then set up a daily lunchtime drop-in

TABLE 2.4.4 CHANGING THE BEHAVIOUR OF **PROVOCATIVE/AGGRESSIVE VICTIMS**

- Parents and teachers need to co-operate in identifying behaviour patterns that lead to negative reactions on the part of peers. It will help greatly if the pupil learns to improve their social skills and to understand the social rules of the peer group. Assertiveness, conflict resolution and stress management are all helpful skills for these pupils to develop in order to cope more effectively or to become more aware of their own reactions to others. In persistent situations these need to be combined with other interventions to help these pupils develop more constructive relationships with their peer group.
- If the pupil has friends, they could be enlisted to give feedback on inappropriate behaviour that is annoying to the peer group. Adults can help by monitoring the quality of the friendships of provocative victims and creating opportunities for these young people to experience warm relationships in a supportive context. The methods described in this chapter (for example, assertiveness training, the No Blame Approach, befriending) and from other chapters (for example, Circles of Friends) are particularly helpful for the provocative victim.
- Where the behaviour of the provocative/aggressive victim is particularly difficult to change, additional help from other professionals, for example from an educational psychologist with specialist expertise or the CAMHS team, or work with the pupil in the context of the family, may be necessary.

for younger pupils. The drama department wrote and performed the musical *Why Me?* which was performed in their school to raise awareness.

WHO NEEDS TO BE INVOLVED IN PEER SUPPORT?

Since then other pupils have become involved with the programme, either by volunteering, or in response to a suggestion from the Head of Year 10. At the present time the peer supporters consist of one member of the upper sixth who is about to leave, four from the lower sixth and a number from Year 10. The Head of Year 10 provides backup but is rarely consulted over pupils presenting to the service. The older sixth-former has helped substantially to develop the scheme. Two years ago, when he started in the lower sixth, he ran a poster campaign to increase awareness throughout the school, and organized teams of peer supporters to visit the Year 7 and 8 classes during registration once a week. He structured quizzes and games to be used during this time. He also organized the peer support team to take regular assemblies.

There continues to be a daily drop-in clinic run by a rota of peer supporters. The supporters have a weekly supervision/support meeting facilitated by the older peer supporters. There is no regular note-keeping.

BENEFITS FOR THE YOUNGER PUPILS FROM PEER SUPPORT

The younger pupils are enthusiastic about the presence of CHIPS in the school. None of those that were interviewed had attended the drop-in clinic but they liked the fact that it is there since it provides role models for the younger ones.

I think that they feel that they know someone older in the school and if they did have a real problem they could collar us on the street. I think that it has been a really positive thing because it has provided an older figure in the school that they can look up to. (Peer supporter)

It's good to know someone is there even if you wouldn't go. (Year 7 girl)

It bonds the upper school with the lower school. When the scheme works it makes the younger ones realize that they will be able to take this sort of responsibility when they are older. (Year 10 parent)

BENEFITS FOR THE PEER SUPPORTERS

The peer supporters have gained in confidence and self-esteem through training in skills of communication, presentation and listening. Some have been given the opportunity to present their work outside school at a ChildLine conference. Parents acknowledged the benefits and recommended this intervention to other schools.

Everyone who has taken part has gained in confidence or the feeling that you have helped someone ... The initial training was excellent. I have still got the notes and I refer to them. They have helped me in life generally. (Male peer supporter)

I wouldn't mind being a teacher and it's given me good experience about what children go through at school. If you have seen someone who is sad and they come back happy then that gives you a good feeling. (Female peer supporter)

I didn't have much confidence at all but now I can lead assemblies. (Female peer supporter)

I think that such initiatives are vital – I know of many pupils at my daughter's school with alcohol problems and eating disorders. There is too little support. If the school has one – make it as high profile as possible. (Year 10 parent)

POSSIBLE PROBLEMS

A recurring issue for potential users of the system was about confidentiality with older pupils concerned about how safe the information they shared with peer supporters would be, though this is less of a worry in Year 7 where the CHIPS teams have been building up relationships in the classes. One or two of the younger peer supporters felt daunted by the possibility of being confronted by a major problem and unsure of where they could turn to due to the issue of confidentiality. The weekly meeting aims to provide support for the younger members of the teams. CHIPS co-ordinators suggest that leaflets or posters might be distributed throughout the school outlining the sorts of issues (to include loneliness, issues with friends, relationship advice) that peer supporters would be most skilled to address and recommending other agencies, such as ChildLine, for more difficult issues beyond the expertise of a peer supporter.

It was also difficult for boys to use the service for fear of being ridiculed, but again Year 7 boys felt more confident about approaching peer supporters than did Year 10 boys:

> I think that the image is improving generally. The people in Year 7 and Year 8 who have grown up with us visiting their classes, as they get to be our age, maybe the boys will be more interested because they have seen the respect that I've got. (Male peer supporter)

Peer supporters expressed some concern about their image though they were dealing with this issue themselves:

> Being in the sixth form and just having a different uniform on. It made a lot of difference. I got much more respect. (Male peer supporter)

> Some people see you as being a swot for doing it but others say, 'Oh well, somebody has got to do it.' and so they are fine about it. (Female peer supporter)

■ TIME COMMITMENT

Some considered that the administration of the scheme is a significant burden, especially with examinations in the lower sixth as well as the upper sixth. A scheme could consider looking for a volunteer parent or pay for a small amount of administrative support for photocopying materials, organizing the peer supporter rotas and assemblies, and reminding people about the support meetings. It was also felt that there should be a definite time for handing over responsibilities by the older student supporters to new recruits, say at the beginning of the spring term, so that the more senior and committed pupils can feel positive about the work that they have achieved within the scheme, rather than being left with guilt at having to devote increasing time to studies. A committed pupil without regular supervision cannot be expected to institute a passing over of authority without help from an adult with some respect within the scheme. It also allows for some appreciation of the part that the older student supporters have played. If the transition is made in the spring term it allows the more experienced members to plan and carry over into the autumn term, which could be argued as being the most important for providing peer support especially for the new Year 7s.

■ PUBLICITY

Peer supporters and staff facilitators expressed a need for publicity so that awareness remains high throughout the school. There is also an issue about keeping staff informed.

■ PRACTICE POINTS

- Training can be lengthy. It is usually recommended that peer supporters receive a minimum of 30 hours of training by a facilitator who is experienced as a counsellor or who has training in peer support. There are a number of good training courses in the UK, by CHIPS and at Relate. The Peer Support Forum website gives a list of current training programmes.

- Resources: the peer supporters need a room in which to see pupils individually or in groups, and where they can have ongoing training and supervision meetings. They will also need a secure place in which to store confidential material.

- Peer support enhances the emotional well-being of young people and is widely acknowledged to be an effective method for helping young people with peer group relationship difficulties such as bullying. It also benefits the peer supporters in terms of personal development, communication skills and confidence.

The approaches that we have reviewed in this chapter can help in many cases of bullying but there are some pupils who repeatedly get victimized at school and elsewhere, and some bullies who have severe patterns of aggressive anti-social behaviour. While small in numbers, these young people have marked problems and can cause immense difficulties for peers and teachers in the school community.

BOX 2.4.1 SETTING UP A PEER SUPPORT SYSTEM

- Secure the support of senior management, staff and pupils.
- Network with outside experts (counsellors, psychologists) who could recruit and train peer supporters.
- Select peer supporters who are mature and who have credibility with pupils.
- Training should be ongoing, with regular opportunities for debriefing.
- Choose a room which feels welcoming and comfortable and offers privacy.
- Promote the service through posters, assemblies, leaflets, lessons and talks.

SUMMARY

In this chapter we have identified the nature of young people in a range of participant roles with regard to bullying. We have also described strategies that have been evaluated and found to be effective in addressing this complex problem. These include whole-school policies, co-operative group work, peer support, the Method of Shared Concern, the No Blame Approach, assertiveness training and particular interventions for persistent bullies and provocative/ aggressive victims.

RESOURCES

Besag, V. (1999) *Coping with Bullying*. CD-ROM. The Rotary Coping with Life Series, distributed by SMS Multimedia, PO Box 40, Ashington, NE63 8YR.

Cowie, H. and Wallace, P. (2000) *Peer Support in Action*. London: Sage.

Department for Education and Skills (DfES) (2000) *Bullying: Don't Suffer in Silence: An Anti-bullying Pack for Schools*. London: HMSO.

European anti-bullying project at http://www.gold.ac.uk.tmr/

Peer Support Networker at http://www.peersupport.co.uk

Strategies Against Violence in Education (SAVE) at http://www.savecircle.co.uk

Sullivan, K. (2000) *The Anti-Bullying Handbook*. Oxford: Oxford University Press.

Varnava, G. (2000) *Towards a Non-violent Society: Checkpoints for Schools*. London: NCB.

ChildLine (2000) ChildLine Teacher's Pack. London: ChildLine, Studd Street, London N1 0QW.

UK Observatory for the Promotion of Non-Violence at www.ukobservatory.com

Sexual Health

[Y]oung people … told us that no-one really talks to them about sex itself. They said time and time again, we want clear and honest information. (Orpin, 2003: 10)

WHAT BEHAVIOURS ARE WE TALKING ABOUT?

According to a recent government report (Select Committee on Health, 2003) England is currently witnessing a rapid decline in sexual health in terms of sexually transmitted infections, teenage pregnancy and human immunodeficiency virus (HIV). For example, around one in ten sexually active young women, and many men, are infected with chlamydia, a sexually transmitted infection which, if left untreated, can lead to infertility. In the last six years, syphilis rates have increased by 500 per cent and those for gonorrhoea have almost doubled. In addition, teenage pregnancy rates in Britain are the highest in Europe: five times as high as those found in the Netherlands, Sweden, Switzerland or Italy. Furthermore, while mortality rates for HIV have decreased, the number of people living with HIV has risen. The report suggests that young people are being failed by an education system that delivers too little, too late due to a lack of time and resources, often placing a mistaken emphasis on the biological facts rather than young people's wider concerns about relationships and emotional issues (Select Committee on Health, 2003).

The World Health Organization (WHO, 2003, p. 2) defines sexual health as

> a personal sense of sexual well-being as well as the absence of disease, infections or illness associated with sexual behaviour. As such, it includes issues of self-esteem, self-expression, caring for others and cultural values. Sexual health can be described as the positive integration of physical, emotional, intellectual and social aspects of sexuality.

A review of the literature suggests that young people are becoming sexually active at an earlier age. For example, a recent study (Wight et al., 2000) reported that at mean age 14 years, 18 per cent of boys and 15 per cent of girls reported having had intercourse. The most important correlate of sexual experience was low level of parental monitoring. Sixty per cent reported that condoms were used throughout their last sexual episode. The key predictor for condom use was whether or not the respondent talked to their partner about protection before having sexual intercourse. At follow-up (mean age 16 years, 1 month) these figures had increased, with 31 per cent of boys and 41 per cent of girls reporting that they had had intercourse (Wight et al., 2000).

Sexually transmitted infections (STIs) and HIV are infections whose primary route of transmission is through sexual contact. Sexually transmitted infections and HIV cause a wide range of illnesses and are a significant cause of long-term and serious disability in the UK. HIV is uncommon among young heterosexual people in the UK. Less than one in 1,000 UK-born teenagers attending sexually transmitted disease (STD) clinics were infected with HIV in 1999 (Public Health Laboratory Service [PHLS], 2003a). Among young people who are sexually active in the UK, homosexual young men are at greater risk than heterosexuals. For heterosexual young people, the risk of catching chlamydia, gonorrhoea or another STI is far higher than catching HIV.

Chlamydia is the commonest sexually transmitted infection in the UK with over 70,000 diagnoses in 2001 (PHLS, 2003b). The highest rates are found in young people; in 2001, 1 per cent of the 16–19-year-old population was diagnosed with chlamydia. Gonorrhoea is the second most common form of sexually transmitted infection in the UK. In 2000, there were over 20,500 cases diagnosed in STD clinics, with the highest rates observed in the 16–19-year-old age group. While sexually active young people of any age can catch syphilis, genital herpes and genital warts, the highest rates of these sexually transmitted infections are recorded for the 20–24-year-old age group (PHLS, 2003c).

The UK currently has the highest rate of teenage pregnancy in Europe. In the year 2000, there were almost 98,000 conceptions to teenage girls aged under 20 in England and Wales; 39 per cent of these led to abortions (Select Committee on Health, 2003). Eight thousand of these conceptions were to girls under the age of 16; of these, almost 400 were to girls under the age of 14, 240 of which led to abortions. These statistics reveal that in England and Wales, conceptions for under 16-year-olds fell by 4.5 per cent between 2000 and 2001; in the same period conception rates for under 18-year-olds fell by 3 per cent.

Some young people, for example, girls with attention deficit disorder, may be more at risk because of the impulsive nature of the attention deficit and the low self-esteem from which these children suffer. In the first instance, it is important that this group of children are recognized and treated with medical help.

According to Alcohol Concern (2002a), anecdotal evidence suggests that alcohol is often involved in teenage pregnancy and risky sex in general. In this context, risky sex is defined as sexual intercourse without a condom, without contraception, with lots of different partners within a specified time frame, with someone they have just met, early (under 16 years of age) and/or that is unintended. The relationship between alcohol and risky sex is complicated. Studies suggest that young people are more likely to have risky sex when they are under the influence of alcohol (Alcohol Concern, 2002a). For example, among 15–16-year-olds, one in 14 said that they had had unprotected sex after drinking, while one in seven 16–24-year-olds said the same (Health Education Authority, 1998a).

Young people state that alcohol is a main reason for having sex, especially early sex with someone they had not known for very long (Alcohol Concern, 2002a). For example, 40 per cent of sexually active 13- and 14-year-olds were 'drunk or stoned' at first intercourse (Wight et al., 2000). Young people say they are more likely to have sex they regret when they have been drinking (Alcohol Concern, 2002a). For example, 10 per cent of 15–16-year-olds said that they had sex that they later regretted (Hibbel et al., 2001).

WHAT BENEFITS ARE THERE TO BE GAINED BY TACKLING BEHAVIOURS WHICH LEAD TO POOR SEXUAL HEALTH?

Given that the statistics suggest that young people are becoming sexually active at a younger age, it is essential that they are equipped with the information and skills necessary to negotiate the highly sexualized adult world in which they live, and schools can play an important part in this process. The Sex Education Forum based at the National Children's Bureau (NCB) defines the purpose of sex education as supporting young people to manage adolescence and prepare them for adult life. A greater emphasis on the importance of handling relationships, as opposed to basic biological facts, would enable young people to achieve more positive attitudes to sexual health in the following ways:

- developing positive values and a moral framework that will guide decisions, judgements and behaviours;
- developing confidence and self-esteem to value themselves and others;
- developing responsible behaviour within sexual and personal relationships;
- developing effective communication skills;
- developing sufficient information and skills to protect both themselves and their partner from unintended/unwanted conceptions, sexually transmitted infections and HIV.

WHAT ARE THE POSSIBLE INTERVENTIONS?

As with many of the chapters in this book, interventions that improve the self-esteem of youngsters, their ability to communicate effectively, their wisdom in choosing friends, their ability to understand and modulate their feelings all play an important part in developing healthy sexual practices. Interventions outlined in other chapters in this book which help with this include Circle Time, Circle of Friends, peer support and the No Blame Approach.

The basic biology of sex and relationship education has a statutory framework as part of the science element of the National Curriculum (NC, 2003). By Key Stage 3 children should have learnt about how babies are made, and the changes that they will go through at puberty (see Box 2.5.1). By Key Stage 4, young people should have learnt more detail about the process of conception, and about how hormonal methods of contraception, such as the pill, work to prevent it. The theory of sexually transmitted infections should also be referred to as young people learn about viruses and how they are transmitted as part of the National Curriculum in science.

BOX 2.5.1 PUBERTY AND MENTAL HEALTH

Secondary schools have to deal with young people experiencing the changes of puberty. The timing of puberty may be either a risk or a resilience factor for mental health. Boys who mature later are more likely to be victims of bullying and have less physical success. However, there is some evidence that early maturation is associated with increased depressive thinking and anxiety (Alsaker, 1992; Petersen and Crockett, 1985). Girls with precocious puberty associate with older girls, and are more likely to have an earlier onset of alcohol use, shorter education and earlier pregnancies, and they are more likely to score highly for depressive feelings and sadness (Alsaker, 1992; Brooks-Gunn and Warren, 1989; Stattin and Magnusson, 1990). Going through puberty with the majority of your peers increases your resilience to mental distress.

However, there is considerable variation in sex education provision, attributable primarily to a school's ethos, the role of key individual teachers with responsibility for sex education, the cohesion of the senior management team and the characteristics of individual classroom teachers, not to mention time and resources. Teachers have varied approaches to dealing with sexual orientation and identity. Inclusive approaches can be constrained by teacher discomfort, lack of support from senior management, worries about perceived lack of neutrality and fear of negative pupil reactions. In a study by Wight et al. (2000), interviews with female pupils in six schools found that nearly all cited school as a useful source in learning about sex, though it tended to be seen as an introduction or supplement to other sources (for example, friends, magazines and mothers). Lessons to develop relationship skills were particularly valued and thought likely to influence behaviour positively in the future, though sex education was commonly thought to have been delivered 'too late'. Interviews with both male and female pupils found that the majority felt uncomfortable in sex education lessons, with gender dynamics in the mixed-sex lessons being the main problem. Discomfort manifested itself in reluctance to ask questions and/or to participate actively in lessons, as well as in disruptive behaviour. Four factors that reduced pupils' discomfort were a protective teacher, a friendly teacher, trust between pupils and fun sex education (Wight et al., 2000).

Working in single-gender groups can be a useful way of planning and organizing sex and relationship education (SRE) to meet the needs of both genders. This may be because the issue is particularly relevant to or sensitive for either gender, for example puberty, menstruation and gender roles. However, it is imperative that both genders learn about each other and, where possible, have the opportunity for group discussion.

Issues that need consideration include confidentiality, boundaries and use of health professionals. For example, schools need a clear and explicit confidentiality policy that teachers, pupils and parents understand. Teachers cannot offer or guarantee pupils unconditional confidentiality: this needs to be explained before individuals/groups make personal disclosures. Schools must be sure about the boundaries of their legal and professional roles and responsibilities. When working in the classroom health professionals must work within the school SRE policy. When they are working on a one-to-one basis they can offer different levels of confidentiality and need to work within their professional guidelines.

The National Healthy School Standard offers schools guidelines on how a school can approach sex education effectively, thus overcoming some of the problems outlined above. The guidelines state that school policies should:

- be delivered in partnership with local health and support services (see Case study 2.5.1);
- consult with the whole-school community including young people and parents on its development (DfEE, 2001).

Good practice in sex education and relationships should:

- include useful information;
- develop social skills;
- discuss morals and values;
- have identified learning outcomes and be designed to match pupils' age, gender, ability and maturity;

- involve pupils' own assessment of their needs (see Chapter 1.6) (DfEE, 2001).

In addition, staff themselves need a good knowledge of sex and relationship issues. They should be aware of the role that schools can play in addressing issues such as sexually transmitted diseases and unwanted teenage pregnancy. Staff need to feel comfortable talking about sex and relationships with pupils.

The aim of a whole-school approach to sex and relationship education is to provide a supporting school ethos and committed management structure that ensures adequate resources and consistency of practice. Central to this are the PSHE framework and the Citizenship curriculum. A whole-school approach will ensure that sex education is not just confined to planned curriculum provision, but disseminated across:

- the school's culture and ethos;
- the values and morals underpinning positive sexual health;
- the sex education policy;
- parents/carers and the local community (see 'Teens and Toddlers', p. 116).

Locating sex and relationship education firmly within the PSHE framework and the Citizenship curriculum offers the opportunities to involve young people in:

- developing school policies on sex education issues;
- conducting a needs analysis;
- consulting on what they already know about sex education issues;
- researching information about sex education and relationship issues for themselves and presenting the results to their peers;
- peer education and projects to improve their school and their local community;
- establishing links with parents/carers, the wider community and outside agencies;
- debating the moral, social and legal issues around sex education;
- establishing personal responsibility.

Resources and information for planning sex and relationship education are available from the Society for the Advancement of Sexual Health (SASH) and the Sex Education Forum at the National Children's Bureau (see Resources at the end of the chapter).

CASE STUDY 2.5.1 A PAUSE

One example of a programme that has been extensively developed and involves a liaison between the health and education sectors is the A PAUSE (Adding Power And Understanding to Sex Education) programme. A PAUSE is an innovative and effective schools-based sex education programme with a balanced, multi-agency approach. Different components of the programme are facilitated by teachers, health professionals and slightly older peers. The programme provides training and curriculum support materials for students, PSHE advisers, health professionals, co-ordinators and education authorities. Based on extensive research at Exeter University's Department of Child Health, it focuses not just on the physical aspects of sex, but also addresses the emotional and relationship issues. The approach stems from a psychosocial concept called Social Learning Theory (SLT), which suggests that we learn behaviour most effectively by copying people we value and respect. Teachers and health professionals deliver the 'technical' aspect of the programme, while peers or slightly older teenagers create social norms. This allows the A PAUSE scheme to overcome one of the biggest obstacles to effective sex education – the generation gap. It can be difficult for adults and young people to appreciate each other's viewpoint when it comes to the emotional aspects of sex. As one teacher puts it: 'I don't think they should be doing it and they don't think I should be doing it.'

The idea for peer-led sex education initially came from similar successful programmes in the USA, where escalating teenage pregnancy rates forced sex education experts to change their approach. The 'just say no' approach was not working on its own. 'Peer educators' (16- to 18-year-olds) undergo a 25-hour training programme, which enables them to run four classroom sessions with Year 9 students. The sessions focus on dispelling myths about sex and building self-esteem and, although a teacher or an A PAUSE supervisor must be present, the peers themselves lead the discussions without intervention.

Dr John Tripp, a consultant paediatrician who is a member of the team behind the A PAUSE programme, says that teenagers should not be pressured into having sex. They may find it difficult to say 'no' without help. He says: 'Young people should not feel pressured, and should be prepared to deal with the dangers and manage them safely.'

On the negative side, the peers can be unreliable, the programme is time-consuming for both teachers and peers, and it is more expensive to run than traditional approaches to sex education. However, savings to the National Health Service (NHS) in terms of preventing sexually transmitted infections and unwanted pregnancies should be considered.

Luke Murray (17) received the A PAUSE lessons when he was a Year 9 student and was so taken with them that he decided to become a peer himself. 'I really enjoyed the lessons. You could laugh with the peers and they spoke a language that I was familiar with.'

TEENS AND TODDLERS

WHAT IS IT?

Teens and Toddlers is an innovative, practical teenage pregnancy prevention and mental health programme which fosters greater awareness of the reality of conception and parenting for young people, long before unwanted pregnancies occur. This approach looks at how practical parenting skills can be encouraged in such a way that they have a positive impact on the emotional health of the young people involved. Teens and Toddlers is an example of a programme for at-risk youngsters that enables them to experience intensive interaction with toddlers in a safe nursery environment and with classroom instruction that is highly interactive. 'One of the great strengths of teens and toddlers is the personal development and the self-esteem they acquire won't go away' (Parillon, Head of Learning Mentoring, Warwick Park).

The project includes three key elements:

- regular one-to-one contact between the young adolescent and the toddler;
- classroom time focusing on child development, parenting skills, and sex education and relationships;
- counselling for young people identified most at risk and need.

To date, Teens and Toddlers has been piloted four times in Greenwich since 2001, with two pilots in Southwark recently completed (2002). The intervention draws at-risk adolescents ranging in ages 14–17-years-old from schools, to work with 3- to 5-year-olds in nurseries. In four years of running Teens and Toddlers in Grass Valley, California, where the national average for teenage pregnancies is 10 per cent, no pregnancies have been reported among the students, suggesting that the intervention has had a positive impact (Whitmore, 2003).

WHO NEEDS TO BE INVOLVED IN TEENS AND TODDLERS?

The Greenwich project worked with 34 teenagers from seven schools and was funded by the Education Department and the Education Action Zone. The teenagers were recommended by schools and selected by the scheme because of their troubled backgrounds and difficulties with school. The intake of teenagers also included pregnant teenage girls and teenage mothers because there is a strong tendency for teenage parents to conceive again.

COST

At the present time each project costs approximately £18,000 to fund.

HOW LONG SHOULD TEENS AND TODDLERS LAST?

The course lasts 12 weeks. As soon as the students arrive each week, they attend a touchdown session to discuss with a counsellor how they are feeling and any problems that are bothering them. Only then are they allowed into the nursery.

The nursery staff treat teenagers as co-workers. For two hours, twice a week, the teenagers adopt a toddler and work with them, deal with their problems, tantrums and accidents, and spend time playing with them. After each session the teenagers attend a one-hour class discussing a range of subjects including caring for toddlers, contraception, child development and parenting and relationship skills. They learn about non-violent communication, self-esteem and boundary-setting with a small child. Additionally, students have the opportunity for an individual, 40-minute weekly session of life coaching with one of the student counsellors which may continue for up to six months.

WHAT ARE THE BENEFITS OF TEENS AND TODDLERS?

The benefits to participants include:

- prevention of teenage pregnancy;
- learning more effective communication skills, including anger management and conflict resolution;
- increasing emotional literacy, self-reflection skills, and self-management skills;
- learning skills for future parenting relationships;
- engagement with the wider community in terms of working in and contributing to local nurseries and supporting nursery staff;
- discovering possible career opportunities in childcare;
- creating a sense of achievement by developing a successful relationship with the assigned toddler and by an in-depth work experience where participants are treated as responsible young people by nursery staff, their own peer group and project leaders;

- facilitating and eliciting a capacity to reflect on the impact of words and behaviour of others, particularly small children, and developing new, more helpful forms of behaviours around such issues as communication and discipline;

- developing alternative goals to being pregnant such as education and career opportunities.

I could share stuff I wouldn't have shared by friends it also built up awareness of how my mind works. (Borondi)

It's a good experience working with little kids. When you are with them you can't swear because you need to be teaching them manners. It makes me behave better. I feel calmer when I'm here. Ibrahim's my special friend. I think about him a lot. (Fatou)

We would have no hesitation in recommending the Teens and Toddlers project to any local authority who is serious about addressing the issue of teenage pregnancy in a rigorous and comprehensive way. The secondary benefits of this project are in the area of emotional literacy and we've seen its effectiveness on this level as well. (Martin, Officer For Reintegration and Teenage Pregnancy and Gyte, Director of Education, Greenwich, 2002)

POSSIBLE PROBLEMS

The pilot studies have suggested that this is a very effective way of targeting an at-risk group of young people. There are obviously considerable cost and resource implications that need to be debated at local education level.

SUMMARY

- In this chapter we have been talking about risky sex that can result in sexually transmitted infections and unwanted teenage pregnancy.

- Reducing and preventing risky sex is necessary to enable young people to lead healthy, fulfilling and satisfying lives.

- Possible interventions include sex education programmes and projects that involve collaboration with outside agencies and the wider community.

- Teens and Toddlers uses an innovative approach aimed at raising awareness of the reality of conception and early parenthood.

- The benefits of this approach work towards increasing self-esteem, self-awareness and effective communication skills, as well as decreasing teenage conception rates.

RESOURCES

A PAUSE, Exeter University, Department of Child Health, at www.ex.ac.uk/sshs/apause

Society for the Advancement of Sexual Health (SASH) at www.a2zsexualhealth.net The objectives of the site are to provide an independent forum for delivering sexual health news, promoting improved communication, shared perspectives and cumulative learning between the various disciplines and services that make up Sexual Health within the UK; to facilitate the development and evaluation of strategies, exchange of expertise and dissemination of new ideas and practices, research projects, events, training, employment opportunities, resources and collaborative working leading to quality Sexual Health services and promotion; to serve the information needs of the professional UK health care and educational communities (opinion formers, practitioners, purchasers, providers, suppliers, policy makers and information providers) and beyond.

Sex Education Forum, National Children's Bureau, 8 Wakley Street, London EC1 7QE. Tel: 020 7843 6000. At www.ncb.org.uk/sexed.html.

Teens and Toddlers further information from Children Our Ultimate Investment UK, Southfield, Leigh, Kent TN11 8PL.

Alcohol, Drugs and Substance Abuse

Research in Britain, the United States and other Western countries has shown that there are influential factors in children's lives associated with an increased risk of developing a range of health and behaviour problems as they grow older – notably: … misuse of drugs, alcohol and other substances … (Beinart et al., 2002, p. 3).

WHAT BEHAVIOURS ARE WE TALKING ABOUT IN THIS CHAPTER?

The authors of a publication entitled *Youth At Risk?* (Beinart, et al., 2002), which describes the results of a questionnaire survey about young people's problem behaviours, suggest that substance use, in particular alcohol, gives the most cause for concern. The following section will outline behaviours in respect of alcohol use, tobacco use, illegal drug use and solvent abuse.

In terms of policy and curriculum, drug education is meant to include alcohol and other substances, yet alcohol education has been increasingly marginalized, according to Alcohol Concern (2002). One of the reasons for this might be that, compared with other drugs, alcohol is a legal, socially acceptable drug, occupying an important, deep-rooted place in our culture. While only legally available for consumption by adults, alcohol is readily available to all, including young people (see below). The government's recommended daily limits are no more than three or four units per day for men, and no more than two or three units per day for women. One unit equates to one glass of table wine, one glass of sherry or port, one single whisky, gin or brandy, a half pint of beer or cider, or a quarter-pint of superstrength beer or cider (pub measures) (Institute of Alcohol Studies, 2002). The acceptability of alcohol in our society, in legal, cultural and social terms, coupled with the fact that roughly 40 per cent of males and 20 per cent of females drink above the recommended daily levels of alcohol, has implications for the teaching of alcohol education; not least, it requires the adults involved to challenge their own drinking habits.

Alcohol has only become a significant part of youth culture since the 1960s. By the 1980s, 18- to 24-year-olds had become the heaviest drinkers in the UK population, and the group least likely to abstain. By 2000, hazardous drinking, that is drinking associated with the risk of physical and/or psychological harm either now or in the future, was most prevalent in young people and young adults. In females, hazardous drinking peaks in the 16- to 19-year age group, with 32 per cent having a risky drinking pattern. In males, hazardous drinking peaks later, with 62 per cent having a risky drinking pattern in the 20- to 24-year age group. In addition, over the past 40 years there has been a decrease in the age at which regular drinking starts (ONS, 2001a).

Among 11- and 12-year-olds, over half have tried alcohol at least once, while one in ten boys and one in 20 girls describe themselves as regular drinkers (Beinart et al., 2002). By Year 10, one-third of males and females describe themselves as regular drinkers. Furthermore, substantial numbers of 15- and 16-year-olds take part in 'binge' drinking, i.e. consuming five or more alcoholic drinks in a single session.

According to the Office of National Statistics (ONS, 2001b), home, or the homes of relatives and friends, is the major source of alcohol. Young people continue to drink at home as they get older, but the venue shifts to parties, then to clubs and discos, and finally to pubs. Although it is illegal for under-18s to purchase alcohol, the Youth Lifestyles Survey (Flood-Page et al., 2000) found that 63 per cent of 16–17-year-olds and 10 per cent of 12–15-year-olds who had drunk in the last year, had bought the alcohol themselves.

Research suggests that young people drink for a variety of reasons, including individual, for example, to change mood, to cope with stress and to feel happy; social, for example, to develop trust with friends, and to explore sexual relationships; and, peer influence, for example, the social expectation that certain kinds of events involve drinking sometimes involving peer pressure. Alcohol is viewed as having both relaxing and bonding functions within an individual's peer group, as well as providing an excuse for 'bad behaviour' (Honess et al., 2000). Furthermore, surveys suggest that there is a growing trend of drinking for effect and drinking to intoxication. Related to this is the partial merging of the alcohol and drug scenes in the context of youth culture, with alcohol being one of a range of psychoactive products now available on the recreational drug market (Honess et al., 2000).

Compared with alcohol, the figures suggest that smoking is a less attractive or acceptable activity (Beinart et al., 2002). Very few young people are smokers when they start secondary school. Indeed, government surveys show that the prevalence of smoking is strongly related to age with the numbers of young people who experiment with smoking increasing significantly for each year group (ONS, 2001b). Over three-quarters of young people in Year 7 reported that they had never had a cigarette (75 per cent of males and 77 per cent of females). Whereas almost half of males in Years 10 and 11 (49 per cent and 47 per cent respectively) said they had never smoked, only a third of females said the same (36 per cent and 35 per cent respectively). Similarly, females outnumbered males in terms of describing themselves as regular smokers in all five age groups, rising from 1 per cent in Year 7 to 17 per cent in Year 11 (ONS, 2001b).

With regard to illegal drug use, the drug that most young people reported using was cannabis. In Years 10 and 11, most of those young people who had smoked cannabis only did so once or twice. Nine per cent of males and 5 per cent of females reported using the drug on three or more occasions in the four weeks preceding the survey. The reported use of more harmful illegal drugs was reported at much lower levels. For example, in Year 11, 5 per cent of males and 4 per cent of females said they had ever used the drug ecstasy, while similar percentages reported using amphetamines or 'speed' (4 per cent of males and 4 per cent of females). In Year 11, the use of cocaine was reported by 4 per cent of males and 3 per cent of females; these levels were double those reported for the use of heroin (2 per cent and 1 per cent respectively) (Beinart et al., 2002).

Probably the most disturbing findings relate to the abuse of glue and other solvents. Solvent abuse is the deliberate inhalation of household products, such as lighter gas refills, aerosols containing products such as hairspray, deodorants and air fresheners, tins or tubes of glue, some paints, thinners and correcting fluids, to achieve intoxication. The most common method of abuse of butane lighter fuels is believed to be by squirting directly into the back of the throat (Adfam, 2002). Most aerosols are sniffed or breathed into the lungs through a cloth or sleeve, while most glues are abused by inhalation of the fumes/vapours from a plastic bag (Field-Smith et al., 2002). Beinart et al. (2002) show that 7 per cent of males and 6 per cent of females in Year 7 reported that they had sniffed solvents at least once. This rose to 9 per cent of males and 11 per cent of females in Year 10 with a decrease in Year 11. Levels of solvent abuse reported for the past month were lower, fluctuating between 2 per cent of females and 3 per cent of males in each age group. Figures for females ranged from 2 per cent of 11- and 12-year-olds in Year 7 to a peak of 5 per cent among 13- and 14-year-olds in Year 9.

Excluded children appear to have more experience of alcohol use and drug-taking than school pupils. Nearly two-thirds (61 per cent) have been offered alcohol and over half have been offered tobacco (52 per cent) and cannabis (53 per cent) (Youth Justice Board, 2002). Excluded young people are significantly more likely to drink regularly than their non-excluded peers, with 46 per cent saying they drink alcohol at least once a week compared with 26 per cent of school children (Youth Justice Board, 2002). There is an even larger distinction between ethnic groups, with three in ten white excluded young people drinking at least once a week compared to just one in ten from ethnic minority backgrounds. Similarly, excluded young people who have tried cannabis report a significantly higher level of usage on a weekly basis than their peers in school. Nearly half (45 per cent) of cannabis users have used the drug in the last month, with 38 per cent having used it in the last week. Figures for the use of other drugs show less of a contrast between excluded and non-excluded pupils. For example, mainstream pupils using drugs appear to be using cocaine and ecstasy on a more regular basis than excluded users (Youth Justice Board, 2002).

WHAT BENEFITS ARE THERE TO BE GAINED BY ADDRESSING ALCOHOL/DRUG ABUSE?

With regard to alcohol abuse, the World Health Organization's European Charter on Alcohol states that 'All children and adolescents have the right to grow up in an environment protected from the negative consequences of alcohol consumption' (WHO, 1995). The negative consequences of young people consuming alcohol include the effects of drinking on health, the links between alcohol and crime and disorder, the links between alcohol consumption and unsafe/unwanted sex, and the links between alcohol and school exclusions.

According to Alcohol Concern (2002b), the link between heavy drinking and physical health is complicated. For example, heavy alcohol consumption can directly cause some diseases, such as, liver disease, or it is indirectly linked to other physical problems including, high blood pressure, heart disease, and oral and upper digestive cancers. There is also a possible link between binge drinking and heart attacks. Between 1985 and 1996 there was a tenfold increase in admissions to Accident and Emergency Departments among under 15-year-olds due to alcohol overdoses and other accidents or violence related incidents (Robson, 1998). Physical health is not the only issue; one person in 20 is dependent on alcohol compared with one in 45 dependent on drugs, including prescribed drugs. Alcohol dependency is closely linked to mental health problems including depression and suicide. Indeed, alcohol and/or drug abuse is a risk factor for developing mental health problems (Mental Health Foundation, 1999).

With regard to alcohol and crime and disorder, the government has stated that alcohol-related crime is a significant problem in UK society. There is a strong link between alcohol and youth offending, with arrests for drunkenness peaking at 18 years of age. One study suggests that 25 per cent of weekly drinkers aged 14 to 15 years had a criminal record compared with 6 per cent of occasional drinkers (Newcombe et al., 1995). A report by the Chief Inspector of Prisons suggests that a quarter of young offenders had been drinking when they committed their crime (Ramsbottom, 1997).

Research suggests that young people combine alcohol and sex. After drinking alcohol, one in seven 16- to 24-year-olds have had unsafe sex, one in five have had sex that they later regretted and one in ten had been unable to remember whether they had had sex the night before or not. In addition, 40 per cent thought they were more likely to have had casual sex after drinking (Health Education Authority, 1998a). In addition, the Social Exclusion Unit's (1999) report on teenage pregnancy highlights the links between alcohol and unprotected sex, which in itself can lead to unplanned pregnancy, and sexually transmitted diseases.

There are also links between alcohol consumption and school exclusions. While there are many factors that contribute to truancy and exclusions, a problem-drinking parent or young person can contribute significantly to the likelihood of truancy, according to a study by the Youth Justice Board (MORI, 2000). Alcohol has been identified as a direct cause of school exclusion with 20 per cent of young people suspended for drinking alcohol in school. Indirectly, the study suggests that 16 per cent of excluded pupils are drinking alcohol every day compared with 3 per cent of non-excluded pupils, and 20 per cent of excluded pupils drink alcohol three to four times a week, compared with 3 per cent of non-excluded pupils.

The use of any illegal drug involves health risks. For example, the user can never be sure of exactly what they are taking; what is purchased is unlikely to be pure but mixed with something else. Not knowing the strength of what has been purchased is more likely to lead to an accidental overdose and the user cannot be sure what effect a drug will have, even if they have taken it before. It is very often dangerous to mix different drugs, including alcohol. If needles, syringes or other injecting equipment are shared there is a serious risk of dangerous infections being spread such as HIV and hepatitis B or C. Injecting can also damage veins. In addition, unlawful possession of an illegal drug is a criminal offence. The Youth Lifestyles Survey (Goulden and Sondhi, 2001) found that 75 per cent of serious and/or persistent young offenders (committing three or more minor offences and/or at least one serious offence in the last year) had used an illicit drug in their lifetime and nearly three-fifths had done so in the past year compared to 25 per cent and one-seventh respectively for non-offenders. A prospective employer may check if an applicant has a criminal record or any past convictions, therefore, affecting job prospects. A drugs conviction can also cause problems obtaining a travel visa to enter some countries (Department of Health, 1998).

Smoking increases the risk of premature death from cancer and heart disease. Children who smoke are two to six times more susceptible to coughs and increased phlegm, wheeziness and shortness of breath than those who do not smoke, according to the Royal College of Physicians (1992). A recent study in the USA found that smoking during the teenage years causes permanent genetic changes in the lungs and increases the risk of lung cancer for ever, even if the smoker subsequently stops (Weincke et al., 1999). The earlier young people become regular smokers and persist in the habit, the greater the risk of dying prematurely as adults. It is estimated that each year in the UK, over 120,000 people die as a result of smoking. Most die from one of the three main diseases associated with tobacco use, namely lung cancer, lung disease and heart disease (Health Education Authority, 1998b). Furthermore, one study suggests that children who smoke are three times more likely to have time off school (Charlton and Blair, 1989).

The immediate health risks of solvent abuse are severe, including nausea, vomiting, black-outs and heart problems that can be fatal; long-term abuse of glue can damage the brain, liver and kidneys. Squirting gas products down the throat may cause the body to produce fluid that floods the lungs and this can cause instant death. In addition, indirect causes of death include plastic bag suffocation, inhalation of stomach contents, and accidental death such as drowning or hanging (Field-Smith et al., 2002). A longitudinal study currently in progress is looking at deaths associated with the abuse of gas fuels, aerosols, glues and other solvent-based products since 1971 (Field-Smith et al., 2002). Deaths from solvent abuse comprise an important proportion of all deaths in young people, as death from any cause in this group is rare (Field-Smith et al., 2002). Key findings for 2000 (the latest figures available) show that while the youngest child to die was aged 12, the highest number of deaths was among 14–18-year-olds (28 per cent). This group accounts for 54 per cent of all solvent abuse deaths from 1971 to 2000. Solvent abuse deaths continue to be much more common among males than females, with the majority of deaths associated with solvent abuse over the past ten years being male (85 per cent). However, it should not be inferred from this that solvent abuse is more common among males than females; as we saw earlier in the chapter, similar percentages of males and females are abusing solvents.

Clearly, addressing the issues of young people and substance abuse has implications not only for individual physical, mental and sexual health, but also for the reduction of crime and school exclusions.

WHAT ARE THE POSSIBLE INTERVENTIONS?

Schools are well placed to address the issue of young people and substance use. A publication written by Alcohol Concern and Drugscope (Sinclair et al., 2001) offers a practical guide to the opportunities for drug and alcohol education across the whole-school curriculum, including guidance on key policy and practice issues.

School policies should:

- include both alcohol and drug issues;
- clarify the use of alcohol on school trips;
- address residential settings and social occasions;
- address teachers' own drinking behaviour.

Good practice in alcohol and drug education should:

- start early;
- take account of young people's current knowledge;
- accept the reality of young people's lives;
- be sensitive to culture and gender;
- be non-judgemental;
- be carefully planned within the curriculum and supported by a whole-school approach;
- involve parents/carers and the wider community;
- use active, participatory learning methods.

The aim of a whole-school approach to drug and alcohol education is to provide a supporting school ethos and committed management structure that ensures adequate resources and consistency of practice. Central to this are the PSHE framework and the Citizenship curriculum (NC, 2003). A whole-school approach will ensure that drug and alcohol education is not just confined to planned curriculum provision, but disseminated across:

- the school's culture and ethos;
- the values underpinning drugs and alcohol education;
- the drug and alcohol policy;
- parents/carers and the local community.

Locating drug and alcohol education firmly within the PSHE framework and the Citizenship curriculum offers the opportunities to involve young people in:

- developing school policies on alcohol- and drug-related issues;
- conducting a needs analysis;
- consulting on what they already know about drug and alcohol issues;
- researching information about drug and alcohol issues for themselves and presenting the results to their peers;
- peer education and projects to improve their school and their local community;

- establishing links with parents/carers, the wider community and outside agencies;

- debating the moral, social and legal issues around drugs and alcohol;

- establishing personal responsibility.

Case study 2.6.1 offers an example of how alcohol education can be addressed through the National Curriculum.

CASE STUDY 2.6.1 BNTL FREEWAY

The British National Temperance League (BNTL) is a proactive charity within the field of drug and alcohol education providers. Following the success of their resource 'Thinking About Drinking, Key Stage 2' which was sent free to all primary schools in the UK, they produced 'Thinking About Drinking, Key Stage 3' as a series of nine lesson plans linked to the National Curriculum. The programme of lesson plans and resources is designed to inform young people about the consequences of alcohol consumption, enabling them to make informed lifestyle choices. The lesson content is signposted to the Key Stage 3 National Curriculum and includes links with PSHE, Science, Maths, Design and Technology, Citizenship and English/ICT. The straightforward materials are designed to be easy and attractive to use in lively and active lessons and the Activity Sheets can be photocopied. 'Thinking About Drinking for Key Stage 3' has become the recommended resource in the Qualifications and Curriculum Authority's 'Drug, alcohol and tobacco education – curriculum guidance at Key Stages 1–4' and in Unit D – alcohol, tobacco and the law.

Within the whole-school context the National Healthy School Standard (NHSS, 1999) offers a useful framework for drug and alcohol education. The NHSS is part of the Healthy Schools Programme, led by the Department for Education and Skills and the Department of Health. The overall aim of the Standard is to offer support to schools, based in education and health partnerships, to become healthier places in which young people and staff can learn and work. The Standard can be used as a baseline for ongoing assessment of current practice or as a starting point for review of policy and offers a list of criteria against which whole-school achievements and specific themes can be assessed. One of the specific themes is drug education, including alcohol and tobacco, which is assessed on the following criteria:

- a named member of staff and a governor responsible for drug education provision;

- a planned drug education programme;

- a policy for managing drug related incidents, owned and implemented by the whole school including parents/carers;

- staff support;
- links with outside agencies, including the police, youth service and local drug services (NHSS, 1999) (see Case study 2.6.2).

At a local level, the Wirral Health Promoting Schools Scheme is one such initiative that aims to enable schools to have a positive influence on young people's health by offering a framework for a needs assessment that involves working through eight key themes, including drugs, alcohol and tobacco. The aim of this theme is to enable young people to access up-to-date information and skills, to assess and resist the risks to their health and alert them to the dangers of abuse and addiction, thus ensuring they know how and where to find support for themselves and others to protect their health and well-being.

CASE STUDY 2.6.2 DRUG AND ALCOHOL SERVICE FOR LONDON

Drug and Alcohol Service for London (DASL) (formerly Alcohol East), offers a range of services across East London to people with alcohol-related problems. It also provides a high-quality pragmatic and rational approach to alcohol education for primary and secondary schools. Their aim is to work closely with a school's own approach to drugs and alcohol and develop a series of lessons that best reflect the requirements of the National Curriculum and the Key Stages. Drug and Alcohol Service for London adopt a number of different learning strategies that seek to actively engage young people, including discussions, lectures, role-play, drama, video, quizzes, presentations, games, etc. They seek to impart knowledge, skills and attitudes and cover the following topics: alcohol and the law, binge drinking, alcohol dependency, healthy living, sexual health and alcohol, alcohol and other drugs, the physical effects of drinking, drink driving, brief intervention and substance misuse.

In addition, DASL provides Peer Education Programmes as one aspect of its work with young people. For example, a sexual health, drug and alcohol project currently operating in Swanlea School involves young people as peer educators. It is commonly acknowledged in the field that a lot of the benefits of peer education are experienced by the peer educators themselves. The students (largely Bengali Year 8 students) feel comfortable and relaxed about discussing the sensitive issues in the project – an essential element of what peer education is all about. Another important reason for using peers as educators is that young people can relate to them, and perceive them to be 'in touch' with the pressures and the 'scene' in a way they perceive adults not to be. This means that the education work that peer educators carry out has more of an impact than traditional forms of educating. Verbal feedback suggests that students find peer educators approachable, knowledgeable and enjoy having them in their school.

BIG FISH THEATRE COMPANY

▓ WHAT IS IT?

Big Fish Theatre Company aims to provide a professional, educational performance art training and active learning programme that engages participants with a range of contemporary social, spiritual and cultural concerns, including drug awareness. They work with a variety of youth and community organizations, including schools, and provide service training for teachers. All the performances and training programmes are interactive and provide a safe, fun and exciting opportunity to learn through group work and an exploration of knowledge and experience.

More specifically, Big Fish Theatre has developed and implemented a drugs awareness initiative for schools entitled Safe and Sound. Based upon the success of a two-year pilot project, the Company has developed an exciting PSHE training programme. The Safe and Sound project currently runs in schools in South London and consists of teacher training on PSHE issues, a drugs awareness information session for parents and an interactive theatre production for young people and their carers.

The aim of the teacher training module is to help schools maximize the effectiveness of the touring production and deliver an effective and comprehensive drugs education programme to young people aged 9–13 years. The training provides practical examples of lesson plans, active learning strategies that can be used and adapted for either the classroom or school hall, and single lessons or longer-term project work. The programme also addresses individual fears, concerns or barriers associated with implementation of PSHE lessons.

The drugs awareness information session for parents and carers provides an opportunity to become informed on the 'What, Why, When and How?' of PSHE. The session provides an opportunity to explore the National Curriculum guidelines and developments on drug education. This session also provides parents and carers with the opportunity to share experiences of their children and parenting, to build new relationships and to assist their own and their child's personal development.

Big Fish Theatre visits all schools with an interactive performance workshop for young people and their carers to watch together. There are other touring theatre companies who provide contemporary theatre for young people on a range of issues, including drugs, bullying and self-esteem (for example, Box Clever Theatre Company, Pop-Up Theatre Limited).

▓ WHO NEEDS TO BE INVOLVED?

In the school that we interviewed, all Year 7 pupils, Year 7 tutors, the PSHE co-ordinator and Year 7 parents were involved in the three stages of the intervention.

◼ COST – OVERT AND HIDDEN

The main cost is for Big Fish Theatre, and quotes are provided on application. In addition to these costs there are other costs in terms of taking the PSHE co-ordinator off timetable to attend the teacher training module, taking young people off timetable to allow them to participate in the interactive performance workshop and staff time in terms of organization and administration of the intervention.

◼ HOW LONG SHOULD IT LAST?

In one school the intervention has been running for at least the last five years for each Year 7 at the end of the summer term. Ideally, the teacher training module, the drugs awareness session for parents and carers, and the interactive performance workshop all occur within a couple of weeks of each other.

◼ BENEFITS

The PSHE co-ordinator in one school said that all three elements of Safe and Sound worked well together. She found the approach sensitive yet challenging, and the provision for teaching staff extremely supportive. The active learning strategies were very helpful in gauging the extent of young people's knowledge and awareness of drugs. The fact that the intervention has been running for 'as long as I can remember' is testimony to its success.

◼ POSSIBLE PROBLEMS

One of the possible problems is that it has been suggested that providing young people with information about drinking, smoking and drug taking actually encourages early and potentially unsafe behaviour in children who would not otherwise have considered it. The other is that ignorance of the issues means that pupils experiment because they do not understand the potential consequences. In theory, an increased awareness of alcohol and drugs might serve to normalize the idea of abuse long before most young people would have engaged in it. In reality, research suggests that there is no significant difference between the prevalence of regular smoking for pupils who remembered lessons about smoking compared with those who did not. Similarly, there was no difference for prevalence of drinking in the previous week, or ever trying drugs (ONS, 2001b). However, the survey did not take into account other factors such as frequency and quality of lessons. With this in mind, the findings of the Office for National Statistics (ONS, 2001b) survey do not support the view that having lessons about smoking, drinking and drug use encourages these behaviours, but neither is there any indication that lessons discourage them.

SUMMARY

- In this chapter we have been talking about alcohol use, tobacco use, illegal drug use and solvent abuse.

- Reducing and preventing alcohol, drug and substance abuse is necessary to enable young people to lead physically, mentally and sexually healthy lives, and also to reduce crime and school exclusions.

- Possible interventions include drug and alcohol education across the whole curriculum; health promoting school schemes, peer educators and touring theatre companies for schools.

- Big Fish Theatre uses teacher training, parent awareness sessions and interactive performance workshops to explore issues around drugs and drug abuse.

- The benefits of this approach include an integrated intervention involving staff, pupils and parents in a programme that confronts issues that some teachers and parents would otherwise find difficult to address.

RESOURCES

Alcohol Concern, Waterbridge House, 32–36 Loman Street, London SE1 0EE. Tel: 020 7928 7377. Website at www.alcoholconcern.org.uk Provides comprehensive information on alcohol and a local service finder.

BNTL, Westbrook Court, 2 Sharrow Vale Road, Sheffield, S11 8YZ. Tel: 0114 267 9976. Website at www.bntl.org

Big Fish Theatre Company, 59 Maidstone Hill, Greenwich, London SE10 8SY. Tel: 020 8692 5244. Website at www.spiff.demon.co.uk/bigfish

Box Clever Theatre, website at www.boxclevertheatre.com

Drinkline National Alcohol Helpline. Tel: 0800 917 8282. Provides information and help to callers worried about their own or someone else's drinking. Lines are open 9 a.m.–11 p.m. Monday to Friday and 6 p.m.–11 p.m. Saturday to Sunday.

Drugscope, 32–36 Loman Street, London SE1 0EE. Tel: 020 7928 1211. Website at www.drugscope.org.uk Provides comprehensive information on illegal drugs and a local service finder.

Drug and Alcohol Service for London (DASL), Capital House, 134–138 Romford Road, Stratford, London E15 4LD. Tel: 020 8257 3068.

Pop-Up Theatre Limited, website at www.pop-up.net

Wirral Health Promoting Schools Scheme. Health Links, 49 Hamilton Square, Birkenhead, CH41 5AR. Tel: 0151 647 1702.

The Socially Isolated/Children on the Asperger's/Autistic Spectrum

I can't myself raise the wind that might blow us into a better world. But I can at least put up a sail, so that when the wind comes, I can catch it. (E. F. Schumacher)

WHAT BEHAVIOURS ARE WE TALKING ABOUT?

There are many reasons why a child may be socially isolated including shyness, being a victim of bullying, becoming socially withdrawn as part of a depressive or psychotic illness or because of worries (such as problems at home, child abuse, etc). Some children have an innate problem with social relationships due to an autistic spectrum disorder (ASD).

WHAT ARE AUSTISTIC SPECTRUM DISORDERS?

Young people with autistic type disorders vary considerably in terms of the behaviour symptoms, severity and intellectual ability, i.e. from severely impaired to 'high functioning'. It includes those diagnosed as having autism or Asperger's syndrome. Young people with ASD are characterized by qualitative abnormalities in reciprocal social interaction, in patterns of communication and by a restricted, stereotyped, repetitive repertoire of interests and activities which are persuasive and affect the individual's functioning in all situations. Recent broadening of the diagnostic criteria has led to the identification of a much larger number of affected individuals. One recent estimate (Chakrabarti and Fombonne, 2001) suggested at least one in 250 children may be affected.

For an overview see Altwood's (1998) book *Asperger's Syndrome: A Guide for Parents and Professionals*. A number of books have also been written for young people with ASD including those by Luke Jackson (2002), who has Apserger's

Syndrome, and Gunilla Gerland (2000).

The National Initiative for Autism Screening and Assessment (NIASA), a multidisciplinary, multi-agency working group, was set up to develop a template/set of guidelines for the process of identification, assessment and access to appropriate interventions for pre-school and primary school aged children with ASD. Its final guidelines report 'National Autism Plan for Children' was completed in summer 2002 and will be published by the National Autistic Society (NAS) and available on a number of websites.

The DfES published good practise guidelines on ASD in 2002. The first part provides an introduction to ASD and the educational provision for children with an ASD, the second part outlines pointers to good practise.

WHAT DIFFICULTIES MAY A CHILD WITH ASD HAVE AT SCHOOL? OR, WHY DO CHILDREN WITH ASD FIND SCHOOL SO HARD?

Social skills deficits cause the most problems in daily life. For instance, children with ASD misread the social cues of teachers and other children, and may act in ways that are inappropriately silly, loud, aggressive or, in contrast, withdrawn. Those with special interests and who like to talk at length about them, do not recognize when they are putting other children off. Playground games with unclear rules and boundaries, e.g. how much pushing is acceptable, are another source of difficulty. Problems with friendship and loneliness are common.

CASE STUDY 2.7.1 LAURA

Laura is 12 years old. She was statemented for Asperger's syndrome when she was 8. However she still has considerable difficulties at school. She flies into frequent tempers where she throws books, pens, and even occasionally chairs. She has a one to one helper in the classroom for 18 hours a week. Most arguments start when the class is working in pairs or sharing books. Many of her class were nervous of working with her.

A Circle of Friends was set up which developed into a supportive group for all involved. Although Laura did not always find the feedback from the group easy, she did feel that there were others who she could be with at break times. Her behaviour and academic work improved. Two years later she made a positive transition to a new school.

CASE STUDY 2.7.2 DANIEL

Daniel is aged 14 years. He attends a local comprehensive school but has always found difficulty in mixing with the other pupils. He keeps himself to himself and always goes to the library at break or hangs around the Head of Year's room. He feels uncomfortable and unsure in lessons which involve group work, and will usually wait to be paired with someone else by the teacher. His parents separated six months ago and he often feels lonely and sad. He was recently referred to the child and adolescent mental health service where he had trouble describing how he felt. He did report that he had never been to someone else's birthday party. His mother started writing social stories for him and he found himself becoming more at ease in structured social settings such as science club at school.

The need for routine and order, and tantrums if violated, can also pose significant problems. Some children with ASD have a very clear sense of night and wrong which does not always endear them to other children!

Sensory issues (e.g. not liking being touched, certain textures, raised voices, or a noisy environment) tend to decrease with age but auditory sensitivity, e.g. in the dining hall can remain a major problem. On the other hand these children may have a high pain threshold.

Repetitive behaviours such as spinning, flapping or self-talk tend to disappear at school age, but may re-emerge at times of high anxiety.

Other difficulties such as poor attention, distractability, a pedantic or monotonous way of speaking, inflexibility, reduced awareness of personal space, the treatment of all people equally (even strangers) and poor verbal and non-verbal processing skills may compound the individual's difficulties at school and set him or her apart from his or her peers.

WHAT CAN BE DONE IN SCHOOL TO HELP?

1 A number of organizational strategies can be employed within the classroom, for example:

   (a) Create a low distraction work place within the classroom and a clearly defined space for personal equipment and belongings.

   (b) Make a quiet room available at any time in the school day (in case 'time out' is needed).

(c) Have clear signs/symbols/photographs in school communal areas and subject bases.

(d) To avoid crowded corridors, arrange for a student to leave early, appropriately supervised.

(e) Due to a reduced concept of time, alarms on watches or timed checklists may be used appropriately.

(f) Clear expectations, with attainable goals should be communicated effectively. Calendars, pictorial clues and schedules may all help.

(g) Be aware that sharing a textbook may be particularly stressful.

2 The provision of extra help in school with reading and numeracy and/or handwriting (if required).

3 Approaches to address communication deficits, for example:

(a) A young person on the autistic spectrum will interpret literally what is said and have difficulty with abstract concepts. This can be helped by giving unambiguous instructions and checking that they have been understood. Limit the amount of verbal information that is given.

b) Mind mapping, writing frames, etc. can be used to structure creative work.

4 Approaches to address social skill deficits, for example:

(a) Circle of Friends (see below).

(b) Social skills groups – these may be provided by speech and language therapy services and these groups provide an opportunity for children to meet other children like themselves.

5 Preparing children for new or difficult situations:

(a) Social stories. These are written for a particular child with the intention of providing information on what people in a given situation are doing, thinking or feeling, the sequence of events, the identification of significant social ones and the script of what to do or say (Gray, 1998). A parent or teacher can write these for a particular situation so that the young person can learn the unspoken signals which he or she cannot read him- or herself. The structure of the story is important. For more information see Gray (2000) or the Future Horizons website.

6 Reviewing recent events:

(a) Comic strip conversations can be used to review a particular behaviour. Conversation can be coloured to represent feelings, e.g. red for angry, yellow for happy, blue for sad. The situation can be reviewed in comic strip form so that the feelings of all the people involved can be unpacked. This allows the Asperger's child an increasing understanding of his/her world.

For a practical overview of the educational issues see the DfES report (DfES/DH, 2002). An excellent book which also includes approaches for young people with attention deficit disorder and developmental co-ordination disorder is by Jenkinson et al. (2002)

CIRCLE OF FRIENDS

WHAT IS CIRCLE OF FRIENDS?

Circle of friends is a creative and innovative approach which uses peer support to help troubled and troubling children by means of a peer network for individuals who experience difficulties in their relationships and behaviour. In brief, it involves setting up a Circle of Friends for the focus child. The circle helps them find ways round the difficulties they are experiencing. A facilitator oversees the process.

Experienced facilitators comment frequently on the depth and richness of support offered by Circle members. Children are also ingenious in devising practical strategies for defusing potentially difficult situations involving the target child. Case study evaluations (Whitaker, 1998; Newton and Wilson, 2000; Luckner, 1994; Perske and Perske, 1988) confirm that Circle of Friends is a flexible and creative method for the supportive role that young people can take in helping peers with relationship difficulties and re-integrating them into social circles.

Taylor and Burden (2001), lists six areas where circle of friends can make change:

- *Empowerment* – how well the focus child can take a greater measure of self-control of his or her behaviour and to make optimum choices about that behaviour.

- *Honesty* – how open is the group? Achieving this may be easier with younger children.

- *Belonging* – Cohesiveness is clearly vital to any group but needs to be worked at.

- *Belief in change* – once the focus children see the need for their behaviour to change and see that others think that it is possible, then their confidence grows and the desired changes start to happen.

- *Attributions* – the attributional nature of the Circle can move towards shared rather than the individual bearing all the responsibility.

- *Alliances* – positive alliances, i.e. friendships, can be formed with peers, parents and teachers.

If a young person has particular difficulties and is isolated from his or her peer group, a group of his or her class can be asked to volunteer to help, i.e. set up a Circle of Friends. After preparatory work with the focus child and parents there is a meeting with the class. (This is best facilitated by a trained counsellor or an educational psychologist.) The session leader makes it clear that it is unusual to talk about a person when they are not present in this way but that the focus child has agreed to the discussion. The leader invites the class to give a picture of the focus child stressing that only positive things can be said at this point. The next step is to invite the class to list some of the things that they find difficult about the focus child.

There is a general discussion about the role of friendship. The children are then asked to consider their own relationships, and, in particular, how they would feel if they were isolated or socially excluded. Children typically respond with words like: 'lonely', 'bored', 'frightened', 'unhappy', 'sad', 'unwanted' and 'depressed'. When the children are asked how they personally would behave if they were experiencing those sorts of feelings, usually they will produce responses like get into crime, try to get attention, get into drugs, run away, go and hide, steal people's things.

This is a turning point since the children have begun to show empathy. When they are asked what could be done to help, typically they produce two clear solutions: offer the focus child friendship or find ways to keep the child on track with his or her behaviour. Next the facilitator invites the class to list the things that might make it difficult for the focus child to change.

It is against this background of honest responsiveness that the Circle of Friends can be formed. The group facilitator then enlists the help of volunteers who will form the Circle of Friends for the focus child, usually between six and eight children.

This procedure, with appropriate adjustments for the particular individual, is effective for focus children with a range of problems: those who are aggressive or isolated, who are about to start as a new member of the class after, for example, having been excluded from their previous school, or those with learning difficulties.

Both Taylor and Burden (2001) and Whittaker (1998) suggest that regular reviews and support is necessary for the success of a group. This approach can be easily adapted to fit with almost any school environment. Good backup literature is available (provided by Inclusive Solutions, Derek Wilson and Colin Newton). However, for the Circle to succeed the general environment within the school needs to be constructive and supportive.

In our study one facilitator felt happy to run a Circle with little backup, but, it is generally accepted that the initial meeting benefits from an 'outsider' to lead it. This gives it an importance and validity. Outside support/facilitation can also be helpful when difficulties are encountered putting the intervention into practice.

Although this approach was developed with children it is being adapted and used increasingly in a variety of ways , such as for young people with a disability, to help some young people make the transition from school into the workplace, etc. (See Circles Network and Interact, in the Resources, for more information,) One school has reportedly approximately 30 Circles running at one time for various reasons.

WHAT ARE THE BENEFITS OF CIRCLE OF FRIENDS?

Circle of Friends can be beneficial for the focus child, other children and the teachers:

1 *For the focus child.* It gives direct feedback by supportive peers to children who are struggling with relationships. The literature reviews suggest that it is helpful for children on the Asperger's spectrum. It could be predicted that children with these difficulties would find peer review hard to handle. However they still appear to benefit, both socially and academically.

   A Circle of Friends set up for a young person moving into an established class tends to have more rapid positive effects

   In our study of three Circles (DfES, in press) the focus children benefited from an improvement in self-esteem. Although there were some concerns about an increased sense of self-importance this did not prevent the young people keeping friends or settling down to work.

2 *For the other children.* Other children feel good about being involved. Some Circles can become supportive for all their members. The Circles also give the young people the chance to develop increasing empathy.

3 *For the teachers.* Circle of Friends requires the facilitator to develop skills to allow the group to identify and resolve issues. It is different to a teaching role.

WHO NEEDS TO BE INVOLVED IN CIRCLE OF FRIENDS?

The circles generally function well if an outside person leads the initial meeting. It is a highly skilled facilitative role which, if carried out by someone from outside the school, carries a notion of seriousness and importance. A nominated teacher, or teaching assistant can facilitate the group. The pupils volunteer which is an important part of the process.

■ COST

Most educational psychologists are enthusiastic about Circle of Friends, though this might be patchy throughout the country. Their time might be costed to the school. Inclusive Solutions also run courses for teachers and support staff. These are day courses and cost £115 per day with a reduction for three or more staff. They also provide INSET training for a school at the cost of £500 for half a day and £1,000 for a whole day. There may be concessions available for a small school. There is the time cost in running the group during a break and in providing supervision for the teacher or teaching assistant.

■ POSSIBLE PROBLEMS

Circle of Friends benefits from regular monthly reviews and debriefing. This would allow a number of issues to be easily pre-empted and solved. An assessment of the progress of the group can be made and an ending planned.

BOX 2.7.1 BAD ENDINGS

The Circle for Simon fizzled out over a year change. This was unfortunate for the focus child who had had a number of bad endings in his life due to breakdowns in foster care and enforced changes of school. Children who are considered for Circle of Friends might be more vulnerable to bad endings.

Issues cropped up in the Circles, which were not serious enough to contact the educational psychologists about, e.g. what to do when Simon failed the tasks, when should the facilitator take back control from the group? These could have been talked through, thereby giving more confidence to the facilitators and helping them with their acquisition of skills.

It is also not clear which is the best age to run a Circle. The literature suggests it has been generally used with younger children. However, teenage years are when the peer group is at its most influential, and therefore when Circles may be the most effective. The difficulty may lie in encouraging other pupils to volunteer. The ethos of the school would make a considerable difference in how likely this would succeed in an older age group.

The Circles can also create feelings in those not immediately involved.

BOX 2.7.2 THIRD PARTY EFFECTS

When Simon's group was initially set up, Michael who subsequently volunteered to be in Kris's Circle, attacked Simon in the playground. Most of the Circle got involved and Simon's mother reported that a number of children left with black eyes that day. Later it transpired that Michael had felt angry because he was going through a difficult time at home and struggling with friendships at school . He felt that it was unfair that Simon was handed friends on a plate while he had to work very hard at it. He told me, 'I thought it was a bad thing because people were telling us to be nice to him and that made me feel angry'. However, a term and a half later he joined Kris's circle. 'I wanted to. I wanted to do it because I had seen the other group working for Simon and I wanted to be part of it.'

BOX 2.7.3 HOW TO DO CIRCLE OF FRIENDS

Preparation
- Liaison with outside staff such as an educational psychologist.
- Liaison with focus child and their parents.

Intervention
- Meeting set up with external facilitator and tutor group.
- Circle established with focus child and volunteers from peer group.
- Circle meets regularly each week for about 20 minutes, facilitated by nominated staff member.
- Review set up to decide ending.
- Regular support provided by external facilitator.

Post-intervention
- Appraise effectiveness.

SUMMARY

Children who struggle with their social environment may find school difficult for a number of reasons. Circle of Friends is an effective intervention which can provide both social and academic improvement. It has mainly been used in the younger age group but, providing the ethos of the school is supportive, is an important tool to be considered.

RESOURCES

Circles Network, Pamwell House, 160 Pennywell Road, Easton, Bristol BS5 OTX. Tel: 0117939 3917.

Gray, C. (2000) *The New Social Story Book.* Arlington: Future Horizons Inc.

Inclusive Solutions, 49 Northcliffe Avenue, Nottingham NG3 6DA. Tel: 0115 956 7305. www.inclusive-solutions.com

Interact, Moulsham Mill Parkway, Chelmsford, Essex CM2 7PX. Tel: 01245 608201.

Jenkinson, J., Hyde, T. and Ahmad, S. (2002) *Occupational Therapy Approaches for Secondary Special Needs*, London: Whurr Publishers.

Newton, C. and Wilson, D. (2000) *Circles of Friends.* Dunstable and Dublin: Folens Ltd.

Perske, R. and Perske, M. (1988) *Circles of Friends.* Nashville, TN: Abingdon Press.

Taylor, G. and Burden, B. (2001) *The Positive Power of Friendship.* Calouste Gulbenkian Foundation.

Helping Children Deal with Loss

I wish someone had explained to me about the time when my father died. I wish someone had thought to tell me that a month is not long enough to get used to the death of someone who has been central to your life for eighteen years. It would have helped so much to know that however normal I might appear after a month, a year would not be long enough to begin to feel normal again. (Abrams, 1992, p. 76)

I'm Rob. I was eight when my Mum died. My memory box helps me not to forget … I like to show my memory box to people who didn't ever know my mum. (Teenager, Winston's Wish)

WHAT BEHAVIOURS ARE WE TALKING ABOUT?

There is a growing concern in the UK about the emotional needs of bereaved children and young people, yet for most youngsters in this situation there is very little support. In fact, while there is scientific evidence that children, for example, who have experienced the death of a parent are at increased risk of developing a mental health problem, it is only when the symptoms of grief become complicated that such young people are referred for professional help (Stokes et al., 1999). Many simply have to cope as best they can with the help of family and friends. Parents and teachers may well find themselves trying to deal with changed patterns of behaviour as the child tries to come to terms with the emotional impact of separation and loss. Of course, the majority of bereaved children may not need professional help but that does not mean that they do not need any help at all. Simply to rely on the spontaneous responses of immediate family, friends and teachers may not be enough since in Western culture many people feel too embarrassed to talk about death. As Stokes et al. (1999) point out, professionals have noted an increase in the number of requests from bereaved families for help in dealing with their children's loss.

If a young person experiences prolonged separation from a loved one (for example, from death or from loss through parental divorce), it is necessary for him or her to go through a period of mourning, just as an adult would. Colin Murray-Parkes (1972) described the phases of grief:

- An initial 'stunned' or numb phase when emotions are blunted. This lasts from a few hours to two weeks.

- A mourning phase, characterized by intense mourning and distress, sadness, irritability and preoccupation with the person who has died. Transient hallucinatory experiences are common, e.g. seeing the dead person, as are guilt or denial.

- Acceptance and readjustment, several weeks after the onset of mourning.

The duration of this process varies with culture; on average it takes about six months. A person may develop atypical grief, and abnormal grief reaction such as:

- chronic grief which may turn into depression with excessive guilt and preoccupation;

- inhibited or delayed grief, where the person is slow to grieve or unable to show their grief;

- non-specific and mixed reactions including the development of physical or mental health problems.

Children go through these same phases and experience the same feelings as adults do but may not be able to describe these experiences well. The symptoms they show vary with age: under-5s have somatic symptoms and primary school children primarily have conduct problems. It is only when they become adolescents that they experience their feelings in a more direct way.

Children and young people respond with behavioural changes when they are coming to terms with such a loss. In the case of children, the symptoms can include withdrawal, stealing, sleeping problems, regressive behaviour, attention seeking and eating difficulties (Dent et al., 1996). Some adolescents show their grief through such behaviours but others suppress the symptoms and can give the impression of indifference. However, it is important not to be taken in by a surface appearance of coping. Adolescents are able to understand death and absence at a cognitive level but may be less willing to express their feelings openly. It is possible, too, that the mourning process may not end in the same way as an adult's since it may be reactivated later on in the young person's life (even in adulthood) by related experiences of separation and loss, for example, when an intimate relationship breaks up. For some young people who have lost a parent early in life, the grieving process may be activated as they enter adolescence and begin the psychological process of individuation and separation, as the case study of Emma illustrates.

CASE STUDY 2.8.1 EMMA, WHOSE MOTHER DIED WHEN SHE WAS A BABY

Emma's mother was diagnosed with breast cancer when Emma was 9 months old. She died six months later. Emma was brought up by her father with help from her maternal grandmother and nannies. Her father remarried, which he hoped would help them all. As Emma entered adolescence, she became increasingly sad and preoccupied with thoughts about her mother: what was her mother like, was she like her, what would it be like if her mother was around now? These thoughts interfered with her ability to concentrate at school. She sought help from her form tutor who became a mother figure to her and helped her plan her coursework and revision as well as being there ready to listen. In spite of this, she became increasingly depressed and was referred by her General Practitioner to the local CAMHS. She was treated with antidepressants and offered psychotherapy to help her with issues of loss and identity. She continued to need extra support from her tutor at school. Gradually she improved and sat her GCSEs which she did well in.

Adolescents respond to loss in a wide variety of ways. They may respond with denial, or anger or protest, or with apparent apathy and a studied involvement in their usual activities. Boys are likely to have greater difficulty in expressing their emotions than girls. Girls find it much easier to express grief through crying or by confiding in close friends and family (Dyregrov, 1991). In the early stages of grieving there is often a great deal of denial. The young person may enter into a numbed state that can go on for days or weeks. They may talk to the absent person. Alternatively, they may deny the importance of the loss by saying things like, 'We weren't that close anyway' or 'These things happen!' It is important for adults to be aware that these behaviours represent strategies that young people devise to protect themselves from the pain of loss. Yet adults are often anxious that they may say the wrong thing and are too quick to believe that their children are coping, so leaving them to deal alone with feelings of fear. However, some of the strategies, while they offer short-term relief, may in the longer term be unhelpful or even destructive, as the case study of Phil indicates.

WHAT BENEFITS ARE THERE TO BE GAINED IN TACKLING LOSS?

The difficulty with a withdrawn young person like Phil (p.145) is that, too often, adults fail to notice the difficulties as they would with someone who acted out their distress. As a result, boys like Phil are more likely to be denied the opportunity to get in touch with their own grieving processes. What Phil's mother and teachers had not realized was that his apparent normality was a strategy to protect himself from emotional pain. Understandably, his mother, who was very preoccupied with her own feelings of loss, had failed to notice how disturbed her teenage son had become, in part because of her need for support. His grief emerged through an aggressive reaction to an insensitive remark made by a peer who, again understandably, had not recognized that Phil's academic aspirations were attempts to please his dead father. If there had been more recognition of Phil's need to grieve and to remember his father and what his father would have wished for him, then he would have been enabled to come to terms more easily with the pain of his loss.

CASE STUDY 2.8.2 PHIL'S REACTION TO THE LOSS OF HIS FATHER

Phil, an only child, was 13 years old when his Dad suddenly died of a heart attack. Phil had important mathematics and physics examinations in the week when his Dad died and was encouraged by his mother to try as far as possible to carry on revising as normal. She in turn promised to try hard not to show her upset. As Phil was a good student, he did well in the examinations. In the weeks that followed, he continued to study hard and spent his spare time doing the household chores that his Dad had formerly carried out. Phil's mother praised Phil for his strength during the difficult months following the death and often said how hard it would have been for her to cope if he had not 'stepped so easily into his father's shoes'. His mother said that these things were private and should be kept within the family. Phil coped so well on the surface that most of his peers and teachers did not even know about the family bereavement. What most people did notice, however, was that, while his academic work continued to be good, Phil was becoming increasingly withdrawn from peer group social life. He was uninterested in sport and was too busy with study and domestic tasks at home to go out much. He was a model student in his teachers' eyes and nobody considered him to be a problem until one day, about a year after his Dad died, he behaved in an extremely uncharacteristic way. In class, when Phil was praised as usual by the teacher for his high performance in mathematics, another pupil taunted him for being 'a sad boff'. Phil reacted by punching the boy in the face so violently that he broke his nose. The teacher was astonished that such a quiet student as Phil could have overreacted to such an apparently trivial incident. He was punished for his misdemeanour but no one, least of all Phil, made any connection with the events in his family life.

WHAT ARE THE POSSIBLE INTERVENTIONS?

It is essential for adults to be aware of the different developmental needs of the young person experiencing loss. The most effective intervention is that a sympathetic adult is present and truly listens to what the young person has to say verbally or express non-verbally. It is important to hear the young person's point of view in whatever form it comes. Props such as photographs and mementoes can help. The media of story, poetry, drama or music may give the young person symbolic ways of expressing overwhelming feelings. The adult should be sensitive to behavioural changes in the young person and provide opportunities for the young person to participate in a grieving process.

It is important to give young people clear information about what has happened, why and how it happened, and what may happen next. It is always a mistake to lie about what happened or to attempt to soften the blow by using ambiguous language like 'Dad went to sleep and won't wake up again'. Preparation for the event can help to avoid confusion, even though it can be difficult to find the right words. It can help for parents to say something like:

> At the moment Dad can do lots of things and even though he has this illness he is still your Dad. But when he gets more sick he might not be able to do all the things he used to. That does not mean that he doesn't care about you very much and he feels sad and angry that he is so ill. (Stokes and Crossley, 2001, p. 8)

Worden (1991) identified four tasks that young people must do before the period of mourning can be said to be over:

- Accept the reality of the loss.
- Work though the pain of grief.
- Adjust to an environment in which the dead or absent person is missing.
- Relocate the absent person emotionally and begin to 'move on' in life.

In the Harvard Bereavement Study (Silverman and Worden, 1993) a sample of 125 parentally bereaved children was compared with a control group of non-bereaved children. One finding was that only a third of the children observed were at risk of severe emotional distress and that most adjusted well with the support of family and friends. Worden (1997) devised three possible models of intervention for helping bereaved young people (Table 2.8.1). The aim of these is to facilitate the grieving process.

There are difficulties with each model. In many instances, especially where services are limited, it is likely that Model A will be adopted, so providing help for those young people who are visibly demonstrating disturbed behaviours that require urgent intervention. But the problem with this kind of reactive approach is that only 'acting out' children get attention while those who internalize their pain may be overlooked. The adoption of Model B in the development of community bereavement services is likely to reach a larger proportion of bereaved children who need help but there may be difficulties in finding a sensitive enough screening tool to identify 'at-risk' or 'potentially at-risk' young people. Model C is likely to be considered unviable since it may be viewed as too expensive an intervention to offer, but it may be possible to incorporate it into community-based work with bereaved families.

The Stokes et al. (1999) well-evaluated initiative, Winston's Wish, has linked Model C with the Dual Process Model of Loss, developed by Stroebe and Schut (1999), which identifies a dynamic process of grieving that shifts between focusing on and avoiding the loss experience. Each can occur in close proximity to the other and such a process is confirmed by the experiences of bereaved people. The development of community services that reflect the dynamic nature of the grieving process can be most successful in facilitating effective coping strategies while heightening awareness of the distinctive ways in which different family members express their grief. Here is one example of how the process might work in everyday life. The young person is probably aware that the parent gets upset when talking about a dead family member (focusing on the loss), and so engages in activities that are less upsetting such as cooking a meal together or talking about other topics (avoiding the loss). This kind of behaviour can be healing for the family if the processes of avoidance are acknowledged as positive means of support. However, it can also lead to problems when such behaviour is misinterpreted as a lack of feeling. Winston's Wish is an example of a Model C grief support intervention.

TABLE 2.8.1 MODELS OF INTERVENTION FOR BEREAVED CHILDREN

Model A To offer intervention only where children display levels of emotional and behavioural problems or psychological distress

Model B To offer intervention to those children identified at-risk by use of a screening measure. This preventative mental health model of early screening aims to target potential 'at-risk' groups for early intervention in order to reduce the likelihood of long-term negative outcomes

Model C To offer intervention routinely to all bereaved children and their families, recognizing that the death of a parent is one of the most fundamental losses a child can experience

Source: adapted from Worden, 1997, pp. 150–1.

A COMMUNITY-BASED INTERVENTION: WINSTON'S WISH

Winston's Wish – http://www.winstonswish.org.uk – is a community-based bereavement support programme for children between the ages of 5 and 16 years who have experienced the death of a close family member. The programme consists of the following:

- a careful assessment of each family's needs in their own home;
- 'Camp Winston', a residential weekend for young people;

- 'Camp Winston' for parents;

- a support programme for schools;

- individual work when grief is complicated;

- residential weekends for those affected by suicide;

- social activities to maintain friendships;

- information weekends and evenings for parents;

- telephone advice supported by books and leaflets;

- support for children when a close family member is dying;

- the positive involvement of children in funerals.

This intervention makes constructive use of family involvement and emphasizes the role of peer support in helping children and their parents deal with grief. Stokes et al. view this kind of community-based intervention as a preventative measure that relieves pressure on specialist mental health services. They also conclude that children need opportunities over time to talk about and remember their dead family member in ways that are meaningful. It is an ongoing process through which the young person can come to understand why their parent died and what role the dead person might continue to have in their lives. Model C community-based services aim to facilitate the appropriate expression of emotions and the development of skills and coping strategies that can be used throughout life. Even for a family that might well be considered not 'at-risk', this process of accommodation following bereavement is described as 'for ever' (Stokes et al., 1999, p. 301).

WHO NEEDS TO BE INVOLVED?

On the basis of their observations of over 1,500 bereaved children and their families, Stokes et al. have written a charter of rights for bereaved children which we have reproduced in Table 2.8.2. From this charter it can be seen that adults in the family and community can work collaboratively with professionals to meet the diverse needs of children and young people at different stages of the grieving process. Note, too, the important role that can be played by peers in alleviating the pain of loss. The peer group can also be helpful in alleviating the distress of young people who are bereaved by offering friendship and protection.

PRACTICE POINTS

- Young people respond in a variety of ways to the death of a close friend or family member. It is important to acknowledge this.

- It is important to speak openly and honestly about the death when appropriate and to give young people the opportunity to understand their own strong emotions around the loss. There is likely to be some difficult behaviour during this time since strong emotions are hard to bear.

■ It is helpful to provide accurate information in terms that young people can understand and at a time when they are ready to assimilate it.

■ Support groups within the family, the community and the school can be very beneficial.

TABLE 2.8.2 A CHARTER FOR BEREAVED CHILDREN

1. *Adequate information.* Bereaved children are given answers to their questions about what has happened, why it happened and what will happen next
2. *Being involved.* Bereaved children are asked if they wish to be involved in decisions that have an impact on their lives (e.g. planning the funeral, remembering anniversaries)
3. *Family involvement.* Bereaved children are given support which both includes parents and respects the child's right to confidentiality
4. *Meeting others.* Bereaved children have opportunities to meet other children with similar experiences
5. Telling the story. Bereaved children have the right to tell their story in a variety of ways and to have those stories heard
6. *Expressing feelings.* Bereaved children should be enabled to express all feelings associated with grief, including anger, sadness, guilt and anxiety
7. Not to blame. Bereaved children should be helped to understand that they are not to blame for the death
8. Established routine. Bereaved children should be free to choose to continue with previously enjoyed activities.
9. School response. Bereaved children can benefit from receiving an appropriate response from their school or college
10. Remembering. Bereaved children have a right to remember the dead person for the rest of their lives if they wish, so that the person becomes a comfortable part of the child's ongoing lifestory.

Source: adapted from Stokes et al., 1999.

POSSIBLE PROBLEMS

The main problem is time and willingness to bear/share the pain of the young person's loss. Being there for someone and listening to their experiences and range of emotions can be very draining for those around them. If this occurs, it is important to recognize this and seek support from someone else used to such situations e.g. the school nurse, school counsellor or educational psychologist.

COSTS

The main cost is time and willingness

HOW LONG SHOULD IT LAST?

As long as necessary to facilitate the grieving process and even when this appears to be over some feelings and issues may re-emerge at anniversaries or the time of other significant events or reminders, and the young person may need further support at such times.

SUMMARY

The loss of a significant adult, either by death or divorce can have profound consequences for a young person. This chapter looks at the normal grief process and positive interventions which can provide support and help.

RESOURCES

Winston's Wish. This organization offers a service for bereaved children and young people to include residential weekends, camps for parents, work with individuals and a support programme for schools. http://www.winstonswish.org.uk

Cowie, H. and Wallace, P. (2000) *Peer Support in Action.* London: Sage.

Dent, A., Condom, L., Blair, P. and Fleming, P. (1996) A study of bereavement care after a sudden and unexpected death, *Archives of Disease in Childhood,* 74, 522-6.

Dyregrov, A. (1991) *Grief in Children: a Handbook for Adults.* London: Jessica Kingsley.

Sharp, S. and Cowie, H. (1998) *Counselling and Supporting Children in Distress.* London: Sage.

Stokes, J., Pennington, J., Monroe, B., Papadatou, D. and Relf, M. (1999) Developing services for bereaved children: a discussion of the theoretical and practical issues involved, *Mortality,* 4, 3, 291–307.

Worden, J.W. (1991) *Grief Counselling and Grief Therapy.* London: Routledge.

Worden, J.W. (1997) *Children and Grief – When a Parent Dies.* New York: Guilford Press.

CHAPTER 2.9

Eating Problems

Why doesn't she just eat! (Sam, brother of anorexic girl)

WHAT BEHAVIOUR ARE WE TALKING ABOUT?

There are several different types of eating disorders which usually begin in adolescence: anorexia nervosa, bulimia nervosa, obesity, dysfunctional dysphagia and pervasive refusal syndrome. More young people will be overweight or worried about their looks.

ANOREXIA NERVOSA

The three main features of anorexia nervosa are:

- determined food avoidance;

- weight loss or failure to maintain the steady weight gain expected for the young person's age. The behaviour of the youngster is often designed to produce this weight loss, e.g. by excessive exercise, vomiting or laxative use;

- preoccupation with weight and shape, often with a distorted body image. There can be a morbid fear of becoming fat.

In most cases the disease starts in adolescence or early adult life. It has been known to start in children as young as 8 years old. The prevalence is up to 0.7 per cent in the adolescent populations but less before puberty. It affects many more girls than boys. The incidence of the disease increased from the 1930s to the early 1980s. However, since then the incidence appears to have stabilized. This trend has been attributed to changes in culturally determined attitudes of behaviour patterns during the twentieth century, e.g. attitudes to beauty, desirability, fashion, etc.

Anorexia nervosa is the third most common chronic illness in adolescents. It has a high morbidity and mortality and it may persist for years disrupting many aspects of woman's life and those close to her (Stewart, 1998).

The onset of the illness may be associated with:

- a period of dieting perhaps in response to being called fat;
- an anti-food pact with a friend;
- following an illness such as a viral infection.

The girl may deny feeling hungry, and may try to hide her lack of eating, e.g. by flushing her packed lunch down the toilet. Mealtimes can be very anxiety provoking, and to cope with this she may develop ritualistic eating habits such as cutting food into tiny pieces. She can be obsessed with exercise, e.g. running rather than walking, wriggling her feet while having to sit still during lessons. When the illness gets a hold, much of her concentration will be taken up by her thoughts of food, exercise, anxiety and body appearance.

Psychologically a youngster with anorexia nervosa avoids anxiety by not eating and thus avoids weight gain and being perceived as a social failure. Initial weight loss may well be rewarded by peers. This is compounded by the feeling of satisfaction the individual feels about being in control of at least one area of her life.

Risk factors for the development of anorexia nervosa include:

- problems in the family;
- early feeding problems;
- obsessive compulsive traits;
- death of a close relative early in childhood;
- interpersonal problems;
- low self-esteem at the age of 11–12 leads to a greater risk of developing an eating disorder four years later;
- dieting – 88 per cent of youngsters with an eating disorder have a history of dieting;
- unrealistic expectations as girls struggle to be high achievers as well as beautiful;
- a family history of eating disorders;
- a history of having been teased about one's weight;
- an increased incidence of severe life stresses in the 18 months

prior to the development of an eating disorder;

- a change of school accompanied by other life stresses can lead to a higher incidence of eating problems.

Other illnesses can occasionally present with a picture of anorexia nervosa. They need to be borne in mind particularly the early stage the illness. The differential diagnosis includes:

- *depressive disorders*, which can also present with social withdrawal, irritability, and sleep disturbance. The attitude to food and body image is crucial in the distinction;

- occasionally, *medical disorders* such as Crohn's disease, diabetes mellitus, hyperthyroidism, renal failure and cancer can mimic the condition;

- *recreational drugs* which cause weight loss (including amphetamines and ecstasy) should always be considered.

■ BULIMIA NERVOSA

The three main features of bulimia nervosa are:

- a powerful and intractable urge to overeat, resulting in episodes of recurrent binges. This is accompanied by a sense of lack of control;

- recurrent compensatory behaviour, such as self-induced vomiting, laxative abuse, fasting or exercise;

- self-evaluation is unduly influenced by body weight and shape. As with anorexia nervosa there is a morbid fear of becoming fat.

Bulimia rarely starts before the age of 14 years. The peak age of onset is probably in late adolescence, although binges and vomiting may be kept secret for years. Most cases present in their twenties. The prevalence in the age range 15 to 30 years is 1–3 per cent in females and 0.1–0.3 per cent in males. There is often a great deal of secrecy about this illness and there are probably undetected cases in the community. There appears to be less genetic influence for bulimia than anorexia.

The main risk factors for bulimia are:

- parental history of obesity;

- personal history of obesity;

- parental history of depression;

- personal history of depression;

- critical comments by family about shape, weight or eating;

- negative self-evaluation;

- parental alcoholism;

- impulsive dramatic personality traits.

Psychologically there may be initially dysfunctional attitudes about body weight and shape, facilitated by negative affect such as depression and stress. The youngster may set herself excessively rigid dietary standards which are followed by binges when they are broken. This induces purging behaviour, such as self-induced vomiting, laxative abuse, restricted diet or strict period to starvation, which initially reduces anxiety but is rapidly followed by guilt and depression. In consequence she promises herself to never do it again and sets even more extreme standards for herself. The circle continues.

Bulimia can be associated with self-injurious behaviour such as cutting, alcohol and drug abuse, and sexual promiscuity. Approximately a third of both anorexic and bulimic patients report being sexually abused.

OBESITY

This can be defined as excessive weight in relation to age or height. Obesity can cause considerable problems in school. Being overweight makes you more likely to be either a victim and/or a perpetrator of bullying incidents. Both pupils and staff can have negative reactions to those children who are overweight. These children frequently develop poor self-esteem and self-value. This chapter is not primarily targeted towards this group of children. Interventions to raise self-esteem may have an impact on this group – see Circle Time, Circle of Friends, etc.

EATING DISORDERS, PUBERTY AND GENDER

Changes in body shape and an increasing body fat in puberty can be particularly challenging for girls as their bodies develop in a way which is opposite to the sociocultural norms of beauty as portrayed in the media. Girls who do not mind the physical changes may struggle with the weight gain (Shore and Porter 1990). Some young women may refuse the task of developing womanhood and try to reverse the process. An eating disorder leads to an interruption and even a reversal in maturation as the girls usually stop menstruating and their breasts diminish in size. There is some evidence for a higher rate of eating concerns in early maturing girls (Alsaker, 1996; Brooks-Gunn, and Warren, 1989). The importance of anorexia nervosa that starts before puberty is that it *can* permanently impair growth and gonad development, and has significant long-term consequences.

The situation for boys is quite different since, for them, puberty brings them closer to the cultural idea of masculinity. The proportion of boys with anorexia nervosa is much greater *before* puberty than after. Although only 5–10 per cent of adolescents and young adult cases occurred in males, 20 to 30 per cent of childhood cases are boys.

WHAT BENEFITS ARE THERE TO BE GAINED BY TACKLING THESE BEHAVIOURS?

Many teenage girls struggle with negative self-image, dieting preoccupations and cultural pressures. A space in the curriculum to allow supportive education and open communication may tackle some of these issues before they develop. There will always be a small number of individuals whose particular circumstances and genetic endowment make them more vulnerable to eating disorders. These children, having developed the full-blown syndrome, will probably require outside help from the child and adolescent psychiatric service, psychologists or, possibly, social workers.

Friends may be the first people to pick up the issues and present them to staff. The earlier an eating disorder is taken seriously the easier it is for the eating problems to be resolved. Friends often find dealing with these issues very difficult. Due to the level of secrecy within the disorder, peers may feel very torn between loyalty to their friends and care for them. They may be unsure of the correct course of action. The discussion of difficult and sensitive issues which the teenagers face in their social environment allows them to feel that the adults can be open and realistic about these challenges. The adults can model supportive and non-judgemental communication, relieving some of the peer anxiety and allowing more focus to be on work. Staff may also have a role in discussing the situation with parents and referring if necessary.

WHAT ARE THE POSSIBLE INTERVENTIONS?

Education programmes can play an important part in changing attitudes to mental health problems including eating attitudes. Healthy eating practices are part of education for life. With increasing disintegration of family life, basic life skills need to be seen as a necessary part of school life. Many schools play an active part in encouraging healthy eating habits. Good eating practices which are encouraged from early years can have an ongoing affect as people mature with age, and for future generations.

Other interventions which increase communication within the school, and support the self-esteem of youngsters and staff may have positive benefits both on allowing early presentation of eating difficulties and on preventing their development. There have been a number of studies on the impact of education programmes for eating disorders. Stewart (1998) summarizes previous programmes, which have focused, first, on imparting information about eating disorders and the adverse effects of dieting and, secondly, on developing skills to resist social pressures to diet. All the studies showed increasing knowledge following the programme and some showed an improvement in eating attitudes (Killen et al., 1993; Moreno and Thelen, 1993; Moriarty et al., 1990; Shisslak et al., 1990; Paxton, 1993; Rosen, 1989). They were less likely to show improvements in eating behaviour. Most of the studies only had short-term follow-up, and very few had a control group. The study by Stewart (1998) who presented the intervention in Year 9, found over the 18 months follow-up a significant deterioration in eating attitudes and behaviours in the control group. The group with the intervention showed less deterioration. It is therefore possible that the interventions have more impact than was previously realized by the studies without control groups.

The timing of the intervention appears to be crucial. The intervention needs to be targeted at youngsters who have developed the cognitive and behavioural skills necessary for change. However, those interventions which discuss body image after puberty has started may make youngsters more aware of how they wish to look. Discussing eating disorders and body image in a vulnerable population may only serve to increase the problem (Lask, 2001, personal communication). The key age for intervention appears to be Year 8/9, as eating habits are not as fixed as Years 10 and 11 (Stewart, 2001).

A particular risk for girls developing anorexia nervosa is increasing academic pressure applied to a youngster who is a perfectionist. As GCSEs approach, it is very easy to apply the same amount of pressure indiscriminately across the class. However, there will be some youngsters, possibly the boys, who need strong encouragement to make them take work seriously, whereas others may actually perform less well as increasing anxiety prevents them from remaining focused. Targeting and decreasing the pressure in Years 10 and 11 may increase the emotional health of this age group.

Other less specific things are important for providing a supportive environment in schools:

- an emphasis on the pastoral role of schools in teacher training, so that teachers are aware of the physical and mental health needs of the youngsters;
- a school counsellor who can provide support such as practical cognitive behavioural advice, anger management groups, problem-solving groups and short-term focused work;

- school nurses who can provide drop-in clinics which are accessible for youngsters;

- good links between schools and outside agencies, e.g. drug and alcohol education, health, child and adolescent mental health services;

- a well-functioning PSHE curriculum;

- self-esteem measures which run throughout school;

- pupils and teachers feel listened to within the school community;

- clear anti-bullying policy which is enforced (Stewart, 2001).

EATING DISORDER EDUCATION PROGRAMME

WHAT IS IT?

The education programme below, was developed by A. Stewart and J. Carter. It is described by Stewart in *The Prevention of Eating Disorders* (1998). It aims to look at helping youngsters:

- adjust to the biological changes of puberty;

- develop positive relationships including sexual relationships;

- develop skills, and setting realistic goals for themselves;

- develop independence, and positive relationships with their families;

- develop a sense of personal identity;

- respond well to sociocultural pressures;

- respond sensibly to adverse comments about shape and weight;

- recognize negative thinking and learn to challenge it;

- education about dieting.

The style of the programme is interactive rather than didactic, making extensive use of discussion and role-play. The pupils are actively encouraged to make changes in their eating habits and exercise patterns. Skills are developed using a variety of strategies including cognitive-behavioural techniques, role-play, home activities and self-monitoring. It includes a story of a girl struggling with puberty and eating problems. Description of the programme can be found in Stewart (1998). The programme was delivered over a period of six weeks and consisted of six 45-minute sessions.

WHAT ARE THE BENEFITS?

In general, pupils respond well to the programme particularly valuing the small group exercises, the role-play and the cognitive restructuring, i.e. the reviewing of negative thoughts. In the Stewart study (1998) pupils occasionally brought up personal issues about themselves or a friend, commonly approaching staff at the end of the session. The programme appeared to facilitate disclosure of problems. There is an improvement in eating knowledge and behaviours.

WHO NEEDS TO BE INVOLVED?

The programme has been developed for teachers to use. A key worker needs to research the programme and assess its appropriateness for use in the school and adapt it if necessary. Time needs to be set aside for staff training. It could be used in a regular slot in the PSHE course in Year 8 or Year 9. There may need to be some backup should some of the youngsters disclose significant problems. This should be thought out before the programme starts.

HOW LONG SHOULD IT LAST?

The programme is designed to be implemented over a six-week period. This is felt to be long enough to tackle the issues but continue to hold the youngsters' attention. Stewart mentions the ongoing need to reinforce the tackling of negative thoughts and the raising of self-esteem. Other policies within the school environment could do this.

COST – OVERT AND HIDDEN

The costs include:

- the resource itself;
- time for the key worker to assess the resource and train up staff (this would be true of any PSHE programme);
- liaison with support services needs to be researched and developed;
- some form of immediate backup and support within the school pastoral system for problems which are disclosed needs to be available. This may already be present in your school.

POSSIBLE PROBLEMS

The programme works best when the regular class tutor is responsible for leading the sessions.

There has been some suggestion that the intervention should be carried out in an at-risk population. However this will make the discussions more biased and the facilitator may find him- or herself in a minority position. This will greatly limit the benefits of the programme.

The studies were carried out in girls' schools. In a mixed group the programme will generate a broader discussion and may give the boys more understanding about some of the issues which concern the girls. The length of the course may need to be reviewed as it may be harder to engage the boys for six weeks. The mixed group may be beneficial but be harder work for the facilitator. There has been little research on this.

The programme does not aim to tackle specific family problems raised in the sessions. They should be discussed privately at the end.

The cognitive behaviour element in the programme works well and the youngsters tend to grasp the ideas easily. However, realistically, this work may need to be continued for the teenagers to develop long-lasting skills in challenging negative cognitions. This could be built into other PSHE programmes. Under the resource section are three publications which give advice about dealing with negative thoughts.

BOX 2.9.1 SETTING UP AN EATING DISORDER EDUCATION PROGRAMME

Preparation
> Research resources (see Stewart, 1998)
> Decide on target audience taking into account age and gender:
> – At-risk group (need a good reason for this one)
> – Girls only
> – Mixed group
> Training for teachers/staff
> Set up backup support if necessary
> Research liaison system and local health resources

Intervention
> Designed to run for six sessions of 45 minutes

Review and adapt
> Plan for the following year.
> Develop themes of challenging negative cognitions/improving self-esteem in other PSHE programmes, etc.

SUMMARY

An eating disorder education programme can help to mitigate the increasing risks of developing these disorders during puberty. Research suggests that the benefits are mixed though it needs to be recognized that during Years 9, 10 and

11 body image and eating behaviours deteriorate throughout the girl population. The timing of the intervention is crucial and should take place when the youngsters have some ability to reason but before they are in high-risk years. As boys are most at risk prior to puberty and have a much lower incidence of the disorders, the interventions in the past have been primarily targeted towards girls. Measures which increase the pastoral work in school and improve the self-esteem of pupils also play an important role in decreasing the incidence of eating disorders.

RESOURCES

Tackling negative cognitions:

Beck, A.T. (1976) *Cognitive Therapy and Emotional Disorders.* New York: International Universities Press.
Beck, A.T., Rush, A.J., Shaw, B.F. and Emery, G. (1979) *Cognitive Therapy of Depression.* New York: Guilford Press.
Burns, D. 1990 *The Feeling Good Handbook.* New York: Plume/Penguin.

Deliberate Self-harm

Some guys were puttin' him
down, bullin' him round (round)
now I wish I would'a talked to him
given him the time of day, not turn away
if I would have, then it wouldn't'a maybe go this far
.....
Oh, no no-no
yeah, (his) life was stole
Now we'll never know (stole)

(Written by Dave Deviller, Sean Hosein, Steve Kipner;
performed by Kelly Rowland)

WHAT BEHAVIOURS ARE WE TALKING ABOUT?

Deliberate self-harm can be defined as an act with a non-fatal outcome in which an individual deliberately did one or more of the following:

- initiated behaviour, for example of cutting, jumping from a height, which they intended to cause self-harm;

- ingested a substance in excess of the prescribed or generally recognized therapeutic dose;

- ingested a recreational or in illicit drug that was an act that the person regarded as self-harm;

- ingested a non-ingestible substance or object.

In many cases self-harming behaviour represents a transient period of distress: in others it is an important indicator of mental health problems and risk of suicide.

Deliberate self-harm, self-poisoning or self-injury is rare in children under 12 years, but becomes more common in adolescence, with an estimated 25,000 presentations to general hospitals annually in England and Wales. In an extensive study of 5,000 Year 10 students, Hawton et al. (2002) found that 13.2 per cent of pupils had at some time in their lives committed an act of deliberate self-harm. Seven per cent had done it in the previous year (Hawton et al., 2002). Girls outnumber boys by 4:1 with the number of boys increasing after the age of 14 years.

There were two main methods for harm: the first was cutting (64.6 per cent); the second was overdose (30.7 per cent). Hospital referral occurred more often for overdoses, and rarely for self-wounding such as cutting (Hawton et al., 2002). Multiple acts of deliberate self-harm were reported by 54.8 per cent.

Risk factors include (references are from Hawton et al., 2002, unless otherwise stated):

- Variations in mental health:
  - high levels of depression. Teenagers often report symptoms of depression. (22 per cent of girls and 13 per cent of boys in Year 8). However, the prevalence of a major depressive illness is lower and was found to be 1.8 per cent and equal for the sexes. This syndrome may contain marked and persistent sadness, poor appetite, sleep disorders, anxiety, irritability, self-depreciation, guilt and ideas of persecution (Angold 1988). Impaired social relationships and scholastic failure can be common;
  - high levels of anxiety and panic;
  - high levels of impulsivity;
  - low self-esteem;
  - to some extent conduct disorder (Fergusson et al., 2000).
- Drug and alcohol issues:
  - subscription to the view that alcohol and drugs are a good way of dealing with problems (Shaffer, 1990);
  - increasing consumption of cigarettes or alcohol;
  - increasing number of times drunk.
- Social issues:
  - previous history of being bullied;
  - in trouble with the police;
  - recent awareness of self-harm by peers (more noticeable for

pupils in a co-educational school);

– concerns about personal sexual orientation.

■ Family issues:

– living with one parent;

– self harm by family member;

– physical and sexual abuse.

The factors, in girls particularly, include recent self-harm by friends or family members, drug misuse, depression, anxiety, impulsivity and low self-esteem. The factors in boys were suicidal behaviour in friends and family members, drug use and low self-esteem. These factors act together and at a moment in time a youngster may act because:

■ they feel sad and lonely;

■ they feel that nobody really understands them or likes them;

■ they feel that they are a failure;

■ they feel trapped and want to escape a situation;

■ they are angry but feel unable to say so, leaving them helpless about the future (DfES, 2002).

SELF-WOUNDING

Although cutting is a less risky behaviour than overdosing, it can become a habit and tends to be repeated once begun. Favazza and Conterio (1989) studied 240 young women who regularly wounded themselves. The behaviour had often begun in the early teens and half the sample had wounded themselves on more than 50 occasions. Serious self-wounders typically continue for five to ten years.

The methods used were:

■ cutting,	72 per cent;
■ skin burning,	35 per cent;
■ hitting or punching parts of the body,	30 per cent;
■ interfering with wound healing,	22 per cent;
■ scratching,	22 per cent;
■ hair pulling,	10 per cent;
■ breaking bones,	8 per cent.

The commonest parts of the body to hurt were:

■ the arms, often the wrists,	74 per cent;

- the legs,   44 per cent;

- the abdomen,   25 per cent;

- the head,   23 per cent;

- the chest,   18 per cent;

- the genitalia,   8 per cent.

Damage can be produced with anything, but broken glass, needles, open scissors, razor blades, sharpener blades, knives or cigarettes are commonly used.

WHAT BENEFITS ARE THERE TO BE GAINED BY TACKLING THESE BEHAVIOURS?
■

PREVENTION OF SUICIDE

There has been a substantial increase in the suicide rate between the 1970s and the 1990s in males aged 15 to 19 years, i.e. 101 per million (1990s) and 45 per million (1970s). These figures include undetermined deaths. The female rate aged 15–19 has remained unchanged (33 per million). There has been no similar change in the suicide rate for 10–14-year-olds: 7 per million males and 3.9 per million females (McClure, 2001).

Repeated self-wounding only rarely results in suicide. The assumption of the risk of suicide in someone who self-harms is in the order of 1 per cent (Hawton, 1987) which is about hundred times the risk of the general population. The risk declines somewhat in subsequent years but continues to remain relatively high until at least eight years after an attempt. However, in the same patient cutting may be associated with more lethal self-harm, such as self-poisoning, hanging, or jumping from a height or in front of vehicles. Those self-wounders at greatest risk of suicide have experienced significantly more adverse effects, especially sexual abuse as a child, but also a recent emotionally important loss or chronic peer conflict. Chronic peer conflict is something that may be tackled in school.

Some youngsters with specific mental health disorders are at a higher risk of suicide, e.g. depressive illness, anorexia nervosa, psychotic disorders such as schizophrenia, alcohol and drug abuse. Research has shown that some groups of young people are more at risk of suicide than their peers. Young South Asian women (that is, from India, Pakistan or Bangladesh) who report cultural conflict within the family are at increased risk of suicide compared with others of a similar age (Soni Raleigh and Balarajan, 1992) as are young men who live apart from their families as a result of family difficulties (Keinhorst et al., 1995).

Therefore education, recognition of mental distress, and well advertised routes for seeking help may work towards preventing long-term consequences in those involved and in their friends.

PREVENTION OF THE LONG-TERM EFFECTS OF DELIBERATE SELF-HARM AND ■ DEPRESSION INTO ADULTHOOD

Sixty per cent of those who are depressed as teenagers have subsequent episodes of depression. Schools cannot tackle all the risk factors and genetic predispositions that individuals face, but they can make schools supportive places, working towards minimal peer conflict and an acceptance of individuality. Schools can also provide education as to appropriate sources of help.

■ PREVENTION OF COPYCAT BEHAVIOURS

Risk factors for self-harm include self-harming behaviours in friends. Interestingly there is a much stronger association with self-harm as compared to completed suicide (Hazell and Lewin 1993). Therefore the peer group is very important both in suggesting maladaptive solutions to problems such as cutting, and also in encouraging appropriate help-seeking behaviours (Kalafat and Elias, 1994).

WHAT ARE THE POSSIBLE INTERVENTIONS?
■

Hawton et al. (2002) calls for the need for development and evaluation of school-based programmes for the promotion of mental health. Targets for such programmes include self-esteem issues, depression, anxiety and impulsivity. It may be appropriate to have a different emphasis for each sex (see below). The potential influence of friends on self-harm indicates that their response to suicidal behaviour may be crucial.

■ AT AN INDIVIDUAL LEVEL

As a teacher you can help by:

- recognizing signs of distress and finding some way of talking with the young person about how they are feeling. It is important to make sure that the young person feels that they are effectively listened to. If they cannot get support when they need it, there is a risk they will harm themselves instead;
- offering practical help with solving problems;
- taking a non-judgemental attitude and staying calm and constructive however upset you feel about the self-harm;

- being clear about the risks of self-harm and making sure they know that with help it will be possible to stop once the underlying problems have been sorted out. Ask whether parents and family will be able to give support that is needed. This may be difficult if there are a lot of problems or arguments at home. Suicidal teenagers had particular difficulty in communicating with their parents and feeling accepted by them. However, ironically, effective communication with parents or another significant concerned person is of crucial therapeutic value to the socially isolated adolescent. At least 80 per cent of teenagers who commit suicide first try to communicate their desperation to others (Nelson, 1987);

- making sure that they get the right kind of help as soon as possible. Referral to a specialist service may well be appropriate. If the youngster says they have taken tablets etc., they need immediate assessment by the doctor. Any record or indication of what and how many pills have been taken need to also be reported;

- encourage pupils to let you know if one of their group is in trouble, upset or showing signs of harming themselves. Because friends often worry about betraying a confidence, you may need to explain that self-harm can be dangerous to life. For that reason it is should never be kept secret (Royal College of Psychiatrists Fact Sheet, 1999). Ciffone (1993) argues that front-line prevention lies in the hands of the teenagers themselves. They are more likely to seek help for a friend if they perceive the problem as a mental health issue and not just part of normality;

- self-wounding can be seen as a habit. Therefore encouragement to cope with withdrawal symptoms and to increase the determination to change may help practically.

AT A SCHOOL PLANNING LEVEL

- *The routine screening of adolescents* to identify those are risk.

- *Helping teachers to recognize such pupils.*

- *Advertisement and promotion of helplines, self-referral agencies,* and *school counselling services.* There is evidence that youngsters favour a hotline approach as a resource, particularly if the number is reinforced with credit card handouts. (Kalafat and Elias, M. 1994).

SPECIFIC INTERVENTIONS
EDUCATION PROGRAMMES

There have been a number of specific education programmes to target deliberate self-harm particularly in the USA (Ciffone, 1993; Kalafat and Elias, 1994; Nelson, 1978; Orbach and Bar Joseph, 1993; Overholser et al., 1989; Spirito, 1988; Vieland et al., 1991). The results are not clear-cut, and further research is necessary. The Orbach and Bar Joseph study was based more on finding coping solutions and understanding emotional experiences than on education per se. It had a noted impact on the special education conduct disordered class. The aims of education programmes are (Shaffer et al., 1991):

- to raise awareness of the problem of teen suicide;
- to increase knowledge about clinical features of pre-suicidal youngsters;
- to provide both behavioural and informational advice about how to refer adolescents identified as being at-risk to appropriate help resources;
- to encourage any suicidal youngsters who may be participating, to disclose their preoccupations in order to obtain appropriate help.

More general educational programmes about mental health can be positive and can improve knowledge. It takes more than a short educational workshop to address young people's deep-rooted beliefs and fears about contact with people with mental illness. However introducing the subject of mental illness alongside the PSHE teaching programme that focuses upon other important social and health issues, such as friendship and bullying, healthy eating and contraception, ensures that mental health problems are recognized as an essential concern for young people to understand and self-manage (Pinfold et al., 2003). An example of this type of intervention is described in Chapter 1.2 on the stigma of mental health issues.

SUPPORT PROGRAMMES FOLLOWING SUICIDE

Hazell and Lewin (1993) carried out a counselling intervention in two schools following two separate suicides. Groups of 20–30 youngsters were selected by staff on the basis of friendship with the deceased. A 90-minute group session was carried out by a child psychiatrist within seven days of the suicide. No benefit was found compared to controls, though no harm was done. Analysis of suicide risk factors after the study showed that a considerable number of youngsters at risk had not been referred and the authors suggest that self-referral, or a simple screen might have been a more appropriate way of picking up the at-risk youngsters.

ACCESSING EXTERNAL SUPPORT

The Internet has resources for self-help for people who self-harm. However, not all sites are helpful and should be screened before being recommended. Such sites include www.ru-ok.com. This is an excellent site directed at teenagers enabling them to assess their strengths and problems. It has information for professionals ie teachers about the aims of the site. Another site www.members.tripod.com/~kittn/index.html has information about what to look for in friends who may be suicidal, how to help such persons with telephone numbers, books and other links. Its links are mainly to sites with information about suicide and depression.

Scotland has a volunteer development programme and produced a paper on the prevention of suicide and deliberate self-harm. They mention that low self-esteem is recognized by those working in the field of mental health as an individual risk factor, also suicide and deliberate self-harm. Voluntary help work can help those at risk to develop self-esteem by providing a safe environment in which to gain competence, learn and develop skills, build interpersonal skills, and can help individuals to work within their community and develop a feeling of self-worth (Volunteer Development Scotland, 2002).

BOX 2.10.1 THE EXTRA EDGE PROJECT

The Extra Edge project, based in Australia, is a three-year project focusing on students at secondary school at risk of leaving early, especially those at risk of homelessness and subsequent substance abuse and self-harm. The aim is to bring various supports together, by including an extra edge co-ordinator for each of the 16 schools with a brief to act as a link in bringing all players together.

Source: www.infoxchange.net.au and Mhealth@Vicnet.net.au.

ESTABLISHING GUIDELINES FOR SCHOOL STAFF

As discussed earlier in the chapter, self-harming behaviour is distressing for the individual involved, his or her peers and staff. By establishing a clear school policy and guidelines, along with training staff, appropriate action can be taken. The Oxfordshire Adolescent Self-Harm Forum have developed an excellent set of guidelines for school staff (Adolescent Self-Harm Forum, 2002). These guidelines include information on self-harm, and a detailed suggested description of the ways of providing front-line help. Other issues discussed in the guidelines are: keeping records, setting boundaries for ongoing help by staff, liaison with outside agencies and providing support for teachers who are directly involved. The guidelines also include a draft letter to parents following a self-harm incident, an incident form and a fact sheet for parents and carers. These guidelines can be purchased from the Adolescent Self-Harm Forum.

WHAT ARE THE BENEFITS OF GUIDELINES?

The distressed individual will receive appropriate help at the time of the incident. Further help may be arranged as necessary.

The reaction of staff is more likely to be supportive and controlled. This allows the situation to be more easily contained, and therefore decreases the risk of copycat behaviours.

In a distressing situation, staff will have a clear understanding of the risks of the situation and be able to choose knowledgeably from a variety of actions open to them.

WHO NEEDS TO BE INVOLVED?

A key worker in the school can research various guidelines in use elsewhere, or develop specific school-based information reflecting local service provision. However, there are benefits to be gained by basing new policy on guidelines which are already in place and being evaluated, such as in the Oxford area.

Training for staff could be focused on the pastoral care team, the heads of year or for all members of staff. It is appropriate that both male and female teachers are involved.

HOW LONG SHOULD THE GUIDELINES BE IN PLACE?

The guidelines are set up for the foreseeable future in the school. However, the key worker needs to review them annually and update the information on local and national resources.

Training for the staff, as for any new policy, benefits by being reviewed regularly following the initial programme.

■ COST

There is a cost in the time for the key worker and for training of staff, as well as in the purchase of established guidelines.

■ POSSIBLE PROBLEMS

As with any school policy, success depends on the enthusiasm of the key worker and the backing he or she receives from the senior management team. It helps if the key worker can maintain ongoing contact with local provision.

Staff need to know how to access the guidelines in an emergency .

BOX 2.10.1 HOW TO DEVELOP DELIBERATE SELF-HARM GUIDELINES

Preparation

Select a key worker, e.g. pastoral care co-ordinator.

Research material for guidelines and local/national resources. (see Resource list).

Set up support systems for staff who may be involved with one-to-one counselling.

Decide how widespread the training in the guidelines will be.

Implementation

Train the group of staff involved.

Information for teachers who are not actively involved.

Review

Review resources annually.

Review training needs as appropriate.

SUMMARY
■

Deliberate self-harm and depression are common and can have serious long-term consequences. Chronic abuse from peers is an important risk factor which can be tackled in schools. (See Chapter 2.4 on bullying.)

Friends are often the first to know about someone else's distress. Their reaction and the reaction of staff who they might tell, can make a significant difference to the outcome.

Education of the staff and clear guidelines can ensure help can be accessed appropriately. Occasionally programmes designed to follow a suicide in school might need to be explored. This is an area which needs further research.

RESOURCES

National Self Harm Network, PO Box 16190, London NW1 3WW. Website at www.nshn.co.uk

Royal Children's Hospital Melbourne. Website at www.rch.unimelb.edu.au offers: peer support programme; suicide risk assessment training handouts; and a suicide risk assessment handbook.

The Bridge Youth Health Service, *Dance with Death*, a musical production video available from the Royal Children's Hospital Melbourne at www.rch.unimelb.edu.au

National Youth Suicide Prevention Strategy Resource Guide on Education and Training – contains information on around 50 education and training packages available within Australia at the end of 1998 to allow the user to appraise suitability of programmes to their requirements. In addition the resource guide contains an independent review of each programme by ranking each against certain criteria developed through national consultations. Produced by Health Services Division, Commonwealth Department of Health and Aged Care. Website at www.mentalhealth.gov.au/resources/reports/nysps_guide.htm

The Samaritans (24-hour helpline). Tel. 08457 90 90 90.

ChildLine (24-hour helpline). Tel. 0800 1111.

Adolescent Self Harm Forum (December 2002), *Guidelines for School Staff* are available at price £5.00 from: Adolescent Self Harm Forum, Highfield Family and Adolescent Unit, The Warneford Hospital, Headington, Oxford OX3 7JX.

Young Minds website at Youngminds@Ukonline.co.uk

Campaign Against Living Miserably (CALM) helpline for males 15–24. Tel. 0800 58 58 58 (7 days a week 5 p.m.–3 a.m.).

www.ru.com

www.members.tripod.com

Attention Deficit Hyperactivity Disorder

Rather than trying to organize his days on his own, he relies upon assistants to manage his schedule and keep track of his appointments, meetings and deadlines. As a result this highly successful educator is free to influence the lives of hundreds of children each year rather than live frustrated by his ADHD (Kennedy, 2002, p. 150)

WHAT IS ATTENTION DEFICIT HYPERACTIVITY DISORDER OR ADHD?

A variety of terms including ADD, ADHD and hyperkinetic disorder are used to describe children who are over active and have difficulties concentrating. 'Hyperkinetic disorder' is the World Health Organization term which has been the description of choice in Europe, while the terms 'attention deficit hyperactivity disorder' or ADHD and attention deficit disorder or ADD are American terms which are also used in Australia and many other parts of the world. Hyperkinetic disorder is a stricter category, and therefore applies to fewer children than ADHD. Many parents seem to prefer 'ADHD', perhaps because much of the literature available for parents uses the American terminology, and because of this we shall use the term ADHD in this chapter.

Children with ADHD have problems with attention, hyperactivity and impulsivity. These behaviours are extreme, have been obvious since an early age and affect most areas of life – home, school and friends. Most children with ADHD are of normal intelligence. A few children with learning disabilities also have ADHD.

Teachers' descriptions of behaviour in schools can be a very good indicator of the diagnosis. Some children are not particularly overactive but are inattentive and impulsive – they are said to have ADD. Many children with ADHD are very bad at organizing themselves and often 'lose' or 'forget' things. Children with

ADHD often have other problems (see Figure 2.11.1) including:

- learning difficulties – generalized or specific;
- language disorder;
- autistic spectrum disorders eg Asperger's syndrome;
- dyspraxia (poor motor co-ordination or clumsiness);
- Tourette's syndrome or tic disorder;
- low self-esteem;
- emotional disorders: anxiety, depression, obsessive compulsive disorder;
- oppositional defiant disorder (anti-social behaviour);
- conduct disorder (severe anti-social behaviour).

'DAMP' is a term used to describe a combination of conditions – disorders of attention, motor control and perception. These children have features of ADHD, dyspraxia and other specific learning impairments or autistic features (affecting perception). See Landgren et al. (1998).

Children with ADHD have significant problems with behaviour and performance at school. At home, they are more difficult to parents than a child without ADHD and receive more negative critical comments and less praise and affection. So life at school and home may be hard for them, they frequently fail, feel different from their peers, develop low self-esteem and may give up and drop out. This may, in turn, lead to involvement in anti-social behaviour and substance misuse, so they get even further into trouble.

HOW COMMON IS ADHD?

One in 100 primary school children are thought to meet the diagnostic criteria for hyperkinetic disorder.

WHAT CAUSES ADHD?

The exact cause is unknown, but genetic factors seem to play a large part. ADHD often runs in families and affects boys more than girls. Recent research studies have suggested that parts of the brain (the frontal and parietal lobes and part of the mid-brain) are not performing as well as they should in children with ADHD.

WHAT CAN BE DONE TO HELP A CHILD WITH ADHD?

There is much that parents and teachers can do to help young people with ADHD alongside support from the health professionals.

BOX 2.11.1 DIAGNOSTIC CRITERIA FOR ATTENTION DEFICIT HYPERACTIVITY DISORDER

The child should have six or more of the following nine symptoms of *inattention*:

- failure to pay close attention to detail, so frequently makes careless mistakes;
- difficulty in concentrating on tasks or play activities;
- failure to listen when spoken to directly;
- failure to follow through on instructions and finish tasks;
- lack of organization;
- reluctance to start tasks that require concentration;
- loses items that are necessary to complete tasks;
- distracted by irrelevant activity;
- forgetful in daily activities.

The child should have three or more of the following five symptoms of *hyper-activity*:

- fidgets;
- cannot remain seated;
- inappropriate running or climbing;
- noisy;
- being 'on the go' or often acting as if 'driven by a motor'.

The child should have one or more of the following four symptoms of *impulsivity*:

- blurts out answers before questions have been completed;
- failure to wait in turn;
- interrupts or intrudes on others' conversations or games;
- talks constantly.

There must be some impairment of functioning both at home and at school, which must affect either academic achievement or family functioning.

The symptoms must have started before the age of 7 years.

The symptoms cannot be accounted for by depression or anxiety.

▓ THINK – MIGHT THIS CHILD HAVE ADHD OR ADD?

Sometimes it can be difficult to see what lies behind difficult, disruptive behaviour. It is important to think – could this child have ADHD? Does he or she display any of the features listed under the diagnostic criteria? Do not forget

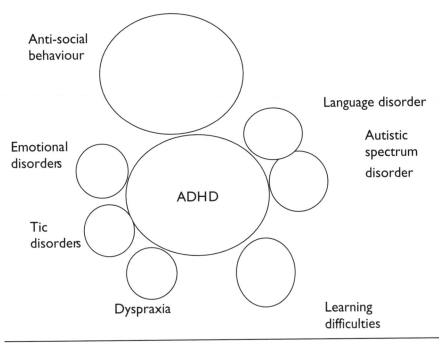

Anti-social
behaviour

Language disorder

Autistic
spectrum
disorder

Emotional
disorders

ADHD

Tic
disorders

Dyspraxia

Learning
difficulties

FIGURE 2.11.1 COMORBIDITY WITH ADHD

that a child with ADD may just be quietly inattentive, daydream a lot and underachieve.

If you think the pupil may have ADHD, discuss the possibility of referral for an assessment with his or her parents and the special needs coordinator, educational psychologist or school doctor. Patterns of referral and service provision vary across the country, so it is important to find out who to refer to locally and how. Some areas have designated ADHD services, in others the local paediatrician and/or child psychiatrist may carry out these assessments. In some areas referrals have to be made via the family's GP, in which case it is important to give the parents the necessary information (reports of concerns at school and copies of any questionnaires administered) so they can take this to their GP who can make the appropriate referral.

■ AVAIL YOURSELF OF INFORMATION AND ADVICE RE ADHD

Being well informed can help you know what you are dealing with. There is a wealth of information available. The following are useful starting points:

- Fact sheets on ADHD and stimulant medication produced by the Royal College of Psychiatrists as part of their 'Mental Health and Growing Up' series of fact sheets;

■ *All about ADHD* – a small booklet produced by the Mental Health Foundation which provides good basic information;

■ one of the books for parents cited in the Resources section at the end of this chapter;

■ try the ADDNet UK website which links to others at www.web-tv.co.uk/.

▓ DOES MEDICATION HELP?

Evidence from a recent large multicentre study (the MTA trials) suggests that the best medication regime is more effective than the best behavioural regime, and that combined treatment has no benefit over medication (MTA, 1999). In the UK, the National Institute for Clinical Excellence 2000 (NICE), carried out an appraisal on the use of methylphenidate for ADHD in childhood. It recommended that methylphenidate be used as part of a comprehensive treatment programme for children with a diagnosis of severe ADHD after a comprehensive assessment by a specialist with expertise in ADHD. This assessment should involve the child, his or her parents/carers and the school.

Although effective in about 70 per cent of cases, in terms of improving attention and reducing activity and impulsivity medication does not solve all the child's problems in school and some children's behaviour will still remain difficult, particularly in terms of conduct problems and peer relations. Some children do not respond well to medication. Additional, non-pharmacological, strategies are required to deal with these.

BOX 2.11.2 HELEN

Helen is a 13-year-old girl who sits quietly in class. Her teachers have occasionally wondered why she has difficulty in keeping friends. She is polite and generally well behaved but often does not seem to achieve the standards which the teachers expect. Her school reports often contain statements such as 'if she tried harder ... ' Her friends report that she is easy to get on with for a short time, but if something upsets her she will storm off. Although she is sorry about this, attempts by her friends to resolve the issue are hard to manage as her impulsive nature means that she frequently leaves the situation.

Her parents were concerned that she had become more oppositional recently and sought advice from their GP who referred her to the local ADHD assessment clinic. Over the last month she has had a trial with methylphenidate which has considerably improved her concentration in school. She takes the tablets only on school days.

BOX 2.11.3 BEN

Ben is an eight -year-old boy who has always had an extremely high activity level. As a toddler he was constantly getting himself into trouble, and putting himself in risky situations. His mother, even now, is unable to let him go and play alone in the park opposite the house because he may run off and remain unsupervised for a few hours.

  At school, he is in a small structured class which he responds to well. He plays for a local football team as a striker. He is generally well accepted by the team because of his footballing skills, however, they get irritated because he cries easily and has been known to storm off in the middle of a match. He also goes to Beavers and tae kwon do. Although the situation at home is frequently quite difficult, particularly as he has two younger siblings and he rarely settles to sleep at night until midnight, his parents have discussed the possibility of medication, but have decided against it at present. They feel that when school life becomes more pressured, or Ben becomes more oppositional, they will reconsider their decision.

Parents may benefit from behavioural management advice to help them cope with their child's behaviour when medication has worn off in the evenings.

SPECIFIC STRATEGIES THAT CAN BE EMPLOYED IN THE CLASSROOM TO HELP THE ■ CHILD WITH ADHD

The educational needs of children with ADHD vary enormously: some children will only require minimal assistance at any particular point in their school career, others have more severe and complex learning difficulties and may need more intensive help throughout their early school years or even most of their school life.

If the child is prescribed medication, this creates a 'window of opportunity' in which the child can learn social and educational skills.

Good behaviour management in the classroom (and home) can improve the performance and behaviour of these children. This is particularly important as medication wears off, and children forget to take their tablets! Some children respond well to behaviour management alone.

Your local educational psychology service may have produced their own guidelines on the classroom management of children with ADHD. Hampshire County Council (1996) has published an excellent guidelines booklet which may be purchased from them.

Behaviour management strategies, when thoughtfully applied, can make a significant difference to the pupil's functioning and the class as a whole. These fall into two main groups, can make the classroom ADHD friendly and maximize the chance of the pupil with ADHD staying on task and achieving his or her potential. These behavioural management strategies may also be beneficial to other members of the class as well. They are summarized in Box 2.11.4. The specific behavioural strategies are listed below. A discussion about altering the classroom environment follows and ends the chapter.

BOX 2.11.4 STRATEGIES TO ASSIST THE PUPIL WITH ADHD

Physical arrangement of classroom
- Minimize distractions.
- Seating positions in class.
- Lesson organization.
- General organization.
- Behaviour management in class.

Strategies to address the particular behavioural problems that pupils with ADHD have
- Dealing with inattention.
- Dealing with overactivity/restlessness/fidgetiness.
- Dealing with poor organization and planning.
- Dealing with impulsiveness.
- Dealing with non-compliance.
- Dealing with difficulties with peers.
- Dealing with poor self-esteem.

STRATEGIES TO ADDRESS PARTICULAR BEHAVIOURAL PROBLEMS SHOWN BY CHILDREN WITH ADHD

DEALING WITH INATTENTION

- Minimize distraction: seating position.
- Think carefully about work assignments.
- Gear to child's attention span, may need to be shortened.
- Break long assignments into smaller parts.
- Give one at a time.
- Give clear, precise instructions and make sure these are understood.

- Write clear, simple instructions.
- Keep page format simple with one or two activities per page.
- Provide frequent, immediate and consistent feedback, cue pupil to stay on task.
- Praise effort as well as attainment.
- Provide written outline of lesson.
- Help pupil set short-term goals.
- Vary type of activities.
- Allow pupil to type or dictate work rather than always requiring written work.

DEALING WITH OVERACTIVITY/RESTLESSNESS/FIDGETINESS

- Choose ADHD pupil to be the one who gets up to write any words or ideas on the board, etc.
- Allow short breaks between assignments and let pupil move around room at certain times.
- Remind pupil to check work if performance is rushed or careless.

DEALING WITH POOR ORGANIZATION AND PLANNING

- Ensure pupil has own personal organizer with individual weekly timetable clearly presented.
- Daily timetable and list of equipment required for each day.
- Homework timetable.
- Get pupil to refer to them regularly (supervised by teacher or parent).
- Give notes or reminders to pupil in lessons if necessary – to act as prompts re lessons, homework, other important things to remember.
- Give assignments one at a time.
- Supervise recording of homework assignments.
- Check homework daily.

DEALING WITH IMPULSIVENESS

- Keep class rules clear and simple.
- Ignore minor inappropriate behaviour.

- Immediately praise or reward appropriate behaviour, e.g. when pupil waits his turn to answer instead of blurting out answer.

- Use careful reprimands for misbehaviour – criticize the behaviour, not the child.

- Sit pupil near a good role model or teacher.

- Consider special techniques such as encouraging pupil to stop and think before they act out or to verbalize what must be done (initially to teacher or other adult, later to themselves).

DEALING WITH NON-COMPLIANCE

- Praise compliant behaviour and any positive behaviour or effort.

- Give immediate feedback about acceptable and unacceptable behaviour.

- Set short measurable goals for behaviour with lesson by lesson reinforcement.

- Tackle only one target behaviour at a time.

DEALING WITH DIFFICULTIES WITH PEERS

- Praise appropriate social behaviour.

- Encourage co-operative learning tasks with other pupils.

- Assign special responsibilities to pupil and praise pupil in front of peers.

- Consider use of Circle Time in class, a social skills group or individual social skills training.

DEALING WITH POOR SELF-ESTEEM

- Try and find something to praise and something pupil can succeed at.

- Spot origins of frustration early and try and intervene to reduce frustration.

CREATING A CALM ENVIRONMENT

Although there are no researched whole-school interventions for children with ADHD, the classroom environment can be manipulated to maximize the ability of these pupils to stay on task and achieve their potential.

▩ WHAT TO DO?

There are a number of elements to consider:

The use of *seating* ideally should be flexible, with several tables for group work and rows for independent work. Tasks which do not require interpersonal contact are better achieved by rows of tables and chairs. Arranging desks in horseshoe can promote discussion without impeding independent work.

Minimizing distractions can help these pupils. Painting walls bright colours can be welcoming but also distracting, displays likewise can be very positive for most pupils, but those with ADHD will benefit from being sat away from them. It is good to keep part of the room free from obvious visual or auditory distractions. Sitting these pupils near the teacher is a frequently applied technique. Students with good study skills are often sat next to those with poor attention and overactivity, however, one always needs to be aware that the same 'good' child may be put in this position in a number of different lessons.

Some schools have introduced the concept of short periods of background music. *Mozart* appears to have a calming effect on concentration which lasts up to half an hour after the music has been stopped. This is an interesting area of research which is at a very early stage. At present it needs to be used with consideration.

School uniform forms the predominant background colour. Some schools have chosen uniforms which are subdued colours (navy/dark green) to help provide a calming environment.

Pupils who suffer from ADHD find *computers* particularly motivating and rewarding. As they often have associated dyspraxias their presentation of work is considerably improved by using IT skills. This helps to give them positive feedback which is often lacking in their individual worlds.

Lesson organization can help. Things to consider are:

- providing an outline, key concepts and essential vocabulary prior to lesson and topic presentation;
- varying the pace of lesson presentation;
- including a variety of activities during each lesson;
- interspersing in-seat tasks with more physical activities when appropriate;
- setting short, achievable targets and rewarding task completion promptly;
- allowing a short break before next target is set;
- actively encouraging pupils to develop mental images of the

concepts or information being presented (ask them about their images to be sure they are visualizing the key material to be learned);

■ using co-operative learning activities, particularly those that assign each child in a group a specific role or piece of information that is needed to complete the group task.

Strategies which involve the *general organization* of the classroom can be considered. *Daily classroom schedules* and routines which are known and practised, are particularly useful for beginnings, endings and transitions. *Five minute warnings* before ending of a session or the completion of the task, *clarity about pupil movement*, and an outside stimulus such as a *kitchen timer* to monitor intense periods of independent work can be helpful structures.

All children benefit from *actively reinforcing desired classroom behaviours and the praising of specific behaviours*, for example, 'I like how you correctly wrote down all the things you have to do' rather than 'well done'. Pupils with ADHD, because they are often brought to the teacher's attention for negative reasons, have to be 'caught being good'.

Children with ADHD are often caught up within a bullying cycle. Interventions discussed in Chapter 2.4 may have a role to play.

■ WHAT ARE THE BENEFITS?

A pupil with ADHD can provide a frequent distraction in class. Because of their impulsivity they are often the children who are seen to be out of their seats, or reacting to another event. Other pupils may provoke a reaction in them. Strategies which are proactive rather than reactive begin to help these pupils put the 'thought before the action'. A calm environment with clear varied activities helps to keep the whole class on task, and can provide a less stressful environment within which to teach.

■ WHO NEEDS TO BE INVOLVED?

Individual teachers are involved in adapting their classrooms to suit their style of teaching, and their pupils. Sometimes a compromise is needed. Other environmental decisions, such as those regarding uniform and colour of walls, are taken by the senior management team.

■ COST

This is very variable. The provision of increasing computer access in lessons other than IT is high, and may give the appearance of inconsistent treatment of different individuals. The organization of the classroom involves knowledge, thought and application of the teacher involved.

PROBLEMS

Constructing a classroom environment for one group of children may mean that other pupils' needs are ignored, e.g. the 'slow to warm up' pupils will benefit from a stimulating environment. A practical, knowledgeable, approach instituted with wisdom and some flexibility will provide the optimum solutions.

SUMMARY

Children with ADD and ADHD can provide an ongoing challenge within school environment. Partly because of the nature of the ADD/ ADHD, and because it is often associated with other difficulties such as Asperger's syndrome, dyspraxias, obsessional compulsive disorders (and, if untreated, with oppositional defiant disorder), it is easy for the environment to be reactive and emotionally charged. Proactive supportive strategies can be beneficial for the whole school community.

RESOURCES

Connors, K. (1973) 'Rating scales for use in drug studies with children', *Psychopharmacological Bullet in Special Issue: Pharmacotherapy Child.*

Green, C. and Chee, K. (1997) *Understanding ADHD*. London: Vermilion. From the author of 'Toddler Taming' – easy to read and humorous.

Greene, R. (2001) *The Explosive Child*. New York: Quill.

Hampshire County Council (1996) *Attention Deficit (Hyperactivity) Disorder. AD(H)D: Information and Guidelines for School*. Winchester: Hampshire County Council Education Department.

Mental Health Foundation (2000) *All About ADHD*. London: Mental Health Foundation.   Useful booklet providing basic information available for £1 from the Mental Health Foundation, 20/21 Cornwall Terrace, London NW1 4QL. Tel: 020 7535 7400. Fax 020 7535 7474. Email mhf@mhf.org.uk Website at www.mhf.org.uk

National Institute for Clinical Excellence (NICE) (2000) *Guidance on the Use of Methylphenidate (Ritalin, Equasym) for ADHD in Childhood*. London: NICE. Books for parents, teachers, young people. Also available at *www.nice.org.uk*

Taylor, E. (1997) *Understanding your Hyperactive Child: The Essential Guide for Parents*. London: Vermilion.   A book full of information by the leading UK authority on the subject.

Accessing Outside Help

Fortunately, schools do not have to deal with young people's mental health problems in a vacuum. There is a plethora of other agencies whose brief it is to do this. The difficulty is often in knowing who is around, what they do (and do not do) and how to access their help. In a similar way, those working in specialist services such as child and adolescent mental health services (CAMHS) need to be familiar with the many, and constantly changing and developing, ways schools can assist young people. Without this mutual understanding and inter-dependency, schools and the individuals concerned can miss out with regard to possible sources of assistance.

Services and agencies vary across the country (and between countries). It is therefore important to find out what services, both statutory and voluntary, exist in your area: who those are, how they operate, what they deal with and what they do not, and how they link in both with schools and other agencies. Many CAMHS services are spending time mapping 'care pathways', i.e. the ways in which adolescents are referred in and around the increasing complex range of services available.

Increasingly, the views of users of services are being sought: how they perceive the help they are offered, ease of access, type of service provided, etc. One study (Clarke et al., 2003) asked 14 to 19-year-olds: 'When asking for help what is important to young people?' The answers given were: confidentiality, to be understood, the advice and information provided, to be listened to, to trust the helper and that the helper is approachable. The Mental Health Foundation (1999) found that young people with mental health problems often found it hard to find their way into services and how, often, when they finally gained access to help, found themselves confronted by professionals who appeared to be both disinterested and intrusive. In contrast, they also found many who spoke highly of those professionals who had reached out to them. The responsiveness of the professionals they came into contact with was a major factor in determining how young people and their parents felt about the service they received. When professionals were felt to be patronizing, to be unwilling to share information with the young people about their illnesses, or appeared not to have any time for the young person, they in turn felt let down by the treatments on offer. A number spoke of the need for psychiatrists to be 'less bow tie and more youth worker'.

A number of barriers prevent young people from accessing help through traditional routes, such as the family doctor. These include difficulty in getting a quick appointment, feeling embarrassed talking about personal issues and concerns about confidentiality. It has therefore been argued that school-based early interventions could meet young people's needs and overcome the barriers to accessing help.

Klinefelter (1994) argues that service provision within schools allows work with adolescents at the time of crisis, reduces stigma and minimizes disruption to academic studies.

How are such services provided within and to schools? By a wide range of individuals and organizations, which are summarized in Figure 2.12.1.

Within schools the *special educational needs co-ordinator* SENCO has an extremely important role, given the overlap between the needs of children with special educational needs and those with mental health problems. Therefore, it may be appropriate for the SENCO to co-ordinate the provision of support for this group. *Learning support assistants* (LSAs) can provide extremely valuable in-class behavioural and learning supports for young people with mental health problems especially when these supports are linked with effective whole-class and whole-school behaviour policies. *Home–school links* are also important and thought should be given to how these are set up and organized. *Pastoral staff* play a role in supporting vulnerable children and those who turn to them for help. *Learning mentors* help young people overcome barriers to learning, both inside and outside school. These have been introduced through the government's Excellence in Cities initiative. Their many functions include developing a one-to-one mentoring relationship with young people who need particular support, maintaining regular contact with the young person's parent(s)/carer(s) and to encourage positive family involvement in learning. *Personal advisers* are being introduced as part of the ConneXions service, to provide one-to-one support for young people and oversee the effectiveness of help offered. Their role is to ensure that 13 to 19-year-olds receive a 'seamless service' in their transition to further learning and adulthood.

Within the education service further, more specialist support is available from

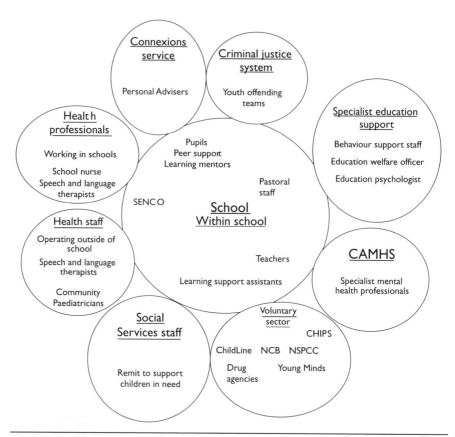

FIGURE 2.12.1 SUPPORT SYSTEMS AVAILABLE

Education Welfare Officers (EWOs), behavioural support staff and the educational psychology service (EPS). *Education welfare officers* play a vital role in supporting those families whose children do not attend school regularly, many of whom have multiple and complex problems and large amounts of unmet need. Many LEAs provide a *behavioural support service* whose job is to support schools in developing whole-school approaches to behaviour plus assisting with interventions for pupils experiencing problems. *Educational psychologists* are trained to promote child development and learning via the application of psychology to pupils, teachers and the school. Their core activity is assessment and intervention work with young people. The intervention may include work with the individual young person or family or advice on strategies that the teacher or SENCO might employ.

Health professionals may work within the school, e.g. school nurses or speech and language therapists (SLT) or operate outside school, e.g. in primary care (health visitors, family doctors) community services (community paediatricians) or hospital/in-patient services.

School nurses are increasingly developing a role in the assessment and management of mental health problems. Clarke et al. (2003) provide an interesting and informative account of a school-based early identification and intervention service for adolescents based on a psychology and school nurse partnership model. Such schemes depend upon partnership at all levels if they are to be effective: partnership between the adolescent and school nurse, the project team, school senior management and the network of school support services, including school nurses. Partnership with teachers is a key relationship.

Child and Adolescent Mental Health Services (CAMHS) have been changing recently. National reports advocate the provision of early intervention services, which are part of a tiered model of care (see Figure 2.12.2).

Tier 1 is a primary level and includes interventions by anyone who comes into contact with young people: for example, teachers, social workers, voluntary agencies, GPs and health visitors.

The *graduate primary mental health care worker's* role is to provide support and consultation to those offering Tier 1 services. He or she is also an integral part of the specialist multidisciplinary mental health service and fulfils some roles at Tier 2 as well as possibly working in Tier 3.

At *Tier 2* more specialist help is offered by a single professional who may be a nurse, clinical psychologist, community paediatrician, educational psychologist or child psychiatrist.

Most young people with mental health problems will be seen at Tiers 1 and 2.

Tier 3 consists of specialist, multidisciplinary teams that provide a service for more severe, complex or persistent disorders. The team includes professionals from a range of disciplines (child and adolescent psychiatrists, social workers, clinical psychologists, community psychiatric nurses (CPNs), child psychotherapists, family therapists, occupational therapists and possibly art, music and drama therapists). They specialize in the assessment and treatment of child mental health disorders as well as providing contributions for training and consultation to Tiers 1 and 2. They can make referrals to Tier 4 if indicated.

Tier 4 consists of highly specialized out-patient and in-patient services that provide assessment and treatment for young people with the most severe mental health problems. These include specialized out-patient teams for young people who sexually abuse, who have complex neuropsychological problems or who are in the criminal justice system, and specialized in-patient units both forensic and for those with severe mental health problems. Access to these is via Tier 3 services.

Social Services teams have a remit to support children in need. Many of the young people known to the Children and Families Teams have marked mental health problems and experience difficulties at school (either with attendance

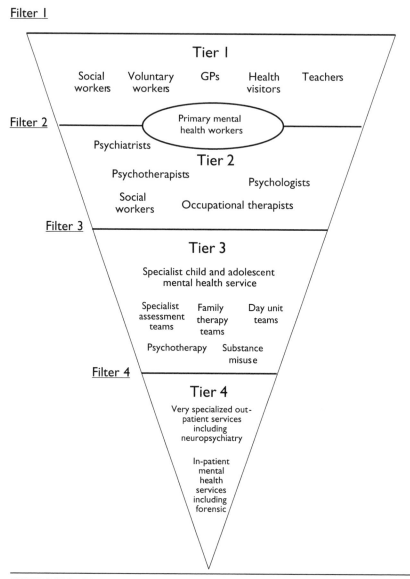

Filter 1

Tier 1

Social workers   Voluntary workers   GPs   Health visitors   Teachers

Filter 2

Primary mental health workers

Psychiatrists

Tier 2

Psychotherapists

Psychologists

Social workers   Occupational therapists

Filter 3

Tier 3

Specialist child and adolescent mental health service

Specialist assessment teams   Family therapy teams   Day unit teams

Psychotherapy   Substance misuse

Filter 4

Tier 4

Very specialized out-patient services including neuropsychiatry

In-patient mental health services including forensic

FIGURE 2.12.2   SCHEMATIC REPRESENTATION OF TIERED MODEL OF CAMHS

or due to their behaviour, or are underachieving for a variety of reasons). Schools need to be aware of the professionals involved with the family and include them in the decisions that are made about the young person at school.

The *ConneXions service* has a role to play, via its personal advisers, as described above.

A young person may be in contact with the *criminal justice system* if his or her behaviour has led to altercations with the law. The *Youth Offending Team* (YOT) consists of a range of professionals who assess the young person's many difficulties and offer appropriate help and support. For some young people, whose behaviour problems have been severe and who usually have attended school little or infrequently, this may be the first time they access help. Others may be known to many professionals in health, education and social services.

Finally, the *voluntary sector* has an important role to play in many ways by campaigning for children's rights, giving young people a voice, providing confidential support and advice or direct work with young people and their families. Many organizations exist, e.g. ChildLine, the National Children's Bureau, Young Minds, the NSPCC and drug agencies, to name but a few. Some have developed particular expertise in a special programme for working with schools, e.g. ChildLine in Partnership with Schools (CHIPS). It is worth finding out who is doing what in your area or more about these organizations via the Internet.

SECTION 3

Predicting the Difficulties

Where there is a shared culture of professional development and action research ... interventions will develop through the process of collective review. Where that culture only partly exists, schools may only stumble across interventions and will end up with a very ad hoc approach to improvement. Interventions need to be systematically mapped, planned, implemented, and evaluated as the prime means of improving schools against their previous best. (Brighouse, 1999, p. 141)

Developing and implementing an intervention requires a transition to new ways of working that can be very challenging and even, at times, disturbing (Cowie and Wallace, 2000). For example, the transition to peer support as a method for alleviating distress in the peer group often involves a major change in the adult's way of relating to young people; it requires a shift towards a more democratic, participatory style of teaching and facilitation. Some adults and young people find it challenging, some are inspired, some become discouraged and others are impelled to sabotage the process (Cowie and Olafsson, 2000). The transition to new ways of working is aided by an attempt on the part of the senior management team to understand the process of change that is taking place, and by working collaboratively over time with the other key parties involved. A crucial aspect of this process is to develop the stance of reflective evaluation from a range of perspectives. It is helpful to view the process of transition as a sequence of stages in a Cycle of Change (see Figure 3.1.1).

In Stage 1, the *pre-awareness* stage, schools are unaware of mental health difficulties experienced by their young people, and are not yet considering change. However, others may be aware of a problem, for example, the outer community.

To move from pre-awareness to *awareness*, a school must become sensitive to the mental health problems experienced by their young people, acknowledge these and take ownership of the problems, confront the issues that are causing the difficulties and begin to see some of the negative aspects of the problem in order to move on to the next stage of seriously activating change. How can this be assisted? Consciousness-raising activities such as those outlined in step 2 of the needs analysis (Chapter 1.6) can help schools become more aware of the causes, consequences and solutions of the problem issues. To move through the awareness stage to the action stage, schools have to become sensitive to the negative consequences of not addressing the problems. While extreme, events such as the stabbing of a boy in an inner London secondary school (see Chapter 2.3) can move schools from the pre-awareness stage to the next stage.

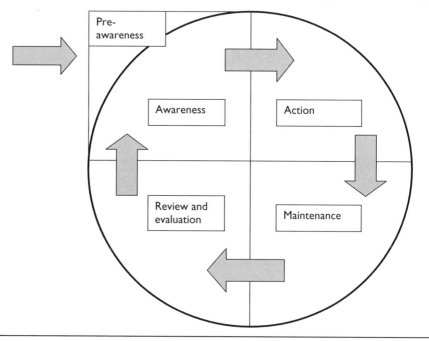

FIGURE 3.1.1 CYCLE OF CHANGE (ADAPTED FROM PROCHASKA AND DiCLEMENTE, 1992)

In the *awareness* stage, the school sees a cause for concern but has ambivalent feelings about wanting to change. A school will recognize some of the negative effects of the mental health difficulties and the benefits of change, however, there may be fear about the *perceived* negative consequences of making the transition for example, concern that changing to new ways of working will alienate some members of staff. Steps 3 and 4 of the needs analysis (see Chapter 1.6) help schools to move from a position of awareness to action.

In Stage 3, the *action* stage, the motivational balance tips in the overall direction of the negative consequences of not addressing the issues and a commitment to change is made. The school is now ready to research a suitable intervention for the goals identified in step 3 of the needs analysis, develop an action plan and implement the chosen intervention (see Chapter 1.6).

In Stage 4, when a school has established an intervention over a period of time, it has entered the *maintenance* stage, when the intervention has become a part of normal school practice. Just as preparation for action is essential for successful implementation of an intervention, so too is preparation for maintenance. Successful maintenance builds on each of the preceding stages and is followed by a process of review and evaluation of the intervention.

Finally, Stage 5 provides an opportunity for *review and evaluation*. All interventions will benefit from an evaluation process that is integrated into the process of change from the beginning. Review and evaluation is essential for gathering evidence to indicate whether the intervention is working, where it is not working and where changes and adjustments are required. Evaluation is also important to establish that the intervention is of benefit to vulnerable young people and not doing them harm and to provide evidence to governors or potential funding bodies of its efficacy.

The transition to new ways of working also requires an understanding of a school's 'readiness' to adopt and sustain an initiative that is determined by certain organizational factors (Dusenbury et al., 1997). Of particular importance are how the school operates as an organization, the quality of leadership and the quality of school culture. For example, a school is more likely to have success in addressing violent behaviour where values are shared, where everyone is involved in decision-making and where the individuals in the school are willing to act within a consistent framework (Roffey, 2000). Good leadership has been identified as a clear vision of the headteacher counterbalanced with the active involvement of staff in decision-making and developing a 'shared ethos' (Sammons et al., 1995). A strong culture is acknowledged as a significant determinant of both effectiveness and of change and is characterized by a commitment to a set of values held by most staff, loyalty to organizational goals and a mutual support system (Robbins, 1994). A school's readiness to change, therefore, will be dependent upon the extent to which elements of these factors will support the introduction of an intervention and whether all staff are empowered to participate meaningfully in its development (Roffey, 2000).

In addition, the Mental Health Foundation (1999) argues that whole-school approaches are necessary to successfully address issues of mental health and well-being. For example, Smith and Sharp (1994) concluded that, properly implemented, anti-bullying policies and practices would reach all young people in the school and most other members of the school community. In a secondary school case study by Roffey (2000), the author identified several difficulties in getting policies established that related to the way that the school was operating as an organization including, who made decisions and decided priorities, how members of the school community communicated with each other, and perceptions of role, rules, status and individual value.

POTENTIAL ROADBLOCKS

The purpose of identifying problems that might undermine the process of planning and implementing an intervention is so that you can think of ways of circumventing such problems at an early stage. Once you are able to identify a potential roadblock, it becomes less of a threat and you can begin to think of possible solutions.

The needs analysis process identified in Chapter 1.6 may help to understand the potential roadblocks that can occur to undermine plans. If potential problems are dealt with from a proactive stance, rather than a reactive position, then the intervention has much more chance of success. For example, the needs analysis may identify a member of staff who is actively blocking the proposed plans for an intervention. The involvement of such a 'saboteur', who more often than not feels threatened in some way by the proposed intervention, in the planning and implementation of the intervention is likely to lead to the intervention's most ardent supporter (see Case study 1.6.2 in Chapter 1.6).

Our own research in schools has identified the following potential roadblocks:

- time;
- funding;
- integration;
- training;
- ownership;
- promotion;
- working with outside agencies;
- closure;
- review and evaluation.

The rest of this chapter will look at each of these potential roadblocks in more detail, and identify some possible solutions.

POTENTIAL ROADBLOCK 1: TIME

In our research with schools, both staff and young people have identified time, in terms of both commitment and administration, as a potential roadblock. The example in Box 3.1.1 highlights the time pressure of young people in the administration of a peer support scheme.

Recommendations

- Be clear about the time commitments for staff and young

people from the outset. A needs analysis will help achieve this.

- Engage volunteers from outside the school, for example, parents or grandparents to help.

BOX 3.1.1 EXAMPLE

Peer supporters in one peer support scheme considered the administration of the scheme a significant burden especially with the pressure of examinations in the lower sixth as well as in the upper sixth. In addition to providing actual peer support, peer supporters were also required to carry out administration tasks such as photocopying materials, organizing the peer supporter rotas, organizing assemblies and reminding people about the support meetings. One potential solution would be to look for a volunteer parent or pay for a small amount of administrative support to handle the administration.

POTENTIAL ROADBLOCK 2: FUNDING

It is important to establish at the outset that there is enough funding to plan, implement and review and evaluate an intervention. For example, the cost of implementing the *Leap* Confronting Conflict in Schools programme is between £25,000 and £30,000 per year. However, due to the seriousness of the issue that Morpeth School were dealing with (see Chapter 2.3), the senior management team decided that they would make the financial investment on an ongoing basis. It is important at the outset that you establish that you have enough funding to initiate and maintain an intervention.

Recommendations

- Carry out a needs analysis.
- Ensure that adequate funds are available on an ongoing basis. A needs analysis will identify available funds.
- If funding is not readily available from the school, consider other options such as fund-raising, sponsorship or grants.

POTENTIAL ROADBLOCK 3: INTEGRATION

Interventions regarded as a 'quick fix', or interventions that are not adopted within a whole–school framework, are liable to cause a potential roadblock. The example in Box 3.1.2 illustrates the benefits of implementing an intervention as part of whole-school development.

BOX 3.1.2 EXAMPLE

One senior management team viewed the implementation of a conflict management programme as an integral part of the whole-school development process rather than as an 'add-on'. As such it was embedded within the school's culture and ethos, and was seen as one factor among several in the management of positive behaviour. The principles underpinning the conflict management programme were based on a desire to include as many students and staff as possible in a clearly structured programme. In this way the programme aimed to ensure that students and staff became more aware of conflict issues and acquired the skills for dealing with them through an understanding of the causes of conflict, working with diversity, working in teams, and learning communication and negotiation skills.

Recommendations

- Do not look for the 'quick fix'; results will only be temporary.
- Be prepared to incorporate your chosen intervention into your School Development Plan and across the curriculum.

POTENTIAL ROADBLOCK 4: TRAINING

It is essential when setting up an intervention that resources are allocated to training, that is, initial training and ongoing training/support. The example in Box 3.1.3 illustrates how ongoing training and supervision is essential for the successful implementation of a peer support scheme.

Recommendations

- Establish in the needs analysis the amount of training and supervision required for teachers and young people to successfully implement an intervention.
- Develop a system of ongoing support for staff and young people.
- Establish a timetable at the outset for the implementation of an intervention.

POTENTIAL ROADBLOCK 5: OWNERSHIP

It is important for staff and students to feel that they 'own' the intervention and the methods for implementing it. For example, in a school that implemented a Circle of Friends, staff were concerned about the extent to which staff facilitators could develop their own ways of running the Circles. While Circle of

Friends requires the facilitator to develop skills to allow the group to identify and resolve issues, which is different from a teaching role, some teachers are happy to run a Circle with little backup, whereas the general view is that the initial meeting benefits from an 'outsider' to lead it.

Another example of lack of ownership is illustrated by the lack of opportunities for young people to practise the skills learned in conflict resolution training. (See the example in Box 3.1.4.)

BOX 3.1.3 EXAMPLE

Training of peer supporters is lengthy. It is usually recommended that peer supporters receive a minimum of 30 hours of training by a facilitator who is experienced as a counsellor or who has training in peer support. In one peer support scheme one or two of the younger peer supporters felt daunted by the possibility of being confronted by a major problem but were unsure of where they could turn due to the issue of confidentiality. Ongoing training and weekly supervision for all members of the peer support team could provide support for younger members and help them gain in confidence. On a practical level, leaflets or posters might be distributed throughout the school outlining the sorts of issues that peer supporters would be most skilled to address, and recommending other agencies, such as ChildLine, for more difficult issues beyond the expertise of a peer supporter. Training and supervision opportunities could also be widened, by setting up visits to other schools for peer supporters and backup staff to share ideas. This would also give peer supporters a greater sense of being part of a wider network.

BOX 3.1.4 EXAMPLE

In one school, the opportunities to practise the skills learned in conflict resolution training were sometimes a challenge because conflicts do not happen in the classroom when you have your peer trainers just lined up ready to deal with them! So, the opportunity to practise is not always available. This can leave young people feeling frustrated as they are not receiving the opportunities to practise their new-found skills, to consolidate their learning or to receive feedback on how they are doing.

Recommendations

- Build in opportunities for ongoing training.
- Provide opportunities for young people to demonstrate their newly learned skills in other arenas, such as, visiting neighbouring schools to demonstrate their work.

POTENTIAL ROADBLOCK 6: PROMOTION

It is clear from our research in schools that marketing and advertising of an intervention, both initially and on an ongoing basis, are essential to successful implementation and maintainance of an intervention. Not only does an intervention need to be initially launched and everyone involved made aware of the scheme, it also needs to receive ongoing publicity so that the high profile of the intervention is maintained (see the example in Box 3.1.5).

BOX 3.1.5 EXAMPLE

In one school the implementation of a conflict management programme involved a whole-school approach. The principles underpinning the programme were based on a desire to include as many students and staff as possible in a clearly structured programme (see Chapter 2.3). However, interviews with staff revealed that there were some difficulties in establishing a higher profile both within the school among less involved staff, and outside in the wider community. Indeed, some staff, particularly newer staff, had little or no knowledge of the intervention. The long-term nature of an intervention such as this requires the need to keep the initial momentum going in terms of marketing and PR, an issue that the school's senior management team had already recognized and were addressing with a relaunch of the intervention in the near future.

Recommendations

- Continually look at ways of promoting your intervention, for example, throughout the school and across the curriculum.
- Harness the media, for example the local press, to promote interest in the intervention.
- Include a rolling training programme for all staff, teaching and non-teaching, an induction training for all new staff and training for groups beyond the school, for example, parents and governors.

POTENTIAL ROADBLOCK 7: WORKING WITH OUTSIDE AGENCIES

While working with an outside agency was considered by some staff and young people to be an advantage, others perceived it as a threat. The example in Box 3.1.6 illustrates this.

BOX 3.1.6 EXAMPLE

In a school that was introducing conflict resolution, the Deputy Headteacher suggested that use of an outside agency meant that the training was accessible for a range of young people and was a means of getting young people who may have had a bad press within the school, or behaviour issues, to be involved. Another strength of using an outside agency was that the trainers were consistent in their approach to training, which meant that the whole school received a similar experience.

However, use of an outside agency was perceived as a threat by some staff. For example, styles of training were perceived by teachers to be different to teaching styles which elicited a different kind of relationship with the young people (e.g. outside facilitators were called by their first names) than they had themselves. Teaching staff were also quite threatened by what they perceived to be the strict nature of the facilitator's approach which they viewed as insensitive.

BOX 3.1.7 EXAMPLE

In one peer support programme it was felt that there should be a definite time for handing over responsibilities by the older student supporters to new recruits, say at the beginning of the spring term, so that the more senior and committed pupils could feel positive about the work that they have achieved within the scheme, rather than being left with guilt at having to devote increasing time to studies while still a supporter. A committed pupil without regular supervision cannot be expected to institute a passing over of authority without help from an adult with some respect within the scheme. It also allows for some appreciation of the part that the older student supporters have made. If the transition is made in the spring term it allows the more experienced new supporters to plan and implement the scheme for the autumn term that could be argued as being the most important factor for providing peer support especially for the new Year 7s.

POTENTIAL ROADBLOCK 8: CLOSURE

Closure, in terms of young people withdrawing from an intervention, for whatever reason, needs to be considered at the planning stage. The example in Box 3.1.7 illustrates the need for older students to officially hand over the reins in a peer support programme and the example in Box 3.1.8 suggests that the ending of a Circle of Friends could have been handled more sensitively.

Recommendations

- Build in a review and evaluation process prior to implementing an intervention.

- Build in opportunities at every stage to celebrate what is already working well.

- When young people move on, mark the occasion with a celebration of achievement.

BOX 3.1.8 EXAMPLE

In one Circle of Friends, the Circle 'fizzled out'. Volunteer pupils stopped turning up towards the end; the educational psychologist was not always available and then the focus child started to say she did not want it to take place. This inappropriate ending reflected a number of bad endings due to breakdowns in foster care and enforced changes of school that the child had already experienced.

POTENTIAL ROADBLOCK 9: REVIEW AND EVALUATION

Several of the case studies mentioned in this book highlight the need for a review and evaluation process which is what the final chapter (3.2) deals with in more detail.

Review and Evaluation

Evaluation is part of a spirit of enquiry that is more effective when there is a climate of trust, a willingness to be open, a genuine concern to be constructively critical and an interest in working co-operatively as part of a team. (Cowie and Wallace, 2000, p. 164)

The major purpose of a review and evaluation is to determine whether the intervention has made a difference. Prior to asking 'Does it work?', however, it is important to establish what 'it' is and that 'it' has actually been implemented. Therefore, before evaluating the intervention's effectiveness, it is important to review its implementation. The review should determine the extent to which the intervention has been implemented, which aspects of the intervention are working well and which aspects of the intervention need attention. The results of the review of the implementation will provide information to make amendments to the intervention prior to its being evaluated for effectiveness.

Effective review and evaluation is not something that happens at the end of a project, rather it is an ongoing process that helps the senior management team and key decision-makers better understand the intervention. Thus, evaluation issues should be considered by staff, young people, parents and governors at Step 8 of the needs analysis process (see Chapter 1.6) in order to clarify thinking about the intervention and its anticipated effects. Review and evaluation is not just about proving that an intervention has worked, it also provides an opportunity to make changes and improve the intervention. In addition to providing information about implementation and effectiveness, review and evaluation also provides the opportunity for supplying information to potential funders and for sharing and disseminating good practice.

Evaluation should therefore have three major purposes:

- reviewing the implementation of the intervention
- evaluating the effectiveness of the intervention

- evaluating key characteristics of the intervention (adapted from Riley and Segal, 2002).

REVIEWING IMPLEMENTATION

The purpose of reviewing implementation is to document the extent to which your school has actually used the intervention. This aspect of the evaluation should look at the extent to which each area of the school has implemented key components of the intervention, which aspects of the intervention are working well, which aspects of the intervention are having problems and what obstacles may be preventing the school from fully implementing the intervention. Issues to consider include:

- To what extent has each area of the school implemented the key components of the intervention?
- What aspects of the intervention are working well?
- What aspects of the intervention are having problems?
- What obstacles are preventing the school from fully implementing the intervention?
- What evidence is there that the intervention is working as intended?
- In what ways can the intervention be improved for ongoing implementation?

EVALUATING EFFECTIVENESS

The purpose of evaluating the effectiveness of an intervention is to determine the extent to which it has had an impact on key indicators of mental health problems. This aspect of the evaluation should provide evidence of the effectiveness of the intervention in reducing, for example, bullying incidents in the playground and violence-related exclusions. It should seek to document what has changed in the school environment since its introduction. For example, it should look to see whether there has been an increase in attendance rates and academic performance or a decrease in exclusion rates and in the numbers of referrals to a behaviour support service. If a standardized questionnaire such as the 'My Life in School Checklist' (Arora and Thompson, 1987, cited in Sharp, 1999) was used pre-intervention then it can be administered for a second time post-intervention to see whether there are any changes in results (see Chapter 1.6).

It is also important to define your own measurement criteria relevant to your school's circumstances. For example, reduced bullying incidents or fewer visits to the school office. Issues to consider include:

- How has the intervention impacted on key indicators such as:
  - number of exclusions?
  - incidence of disciplinary action?
  - number of violent/physical confrontations?
  - peaceful resolutions to conflict?
  - reduction in racist bullying?
- How visible is the intervention in the school?
- How visible is the intervention outside the school?
- Has the school environment become more positive?
- What are the 'real stories' that support the statistics?
- What are the perceived benefits of the intervention for individuals?
- What are the perceived benefits of the intervention for the school as a whole?

EVALUATING KEY CHARACTERISTICS

The purpose of this stage of the evaluation is to describe which aspects of the intervention are working well in which contexts. It should seek to describe which characteristics of classrooms, schools and communities affect intervention outcomes, and which elements key stakeholders value (for example, training, materials, use of outside agency, sense of community, communication, levels of involvement and ownership, etc). Identifying these key factors should prove useful for making amendments to the intervention in order for it to operate successfully. Issues to consider include:

- What are the characteristics of the school that successfully promote the intervention?
- What elements of the intervention are related to success in achieving the goals designed in the needs analysis?
- Which resources and materials provided by the school or the outside agency do staff and young people value?

PREPARATION FOR EVALUATION

If evaluation seems like a daunting task, it might be helpful to carry out the following exercise as a means of preparation for the review and evaluation process:

- Write down a brief history of your intervention.
- Briefly describe your intervention.

- List the intervention's aims and goals as defined in the needs analysis (see Chapter 1.6).

- List the core elements of the intervention.

- Outline the major purposes of the evaluation.

- Identify the anticipated audiences for the evaluation (adapted from Riley and Segal, 2002).

The following examples describe the evaluation of a peer support service from the perspective of users, and the evaluation of a behaviour management package from the perspective of staff.

EVALUATION OF A PEER SUPPORT SERVICE

Naylor and Cowie (1999) elicited the views of 65 users of an established peer support system as part of a survey carried out in 51 secondary schools (see Box 3.2.1). Of the 65 pupils who responded to the question about how helpful they found their school's peer support system, 82 per cent responded 'very helpful' or 'helpful' and 19 per cent 'not helpful'. The three most commonly mentioned benefits for users were that the service provides 'somebody to talk to and who listens', 'the strength to overcome the problem' and that it 'shows that somebody cares'. In answer to the question 'please say what you think the benefits of peer support are', those most frequently mentioned by peer supporters and teachers concerned the acquisition and development of skills and being in a 'caring school'. The three most frequently mentioned benefits of a peer support system to the school as a whole were that 'the school cares', 'bullying is reduced' and 'teachers are freed to do other things'. The idea of a caring school was mentioned by over 40 per cent of the users of these systems. The survey also indicated that the existence of a peer support system was perceived as beneficial to the school as a whole. Many young people who had not used the system still appreciated the provision of the service to protect their safety, and viewed its presence as a sign that the school was caring.

EVALUATION OF A BEHAVIOUR MANAGEMENT PACKAGE

Watt and Higgins (1999) describe the evaluation of a behaviour management package in Scottish schools entitled 'Turn Your School Round' (TYSR). TYSR is a package designed to foster a 'listening' school and address indiscipline in primary and secondary schools using a whole-school or a part-school approach. The package consists of eight components: Circle Time; Golden Rules (which are devised with the help of the pupils and clearly displayed throughout the school); Incentives; Sanctions; Lunchtime Policy; Children Beyond (which addresses issues concerning moral and personal development); Containment

---

BOX 3.2.1 QUESTIONNAIRE TO ELICIT THE VIEWS OF PEER SUPPORTERS

Have you ever used your school's peer support service?   YES   NO

If YES, please say how helpful it was:

Very helpful   Helpful   Not helpful

Please describe your most helpful experience of peer support

....

....

....

....

Please describe your least helpful experience of peer support

....

....

....

....

Are there any ways in which the peer support service could be improved?

....

....

....

....

Please say what you think the benefits of peer support are to:
(a) users ....
(b) peer supporters ....
(c) the school ....

Source: adapted from Naylor and Cowie, 1999.

(which examines whether teachers are given support with difficult circum-stances, and whether colleagues are generally encouraged to support one another); and Support and Review. Circle Time, while a component of the TYSR project, can be implemented as a stand-alone package. The aim of the project was to analyse the extent of usage, and the degree of usefulness of TYSR/Circle Time in Scottish primary schools. All schools in the study cur-rently using the TYSR approach or Circle Time only were invited to complete a questionnaire which focused on a variety of issues regarding implementation and perceived problems and successes of the approach (see the Appendix at the end of this chapter). The main finding suggested that success was reported more frequently among schools that had implemented the entire TYSR package as opposed to Circle Time only. Of the 41 schools that returned questionnaires, none made negative comments about either TYSR or Circle Time. All TYSR staff agreed that their package 'improved parental interest and goodwill towards school' and almost three-quarters of TYSR staff agreed in the most extreme category that pupil on-task behaviour time was increased. More than half of TYSR staff agreed that teachers' stress levels had been reduced and the majority of staff believed that school ethos had improved.

CONCLUSION

This chapter has highlighted some of the ways in which your intervention might be evaluated. Evaluation strategies will vary according to the needs of the individuals and the schools involved, however, it is our argument that all interventions will benefit from a review and evaluation process that is embedded in to the intervention from the outset.

Evaluation should not be viewed as the end of the Cycle of Change (see Figure 3.1.1), rather it could represent a new beginning, as adults and young people reflect on the outcomes and processes of their intervention, and collaboratively plan new strategies and approaches. When adults and young people have become accustomed to regularly taking part in a process of observation, analysis and reflection, they have a choice: they may choose to consolidate their intervention, or they may take the opportunity to renew the cycle by identifying new goals. They can return to the stage of awareness described in Chapter 3.1, but from a different perspective and grounded in actual experience, and so the Cycle of Change continues.

FINAL COMMENTS

In this book, we have offered a variety of ideas and resources to enable secondary schools to create an environment that positively promotes the emotional health and well-being of all. A number of practice points have emerged from the work that we have overviewed in this book. Our fundamental argument is that schools can play a key role in addressing mental health issues in young people. Teachers need to understand when and how to keep a balance between PSHE and citizenship education on the one hand, and active listening/counselling-based approaches to young people's distress on the other. Teachers need to know about and understand the risk factors that underlie mental health difficulties, such as aggression, depression and anxiety. They need to keep a balance between discipline issues on the one hand, and support for young people with behavioural and emotional difficulties on the other. They need to be familiar with the ethical issues about confidentiality that arise when dealing with mental health issues as they affect young people and their families. This does not mean, however, that teachers should act as psychotherapists or counsellors; teachers need to know the limits of their expertise but also to have confidence in the wide range of ways in which they can as educators enhance the emotional well-being of the young people they teach.

Many of these ways have been documented in this book with frequent examples of practice in action. The interventions described are founded on positive relationships and a caring ethos characterized by a willingness to share and a concern for the well-being of others. The creation of a supportive climate in the school setting relies on clear policies and firm but caring management. Supportive behaviour needs to be modelled throughout the school. Guidelines and policies need to be forged through an ongoing process of negotiation and consultation with all concerned, including the pupils.

Teachers also need to examine their own attitudes towards mental health issues and to be honest with themselves about issues that arise when faced with the mental health issues and distress of another if they are to play their part in addressing the stigma of mental health difficulties. In this they need to be supported by a strong school policy with backing from their senior management team. There must also be recognition of the fact that the interventions that we describe in this book need support if they are to be sustained in the long term. The structures and systems within the school must be supportive in order to maintain interest, knowledge and involvement in the complex area of mental health. At the same time, schools alone cannot solve many of the causes of mental distress that arise from issues deeply rooted in the communities or in the wider society. Success will be limited without the involvement of parents, support services and the community in addressing issues like racism, xenophobia or homophobia, that cause such mental anguish to so many young people.

The task is not easy. It has high costs in terms of time and money. But it is hoped that the outcomes will demonstrate that the cost is worth it. The case studies and examples in this book illustrate a range of ways in which schools in different settings have addressed the issue of mental health with their young people.

APPENDIX: QUESTIONNAIRE COMPLETED BY ALL SCHOOLS CURRENTLY USING EITHER TYSR OR CIRCLE TIME

Section 1

Do you operate 'Turn Your School Round' as a *whole-school* discipline package or do you operate 'Circle Time' only?	Yes	No
Do you operate 'Turn Your School Round' or 'Circle Time' with only *some* of your classes?	Yes	No

If so, which classes? ....

Why has this not been implemented in all classes? ....
....

Why did you start using 'Turn Your School Round' or 'Circle Time'? ....
....

For how long have you been using 'Turn Your School Round'/Circle Time?
      Whole-school (......yrs......mths) Part-school (......yrs......mths)

Have you tried any other discipline systems?	Yes	No

If so, which one(s)? ....

Do you continue to use parts of it/them?	Yes	No

If so, which parts? ....
If applicable, why did you not continue to use it/them? ....

Section 2 – Circle Time

Do more than half your teachers practise weekly Circle Time meetings?	Yes	No
Do your lunchtime supervisors hold regular circle meetings?	Yes	No
Do you hold staff circle meetings each term to focus on issues outside the curriculum?	Yes	No

If so, for what purposes?

case conferences	Yes	No
helping each other with difficult children	Yes	No
celebrating success	Yes	No
reviewing personal and school care plans		

Any other purposes ....
....

Do you think the introduction of Circle Time has improved areas of concern in your school?	Yes	No

If so, give examples and evidence ....
....

Section 3 – Golden Rules

Do you use Golden Rules as part of Circle Time?	Yes	No

If so, are the Golden Rules displayed in:

every classroom?	Yes	No
some classrooms?	Yes	Nh
dining room?	Yes	No
the playground?		

Anywhere else? ....

Does Circle Time focus on the moral values within the Golden Rules?	Yes	No
Do parents receive a copy of the Golden Rules?	Yes	No

Section 4 – Incentives

Do all teachers have access to incentives?	Yes	No
Do all supervisors have access to incentives?	Yes	No
Do support staff have access to incentives?	Yes	No
Does your incentive system ensure that all children receive good news about themselves?	Yes	No

Do any of your teachers use a peer support system which involves children nominating others

in Circle Time for rewards or encourages?   Yes   No

What is central to your sanctions system?

withdrawal of a privilege	Yes	No
withdrawal of a treat	Yes	No
withdrawal of Golden Time	Yes	No

    Other ....

Section 5 – Lunchtimes

Has teaching playground games become part of your school policy?   Yes   No

Have you divided your playground into any separate areas of activity, for example:

quiet area?	Yes	No
special activities area?	Yes	No
dressing-up area?	Yes	No

    Other? ....

Have you introduced a lunchtime helper system involving the children?	Yes	No
Has the introduction of Circle Time improved Dining Hall behaviour?	Yes	No

If so, in what ways? ....

Have you introduced a task force for troubled children at lunchtime?   Yes   No

Section 6 – Children Beyond

Is peer support offered to difficult children through Circle Time?	Yes	No
Do your teachers use a Tiny Achievable Tickable Target?	Yes	No
If so, do they contain appropriate self-esteem rewards?	Yes	No
Does your school also operate smaller therapeutic circles for a range of troubled children?	Yes	No

Section 7 – Containment and Review

Are teachers with severely damaged children offered, through the Circle Time, the opportunity

for discussion?   Yes   No

If so, are they also offered a written timetable of support from other members of staff which

guarantees them a break from that child every day?   Yes   No

Section 8 – Evaluation

To what extent do you believe the introduction of Turn Your School Round/Circle Time in your school has helped to

achieve the following:

For the young people's benefit	Strongly Agree	Agree	Disagree	Strongly Disagree
Self-esteem	☐	☐	☐	☐
Reduced 'put-downs' and promoted personal and collective responsibility	☐	☐	☐	☐
Raised self-esteem	☐	☐	☐	☐
Promoted confidence boosting	☐	☐	☐	☐
Personal Development				
Given young people more responsibility for their own behaviour	☐	☐	☐	☐
Given ownership of the system to young people as well as teachers	☐	☐	☐	☐
Given security to young people by providing definite boundaries	☐	☐	☐	☐
Trust is created	☐	☐	☐	☐
Encouraged self-discipline	☐	☐	☐	☐
Developed personal integrity	☐	☐	☐	☐
Improved planning organization, fluency and presentation of ideas	☐	☐	☐	☐
Improved self-control	☐	☐	☐	☐
Social Development				
Built friendships	☐	☐	☐	☐
Developed empathy	☐	☐	☐	☐
Improved relationship skills	☐	☐	☐	☐
Improved listening skills	☐	☐	☐	☐
Integrated SEN young people within the class	☐	☐	☐	☐
Improved participation and communication skills	☐	☐	☐	☐
Improved appropriate responses	☐	☐	☐	☐
Promoted the sharing of ideas	☐	☐	☐	☐
Promoted the sharing of feelings	☐	☐	☐	☐
For the teacher's benefit				
Teacher–young person classroom management				
Increased on-task behaviour	☐	☐	☐	☐
Reduced persistent low-level misdemeanours	☐	☐	☐	☐
Reduced teacher stress	☐	☐	☐	☐
Developed teacher assertiveness skills	☐	☐	☐	☐
Home–school links				
Provided parents with ideas of how to be more supportive	☐	☐	☐	☐
Provided parents with better understanding of children's anxieties	☐	☐	☐	☐
Promoted parents' awareness of belittling or disregarding their child's opinions	☐	☐	☐	☐
Improved parental interest and goodwill towards school	☐	☐	☐	☐

	Strongly Agree	Agree	Disagree	Strongly Disagree
For the young people's benefit				
Encouraged parents to reinforce school policy at home	☐	☐	☐	☐
School/senior management benefit				
Enhanced school ethos	☐	☐	☐	☐
Benefited everyone	☐	☐	☐	☐
Created a sense of belonging	☐	☐	☐	☐
Promoted understanding	☐	☐	☐	☐
Brought playground/lunchtime supervisors' views on behaviour policy in line with the teaching staff	☐	☐	☐	☐
Encouraged support staff to work within school ethos	☐	☐	☐	☐

Please detail, hierarchically, the three most important benefits of Circle Time in your experience as an educator, detailing the most significant benefit first ....
....
....

Please use this space to provide comments on the implementation and/or day-to-day running of Circle Time
....
....
....
....
....

What problems have you encountered? ....
....
....
....

How have you overcome these problems (assuming that you have!)? ....
....
....
....

Thank you very much for taking the time to complete these questions

Source: Watt and Higgins, 1999.

References

Abrams, R. (1992) *When Parents Die*. London: Letts.

Adfam (2002) *Do Your Children Know More About Drugs Than You Do?* London: Home Office Drugs Prevention Advisory Service. Website at www.adfam.org.uk

Alcohol Concern (2002a) *Alcohol and Teenage Pregnancy*. London: Alcohol Concern. Website at www.alcoholconcern.org.uk

Alcohol Concern (2002b) *Information on Alcohol Education*. London: Alcohol Concern.

Alsaker, F.D. (1992) 'Annotation: the impact of puberty', *Journal of Child Psychology and Psychiatry*, 37, 249–58.

Altwood, T. (1998) *Asperger's Syndrome: A Guide for Parents and Professionals*. London: Jessica Kingsley.

Angold, A. (1988) 'Childhood and adolescent depression, epidemiological and aetiological aspects', *British Journal of Psychiatry*, 152, 601–17.

Arkin, A. (2003) 'Massaging figures is one way to improve', *Times Educational Supplement*, 14 March, p. 28.

Armstrong, C., Hill, H. and Secker, J. (2000) 'Young people's perceptions of mental health', *Children and Society*, 14, 60–72.

Aspey, D. and Roebuck, F. (1997) *Kids Don't Learn from People They Don't Like*. Massachusetts: Human Resource Development Press.

Audit Commission (1999) *With Children in Mind*. London: HMSO.

Australian Education Union Report (2003) is at www.aeufederal.org.au/Tafe/documents under VETISFinalReport.pdf

Bailey, S. (1999) 'Young people, mental illness and stigmatisation', *Psychiatric Bulletin*, 23, 107–10.

Ballard, J. (1982) *Circlebook*. New York: Irvington Inc.

Beck, A.T. (1976) *Cognitive Therapy and Emotional Disorders*. New York: International Universities Press.

Beck, A.T., Rush, A.J., Shaw, B.F. and Emery, G. (1979) *Cognitive Therapy of Depression*. New York: Guilford Press.

Beinart, S., Anderson, B., Lee, S. and Utting, D. (2002). *Youth At Risk? A National Survey of Risk Factors, Protective Factors and Problem Behaviour Among Young People in England, Scotland and Wales*. London: Communities that Care.

Bitel, M. (2000) *The Evaluation of Year 2 of Leicestershire Mediation Services Conflict Resolution in Schools Programme*. Leicester: Charities Evaluation Services.

Bliss, T., Robinson, G. and Maines, B. (1996) *Developing Circle Time*. Bristol: Lucky Duck Publishing.

Bloom, A. (2003) 'How to Beat the Baddies', *Times Educational Supplement*, 7 February, p. 20.

Bono, E.de (1992) *Teach Your Child How to Think*. London: Viking.

Brennan R. (1992) *The Alexander Technique Workbook*. Shaftesbury: Elements.

Brighouse, T. (1999) *How to Improve your School*. London: RoutledgeFalmer.

Brooks-Gunn, J. and Warren, M.P. (1989) 'Biological and social contributions to negative affect in young adolescent girls', *Child Development*, 60, 40–55.

Buzan, T. (2001) *Head Strong*. London: Thorsons

Chakrabarti, S. and Fombone, E. (2001) 'Pervasive developmental disorders among preschool children', *Journal of the American Medical Association*, 285, 3093–9.

Charlton, A. and Blair, V. (1989) 'Absence from school related to children's and parental smoking habits', *British Medical Journal*, 298, 90–2.

ChildLine (2000) *Annual Report*. London: ChildLine.

ChildLine (2002) *Setting Up a Peer Support Scheme: Ideas for Teachers and Other Professionals Setting Up and Supporting a Peer Support Scheme*. London: ChildLine.

Children's Rights Development Unit (CRDU) (1993) *The United Nations Convention on the Rights of the Child*. London: UNICEF/Gulbenkian/UNA.

Ciffone, J. (1993) 'Suicide prevention: a classroom presentation to adolescents', *Social Work*, 38 (2), 197–203.

Clarke, A. and Clarke, A.D.B. (2000) *Early Experience and the Life Path*. London: Jessica Kingsley.

Clarke, M., Coombs C. and Walton L. (2003) 'School-based early identification and intervention service for adolescents: a psychology and school nurse partnership model', *Child and Adolescent Mental Health*, 8 (1), 34–9.

Coie, J.D. and Dodge, K.A. (1998). 'Aggression and anti-social behaviour', in N. Eisenberg (ed.), *Handbook of Child Psychology*. New York: Wiley. Vol. 3, pp. 779–862.

Conners, K. (1973) 'Rating scales for use in drug studies with children', *Psychopharmacological Bulletin Special Issue: Pharmacotherapy Child*, 1, 24–84.

Cowie, H. and Olafsson, R. (2000) 'The role of peer support in helping the victims of bullying in a school with high levels of aggression', *School Psychology International*, 21 (1), 79–95.

Cowie, H. and Sharp, S. (1994) 'Working directly with bullies and victims', in S. Sharp and P.K. Smith (eds.), *Tackling Bullying in Your School*. London: Routledge.

Cowie, H. and Smith, P.K. (2001) 'Violence in schools: a perpective from the UK', in E. Debarbieux and C. Blaya (eds), *Violence in Schools and Public Policies*. Issy-les-Moulineaux: ESF.

Cowie, H. and Wallace, P. (2000) *Peer Support in Action*. London: Sage.

Cowie, H., Jennifer, D. and Sharp, S. (2002) 'Violence in schools: the United Kingdom', in P.K. Smith (ed.), *Violence in Schools: The Response in Europe*. London: RoutledgeFarmer.

Cowie, H., Naylor, P., Talamelli, L. and Dawkins, J. (2002a) *The Development of Adolescent Pupils' Knowledge about and Attitudes towards Mental Health Difficulties (Grant Number 1750/197)*. Project report to PPP Healthcare Medical Trust.

Cowie, H., Naylor, P., Talamelli, L., Chauhan, P. and Smith, P.K. (2002b) 'Knowledge, use of and attitudes towards peer support', *Journal of Adolescence*, 25 (5), 453–67.

Craig, W. and Pepler, D. (1995) 'Peer processes in bullying and victimisation: an observational study', *Exceptionality Education Canada*, 5, 81–95.

Crisp, A., Gelder, M.G., Rix, S., Meltzer, H.I. and Rowlands, O.J. (2000) 'The stigmatisation of people with mental illness', *British Journal of Psychiatry*, 177, 4–7.

Cunningham, C.E., Cunningham, L.J., Martorelli, V., Tran, A., Young, J. and Zacharius, R. (1998) 'The effects of primary division, student-mediated conflict resolution programmes on playground aggression', *Journal of Child Psychology and Psychiatry*, 39, 653–68.

Deater-Decker, K. (2001) 'Recent research examining the role of peer relations in the development of psychopathology', *Journal of Child Psychology and Psychiatry*, 42 (5), 565–80.

Dent, A., Condom, L., Blair, P. and Fleming, P. (1996) 'A study of bereavement care after a sudden and unexpected death', *Archives of Disease in Childhood*, 74, 522–6.

Department for Education and Employment (DfEE) (2001) *National Healthy School Standard: Getting Started – a Guide For Schools.* Nottingham: DfES.

Department for Education and Skills (DfES) (2000) *Bullying: Don't Suffer in Silence: An Anti-bullying Pack for Schools.* London: HMSO.

Department for Education and Skills, (DfES) (2002) *Opportunity and Excellence* London: DfES.

Department for Education and Skills (DfES) (2001b) 'Supporting School Improvement Emotional and Behavioural Development', London: QCA.

Department for Education and Skills (DfES) (2002) *14–19 Opportunity and Excellence.* London: DfES Publication.

Department for Education and Skills/Department of Health (DfES/DH) (2002). *Autistic Spectrum Disorders: Good Practice Guidance.* London: DfES Publications.

Department of Health (1998). *A Parent's Guide to Drugs and Alcohol.* London: Department of Health Publications.

Donellan, C. (series ed.) (1998) *Issues: Bullying, Vol. 13; Disabilities, Vol. 17; Mental Illness, Vol. 21; Coping with Eating Disorders, Vol. 24.* Cambridge: Independence Educational Publishers.

Donellan, C. (series ed.) (2000) *Issues: Dealing with Mental Illness, Vol. 21; Coping with Stress, Vol. 21; Self-harm and Suicide,* Vol. 51. Cambridge: Independence Educational Publishers.

Drugscope (2000) *Drug Education for School Excludees.* Website at www.drugscope.org.uk

Drugscope (2001) *Evidence to Home Affairs Select Committee on Drug Policy.* Website at www.drugscope.org.uk

Dusenbury, L., Falco, M., Lake, A., Brannigan, R. and Bosworth, K. (1997) 'Nine critical elements of promising violence prevention programs', *Journal of School Health*, 67 (10), 409–14.

Dyregrov, A. (1991) *Grief in Children: A Handbook for Adults.* London: Jessica Kingsley.

Eskin, M. (1995) 'Adolescents' attitudes towards suicide and a suicidal peer: a comparison between Swedish and Turkish high school students', *Scandinavian Journal of Psychology*, 36 (2), 201–7.

Farrington, D.P. (2002) 'Risk factors for youth violence', in E. Debarbieux and C. Blaya (eds), *Violence in Schools and Public Policies.* London: Elsevier.

Favazza, A., Conterio, K. (1989) 'Female habitual self-mutilaters', *Acta Psychiatrica Scandinavica*, 79, 283–9.

Felsman, J.K. and Valliant G.E. (1987) 'Resilient children as adults: a 40 year study', in E. Anderson and B. Cohler (eds), *The Invulnerable Child.* New York: Guilford Press.

Fergusson, Woodward, and Horwood (2000) 'The risk factors and life processes associated with the onset of suicidal behaviour during adolescence and early childhood', *Psychological Medicine*, 30 (1), 23–39.

Field-Smith, M.E., Bland, J.M., Taylor, J.C., Ramsey, J.D. and Anderson, H.R. (2002) *Trends in Death Associated with Abuse of Volatile Substances.* A report compiled for the Department of Health by the Department of Public Health Sciences at St George's Hospital Medical School, London. Website at ww.sghms.ac.uk/depts/phs/vsa2000

Flood-Page, C., Campbell, S., Harrington, V. and Miller, J. (2000) Youth Crime Findings from the 1998/99 Youth Lifestyles Survey. Home Office Research Study 209. London: Home Office.

Frosh, S., Phoenix, A. and Pattman, R. (2002) *Young Masculinities*. London: Palgrave.

Gale, E. and Holling, A. (2000) 'Young people and stigma', *Young Minds Magazine*, 49–50.

Gelder M. (2001) 'The Royal College of Psychiatrists' survey of public opinions about mentally ill people 2001', in A. Crisp (ed.), *Every Family in the Land: Understanding Prejudice and Discrimination Against People with Mental Illness*. CD-ROM. London: Royal College of Psychiatrists. pp. 28–33. Website at www.stigma.org/everyfamily

Gerland, G. (2000) *Finding out about Asperger's Syndrome, High Functioning Autism and PDD*. London: Jessica Kingsley.

Gill, M. and Hearnshaw, S. (1997) *Personal Safety and Violence in Schools*. DfEE Research Report 21. London: HMSO.

Glover, D., Gough, G. and Johnson, M. (2000) 'Bullying in 25 secondary schools: incidence, impact and intervention', *Educational Research*, 42 (2), 141–56.

Goldberg, D. and Huxley, P. (1992) *Common Mental Disorders: A Biosocial Model*. London: Routledge.

Goleman, D. (1996) *Emotional Intelligence*. London: Bloomsbury.

Goleman, D. (1998) *Working with Emotional Intelligence*. London: Bloomsbury.

Gordon, J. and Grant G. (1997) *How we Feel*. London: Jessicsa Kingsley.

Goulden, C. and Sondhi, A. (2001) At the Margins: Drug use by vulnerable young people in the 1998/99 Youth Lifestyles Survey. Home Office Research Study 228. Home Office Research Development Strategies.

Graham , M. (2002) 'The "miseducation" of black children in the British system – towards an African-centred orientation to knowledge', in R. Majors (ed.), *Educating our Black Children: New Direction and Radical Approaches*. London and New York: RoutledgeFalmer.

Gray, C. (1998) 'Social stories and comic strip conversation with students with Asperger's syndrome and high-functioning austism', in E. Schopler, G. Mesibov and L.J. Kunce (eds), *Asperger's Syndrome or High-functioning Austism? Current Issues in Autism*. New York: Plenum Press.

Gray, C. (2000) *The New Social Story Book*. Arlington, VA: Future Horizons Inc.

Green, C. and Chee, K. (1997) *Understanding ADHD*. London: Vermilion.

Greenberg, M.T., Kusche, C.A., Cooke, E.T., and Quamma, J.P. (1995) 'Promoting emotional competence in school-aged children: the effects of the PATHS curriculum', *Development and Psychopathology*, 7, 7–16.

Hampshire County Council (1996) *Attention Deficit (Hyperactive) Disorder AD(H)D: Information and Guidlines for Schools*. Hampshire County Council Education Department.

Hargreaves, A., Earl, L. and Ryan, J. (1996) *Schooling for Change: re-inventing Education for Early Adolescents*. London: Falmer.

Hawton, K. (1987) 'Assessment of suicide risk', *British Journal of Pyschiatry*, 150, 145–53.

Hawton, K., Rodham, K., Evans, E. and Weatherall, R. (2002) 'Deliberate self-harm in adolescence: self-reports survey in schools in England', *British Medical Journal*, 325, 23 November, 1207–11.

Hayden, C. (2002) 'Risk factors and exclusion from school', in E. Debarbieux and C. Blaya (eds), *Violence in Schools and Public Policies*. Paris: Elsevier.

Hayden, C. and Blaya, C. (2001) 'Violent and aggressive behaviour in English schools', in E. Debarbieux and C. Blaya (eds), *Violence in Schools and Public Policies*. Issy-les-Moulineaux: ESF.

Hayward, P. and Bright, J.A. (1997) 'Stigma and mental illness: a review and critique', *Journal of Mental Health*, 6, 345–54.

Hazell, P. and Lewin, T. (1993) 'An evaluation of postvention following adolescent suicide', *Suicide and Life Threatening Behaviour*, 23 (2), 101–9.

Health Education Authority (1997) *Mental Health Promotion: A Quality Framework.* London: HMSO.

Health Education Authority (1998a). *Sexual Health Matters: Research Survey.* London: HEA.

Health Education Authority (1998b). *The UK Smoking Experience: Deaths in 1995.* London: HEA.

Hewitt, R., Epstein, D., Leonard, D., Mauthner, M. and Watkins, C. (2002) *'The violence resilient school; a comparative study of schools and their environments.* A report to the ESRC, London. Available at www1.rhbnc.ac.uk/sociopolitical-science/VRP/Findings/rfhewitt. PDF

Hibell, B. (2001) *The 1999 ESPAD Report; Alcohol and Other Drug Use amongst Students in 30 European Countries.* Stockholm: Swedish Council for Information on Alcohol and Other Drugs.

Honess, T., Seymour, T. and Webster, L. (2000) *The Social Contexts of Underage Drinking.* London: Home Office.

Hook, S. (2003) 'Closer Links Bind Colleges to Schools', Times Educational Supplement, 24 January, p. 39.

Inclusive Solutions, 49, Northcliffe Venue, Nottingham, NG3 6DA Tel: 0115 956 7305 www.inclusive-solutions.com.

Inman, S. and Turner, N. (2001) *Report on the evaluation of Tower Hamlets Conflict Resolution Project (TH17).* On behalf of the Centre for Cross Curricular Initiatives, South Bank University, commissioned by Tower Hamlets Education.

Institute of Alcohol Studies (2002). *What is Problem Drinking?* Cambridge: Institute of Alcohol Studies. Website at www.ias.org.uk

Jackson, L. (2002) *Freaks, Geeks and Asperger's Syndrome: A User Guide to Adolescence.* London: Jessica Kingsley.

Jaycox, L.H., Reivich, K.J., Gillham, J. and Seligman, M.E.P. (1994) 'Prevention of depressive symptoms in school children', *Behaviour Research and Therapy*, 32, 801–16.

Jenkinson, J., Hyde, T. and Ahmad, S. (2002) *Occupational Therapy Approaches for Secondary Special Needs.* London: Whurr Publishers.

Johnson, D. and Johnson, R. (1992) *Learning Together and Alone: Cooperative, Competitive and Individualistic Learning.* Needham Heights, MA: Allyn and Bacon.

Kalafat, J. and Elias, M. (1994) 'An evaluation of a school based suicide awareness intervention', *Suicide and Life Threatening Behaviour*, 24 (3), 224–33.

Katz, A., Buchanan, A. and Bream, V. (2001) *Bullying in Britain: Testimonies From Teenagers.* London: Young Voice.

Keinhorst, I., De Wilde, E. and Diekstra, R. (1995) 'Suicidal behaviour in adolescents', *Archives of Suicide Research*, 1, 185–209.

Kendell, R.E. (2001) 'Why stigma matters', in A. Crisp (ed.), *Every Family in the Land: Understanding Prejudice and Discrimination Against People with Mental Illness.* CD-ROM. London: Royal College of Psychiatrists. Website at www.stigma.org/everyfamily

Kennedy, D. (2002) *The ADHD Autism Connection*. Colorado Springs, Colorado: Waterbrooks.

Killen, J.D., Barr Taylor, C., Hammer, L.D., Litt, I , Wilson, D.M., Rich, T., Hayward, C., Simmonds, B., Kraemer, H. and Varady, A. (1993) 'An attempt to modify unhealthful eating attitudes and weight regulation practices of young adolescent girls', *International Journal of Eating Disorders*, 13 (4), 369–84.

Klein, R. (2002) 'Special Friends', *Times Educational Supplement*, 6 December.

Klinefelter, P. (1994) 'A school counselling service', *Counselling*, 8, 215–17.

Landgren M., Kjellman B. and Gillberg C. (1998) 'Attention deficit disorders with developmental coordination disorders', *Archives of Disease in Childhood*, 79, 207–12.

Lavikainen, J., Jahtinen, E. and Lehtinen, V. (eds) (2000) *Public Health Approach on Mental Health in Europe*. Helsinki: STAKES.

Leap Confronting Conflict (1999). 'Annual Review 1999'. Unpublished. *Leap* Confronting Conflict, The Leap Centre, 8 Lennox Road, London, N4 3NW.

Luckner, J. (1994) 'Learning to be a friend', *Perspectives in Education and Deafness*, 12 (5), 2–7.

Market and Opinion Research Institute (MORI) (2000) *Youth Survey: Research Study Conducted for the Youth Justice Board*. London: Youth Justice Board.

Masheder, M. (1997) *Let's Co-operate*. London: Green Print.

Maslow A. (1970) *Motivation and Personality*. 2nd edn. New York: Harper and Row.

McCarthy, K. (1998) *Learning by Heart: The Role of Emotional Education in Raising School Achievement*. Brighton: Re : membering education.

McClure, G.M.G. (2001) 'Suicide in children and adolescents in England and Wales 1970–1998', *British Journal of Psychiatry*, 178, 469–74.

McGurk, H. and Soriano, G. (1998) 'Families and social development: the 21st century', in A. Campbell and S. Muncer (eds), *The Social Child*. Hove: Psychology Press. pp. 113–42.

Mehta, S., Mehta, M. and Mehta, S. (1990) *Yoga: The Iyengar Way*. London: Dorling Kindersley.

Meltzer, H. (1999) *Mental Health of Children and Adolescents in Great Britain*. London: HMSO.

Mental Health Foundation (MHF) (1999) *Bright Futures*. London: Mental Health Foundation, 20/21 Cornwall Terrace, London, NW1 4QL.

Mental Health Foundation (MHF) (2000) *All About ADHD*. London: Mental Health Foundation.

Moreno, A.B. and Thelen, M.H. (1993) 'A primary prevention programme for eating disorders in a junior high school population', *Journal of Youth and Adolescence*, 22 (2), 109–24.

Moriarty, D., Shore, R. and Maxim, N., (1990) 'Evaluation of an eating disorder curriculum', *Evaluation and Programme Planning*, 13, 407–13.

Mosley, J. (1988) 'Some Implications arising from a small scale study of a circle based programme', *Pastoral Care*, 10–16.

Mosley, J. (1996) *Quality Circle Time*. Cambridge.

Mosley, J. (1998) *Important Issues Relating to the Promotion of Positive Behaviour and Self Esteem in Secondary Schools*. Trowbridge: Jenny Mosley Consultancies.

MTA Cooperative Group (1999) A fourteen month randomised clinical trial of treatment strategies for attention-deficit/hyperactivity disorder. *Archives of General Psychiatry*, 56, 1073–86.

Murray-Parkes, C. (1972) *Bereavement: Studies of Grief in Adult Life*. London: Tavistock.

National Curriculum (NC) (2003) The National Curriculum Online. Available at www.nc.uk.net.

National Healthy School Standard (NHSS) (1999) *National Healthy School Standard Guidance*. Nottingham: DfEE

National Healthy School Standard (NHSS) (2000) Website at http://www.wired-forhealth.gov.uk

National Institute for Clinical Excellence (NICE) (2000) *Guidance on the Use of Methylphenidate (Ritalin, Equasym) for ADHD in Childhood*. London: NICE.

Naylor, P. and Cowie, H. (1999) 'The effectiveness of peer support systems in challenging school bullying: the perspectives and experiences of teachers and pupils', *Journal of Adolescence*, 22, 1–13.

Neill, S. R. St J. (2001) *Unacceptable Pupil Behaviour: A Survey Analysed for the National Union of Teachers*. University of Warwick, Institute of Education.

Nelson, F. (1987) 'Evaluation of a youth suicide prevention school programme', *Adolescence*, 22 (88), 813–25.

Newcombe, R. Measham, F. and Parker, H. (1995) 'A survey of drinking and deviant behaviour among 14/15 year olds in North West England', *Addiction Research*, 2 (4), 319–41.

Newton, C. and Wilson, D. (2000) *Circles of Friends*. Dunstable and Dublin: Folens Ltd.

O'Connell, P. and Pepler, D. (1999) 'Peer involvement in bullying: insights and challenges for intervention', *Journal of Adolescence*, 22, 437–52.

Office for National Statistics (ONS) (2001a) *Psychiatric Morbidity Among Adults Living in Private Households*. London: The Stationery Office.

Office for National Statistics (ONS) (2001b) *Smoking, Drinking and Drug Use Among Young People in England in 2000*. London: The Stationery Office.

Olweus, D. (1999) 'Sweden', in P.K. Smith, Y. Morita, J. Junger-Tas, D. Olweus, R. Catalano and P. Slee (eds), *The Nature of School Bullying*. London: Routledge.

Orbach, I. and Bar Joseph, H. (1993) 'The impact of a suicide prevention programme for adolescents with suicidal tendencies', *Suicide and Life Threatening Behaviour*, 23 (2), 120–9.

Orpin, L. (2003) 'A fresh approach to sex and relationships education', *Children Now*. London: NCB.

Overholser, J., Hemstreet, A., Spirito, A. and Vyse, S. (1989) 'Suicide awareness programmes in schools: effects of gender and personal experience', *Journal of American Academy of Child and Adolescent Psychiatry*, 28, 925–30.

Papyrus (Prevention of Suicides) (2000) *Don't Die of Embarrassment* (video film) PAPYRUS, Rossendale G.H., Union Road, Rawtenstall, Lancashire, BB4 6NE.

Paxton, S.I., (1993) 'A prevention programme for disturbed eating and body dissatisfaction in adolescent girls: a one year follow-up', *Health Education Research*, 8 (1), 43–51.

Pellegrini, A.D. and Blatchford, P. (2002) 'Time for a break', *The Psychologist*, 15 (2), 60–2.

Pepler, D. and Craig, W. (1995) 'A peek behind the fence: Naturalistic observations of aggressive children, with remote audiovisual recording', *Developing Psychology*, 31, 548–53.

Perry, D.G., Kusel, S.J. and Perry, L.C. (1988) 'Victims of peer aggression', *Developmental Psychology*, 6, 807–14.

Perske, R. and Perske, M. (1988) *Circles of Friends*. Nashville, TN: Abingdon Press.

Petersen, A.C. and Crockett, L. (1985) 'Pubertal timing and grade effects on adjustment', *Journal of Youth and Adolescence*, 14, 191–206.

Pinfold, V, .Toulmin H.R., Thornicroft, G., Huxley, P., Farmer, P. and Graham, T. (2003) 'Reducing psychiatric stigma and discrimination: evaluation of educational interventions in UK secondary schools', *British Journal of Psychiatry*, 182, 342–6.

Pollard, D. and Ajirotulu, C. (2002) 'The African American immersion schools experiment', in R. Majors (ed.), *Educating Our Black Children: New Directions and Radical Approaches*. London and New York: RoutledgeFalmer.

Pretty, J.N. Guijt, I., Thompson, J. and Scoones, I. (1995) *Participatory Learning and Action: A Trainer's Guide*, IIED Participatory Methodology Series. London: IIED, 3 Endsleigh Street, London, WC1H 0DD. 020 7388 2117.

Prochaska, J.O. and DiClemente, C.C. (1992) 'The transtheoretical approach', in J.C. Norcross and M.R. Goldfried (eds), *Handbook of Psychotherapy Integration*. New York: Basic Books.

Public Health Laboratory Service (PHLS) (2003a) *HIV and AIDS: General Information*. Available at www.phls.co.uk/topics

Public Health Laboratory Service (PHLS) (2003b) *Chlamydia: General Information*. Available at www.phls.co.uk/topics

Public Health Laboratory Service (PHLS) (2003c) *HIV and Sexually Transmitted Infections (STI)*. Available at www.phls.co.uk/topics

Ramsbottom, D. (1997) *Young Prisoners: A Thematic Review*. London: Home Office.

Revel, P. (2002) 'Talking Back to Happiness', *Times Educational Supplement*. 26 April. p. 25.

Rey, J. and Tennant C. (2002) 'Cannabis and mental health', *British Medical Journal*, 325, 1183–4.

Riley, P.L. and Segal, E.C. (2002) 'Preparing to evaluate a school violence prevention program: Students Against Violence Everywhere', *Journal of School Violence*, 1 (2), 73–86.

Robbins, S.P. (1994) *Essentials of Organisational Behaviour*. Englewood Cliffs, NJ: Prentice Hall International.

Robinson, G. and Maines, B. (1997) *Crying for Help: The No Blame Approach to Bullying*. Bristol: Lucky Duck Publishing.

Robson, W.J. (1998) 'Alcohol and adolescents', *Journal of Substance Misuse*, 3 (1), 3–4.

Roffey, S. (2000) 'Addressing bullying in schools: organisational factors from policy to practice', *Educational and Child Psychology*, 17 (1), 6–19.

Rosen, I.C. (1989) 'Prevention of eating disorders', *National Anorexic Aid Society Newsletter*, 12, 1–3.

Royal College of Physicians (1992) *Smoking and the Young*. London: RCP.

Royal College of Psychiatrists (RCP) (1996) *Information Factsheets: Mental Health and Growing Up*. Royal College of Psychiatrists, 17 Belgrave Square, London, SW1X 8PG.

Royal College of Psychiatrists (RCP) (1998) *Mental Illness and Stigma*, Module 217. London: Office of National Statistics.

Royal College of Psychiatrists (1999) Fact Sheet: *Deliberate Self Harm in Young People*. Royal College of Psychiatrists, 17 Belgrave Square, London, SW1X 8PG.

Royal College of Psychiatrists (RCP) (2000a) *Changing Minds* Booklets: *Alcohol and Other Drug Misuse; Anorexia and Bulimia; Depression; Anxiety; Challenging Prejudice*. Available at www.rcpsych.ac.uk/public/stigma/htm (accessed 27 September, 2003).

Royal College of Psychiatrists (RCP) (2000b) Factsheets: *Behavioural Problems and Conduct Disorder*, Factsheet 4; *Attention Deficit Disorder and Hyperactivity*, Factsheet 5; *The Child with General Learning Disability*, Factsheet 10; *Specific Learning Difficulties*, Factsheet 11. Available at www.rcpsych.ac.uk/public/newmhgu/htm

Royal College of Psychiatrists (RCP) (2000c) *Surviving Adolescence*. Available at www.rcpsych.ac.uk/public/help/adol/survadol.htm

Royal College of Psychiatrists (RCP) (2000d) *1 in 4* (video film). The Royal College of Psychiatrists, 17 Belgrave Square, London, SW1X 8PG, www.changing-minds.co.uk (launched 10 October, 2003).

Royal College of Psychiatrists (RCP) (2000e) *Headstuff* (video film). The Royal College of Psychiatrists, 17 Belgrave Square, London, SW1X 8PG, www.chang-ingminds.co.uk (launched 10 October).

Royal College of Psychiatrists (RCP) (2002) *Changing Minds*. CD-ROM, London: RCP.

Rutter, M. (2000) 'Psychosocial influences: critiques, findings and research needs', *Development and Psychopathology*, 12, 375–405.

Rutter, M. and Smith, D. (1995) *Psychosocial Disorders in Young People. Time Trends and their Causes.* Chichester: John Wiley and Sons.

Rutter, M., Giller, G. and Hagell, A. (1998) *Antisocial Behaviour by Young People.* Cambridge: Cambridge University Press.

Rutter, M., Maughan, B., Mortimore, P., Ouston, J. and Smith A. (1979) *Fifteen Thousand Hours: Secondary Schools and Their Effects on Children.* Shepton Mallet: Open Books.

Salmivalli, C. (1998) 'Participant role approach to school bullying – implications for interventions', *Journal of Adolescence*, 22 (4).

Salmivalli, C., Karhunen, J. and Lagerspetz, K.M.J. (1996) 'How do the victims respond to bullying?', *Aggressive Behavior*, 22 (2), 99–109.

Salmivalli, C., Lagerspetz, K., Björkqvist, K., Österman, K. and Kaukiainen, A. (1996) 'Bullying as a group process: participant roles and their relations to social status within the group', *Aggressive Behavior*, 22, 1–15.

Samaritans (2003) *Youth and Self-harm: Perspectives.* Report to the Samaritans by Centre for Suicide Research, University of Oxford. London: Samaritans.

Sammons, P., Hillman, J. and Mortimore, P. (1995) *Key Characteristics of Effective Schools.* London: Institute of Education/Office for Standards in Education.

Shaffer, D., Garland, A., Vieland, V., Underwood, M. and Busner, C. (1991) 'The impact of curriculum based suicide prevention programmes for teenagers', *Journal of American Academy of Child and Adolescent Psychiatry*, 30 (4), 588–96.

Shaffer, D., Vieland, V. and Garland, A. (1990) 'Adolescent suicide attempters: Response to suicide prevention programs', *Journal of American Medical Association*. 264: 3151–5.

Select Committee on Health (2003) *Third Report.* London: The Stationery Office.

Seligman, M. (2002) 'Positive psychology, positive prevention and positive therapy', in C.R. Snyder and S.J. Lopez (eds), *Handbook of Positive Psychology.* Oxford: Oxford University Press. pp. 3–9.

Sharp, S. (1999) *Bullying Behaviour in Schools.* Windsor: NFER-Nelson.

Sharp, S. and Cowie, H. (1998) *Counselling and Supporting Children in Distress.* London: Sage.

Sharp, S. and Smith, P.K. (1994) (eds) Tackling Bullying in Your School: a Practical

Guide for Teachers. London: Routledge.

Shisslak, C., Crago, M. and Neal, M.E. (1990) 'Prevention of eating disorders among adolescents', *American Journal of Health Promotion*, 5 (2), 100–6.

Shore, R.A., and Porter, J.E. (1990) 'Normative and reliability data for 11–18 year olds on the Eating Disorder Inventory', *International Journal of Eating Disorders*, 9, 201–7.

Silverman, P.R. and Worden, J.W. (1993) 'Children's reactions to the death of a parent', in M.S. Stroebe, W. Stroebe and R.O. Hansson (eds), *Handbook of Bereavement: Theory, Research and Intervention*. New York: Cambridge University Press. pp. 300–16.

Sinclair, N., Noor, S. and Evans, V. (2001) *Opportunities for Drug and Alcohol Education in the School Curriculum*. London: Alcohol Concern/Drugscope.

Smith, J. (2001) *The Learning Game*. London: Abacus.

Smith, P.K. and Sharp, S. (1994) *School Bullying: Insights and Perspectives*. London: Routledge.

Snow, T. (2003) 'Schools Use Peace to Promote Learning', *Times Educational Supplement*. 31 January, p. 4.

Social Exclusion Unit (1999) *Teenage Pregnancy*. London: SEU.

Soni Raleigh, V. and Balajaran, R. (1992) 'Suicide and self-burning among Indians and West Indians in England and Wales', *British Journal of Psychiatry*, 161, 365–8.

Spirito, A. (1988) 'Evaluation of a suicide awareness of curriculum for high school students', *Journal of American Academy of Child and Adolescent Psychiatry*, 27, 705–11.

Stattin, H. and Magnusson, D. (1990) *Pubertal Maturation in Female Development*. Hillsdale, NJ: Erlbaum Associates.

Steiner, M. (1993) *Learning From Experience: Cooperative Learning and Global Education*. Stoke-on-Trent: Trentham Books.

Stewart, D.A. (1998) 'Experience with a school based eating disorder prevention programme', in W. Vandereycken and G. Noordenbos (eds), *The Prevention of Eating Disorders*. London: Athlone.

Stewart, D.A. (2001) Private communication.

Stewart-Brown, S. (1998) *Evaluating Health Promotion in Schools: Reflections from the UK*. Oxford: Health Services Research Unit, Deptartment of Public Health, University of Oxford.

Stokes, J. and Crossley, D. (2001) *A Child's Grief*. Gloucester: Winston's Wish. Website at www.winstonswish.org.uk

Stokes, J., Pennington, J., Monroe, B., Papadatou, D. and Relf, M. (1999) 'Developing services for bereaved children: a discussion of the theoretical and practical issues involved', *Mortality*, 4 (3), 291–307.

Stroebe, M.S. and Schut, H. (1999) 'The dual process model of coping with bereavement: rationale and description', *Death Studies*, 23, 197–224.

Sullivan, K. (2000) *The Anti-Bullying Handbook*. Oxford: Oxford University Press.

Sutton, J., Smith, P.K. and Swettenham, J. (1999) 'Bullying and theory of mind: a critique of the social skills deficit view of anti-social behaviour', *Social Development*, 8, 117–27.

Taylor, E. (1997) *Understanding your Hyperactive Child: The Essential Guide for Parents*. London: Vermilion.

Taylor, G. and Burden, B. (2001) *The Positive Power of Friendship*. Calouste Gulbenkian Foundation.

Tew. M. (1998) Circle Time: 'A much Neglected Resource in Secondary Schools?, Pastoral Care in Education, 16, 3.

The Chalkface Project, Milton Keynes:

Ball, C. and Hartley, M. (1999a) *Zero Tolerance to Bullying.*

Brown, J. and Fabey, L. (1993) *Overcoming Bullying.*

Freeman, P. and Hartley, M. (1999b) *Effective Learning Through Better Classroom Behaviour.*

Naylor, P. and Eddy, S. (1997) *Equal Opportunities.*

Russell, J. and Rogers, A. (1999c) *Exploring Body Images and Issues.*

The Gatehouse Project published on the web by Royal Children's Hospital Melbourne, 24/6/2002 Enquiries John Hargreaves. www.rch.unimelb.edu.au/gatehouseproject

Tierney, J., Grossman, J. and Resch, N. (1993) *Making a Difference: An Impact Study of Big Brother/Big Sister*, Philadelphia, PA: Public/Private Ventures.

Times Educational Supplement (2002) 'More stressed out staff turn to treatments such as massage'. 26 April, p. 4.

Turunen, H., Tossavainen, K., Jakonen, S., Salomäki, U. and Vertio, H. (1999) 'Initial results from the European network of health promoting schools program on development of health education in Finland', *Journal of School Health*, 69, 387–91.

Tweedale, C. (2002) 'Behaviour: part 3, The Issue', *Times Educational Supplement*, 6 December.

Vandereycken, W. and Noordenbos, G. (1998) *The Prevention of Eating Disorders.* London: Athlone.

Varnava, G. (2000) *Towards a Non-Violent Society: Checkpoints for Schools.* London: NCB.

Varnava, G. (2002a) *Towards a Non-Violent Society: Checkpoints for Young People.* London: National Children's Bureau.

Varnava, G. (2002b) *How to Stop Bullying in your School: A Guide For Teachers.* London: David Fulton.

Vettenburg, N. (1999) 'Violence in schools, awareness raising, prevention, penalties', *General Report*. Council of Europe Publishing.

Vieland, V., Whittle, B., Garland, A., Hicks, R. and Shaffer, D. (1991) 'The impact of the curriculum based suicide prevention programme for teenagers: an 18 months' follow up', *Journal of American Academy Child and Adolescent Psychiatry*, 30 (5).

Volunteer Development Scotland (2002) Scotland's response to the National Framework for the Prevention of Suicide and Deliberate Self-Harm in Scotland, January 30, produced by Volunteer Development Scotland.

Vulliamy, G. and Webb, R. (2003) 'Reducing school exclusions: a multi-site development project', *Oxford Review of Education*, 29, 33–49.

Watt, S. and Higgins, C. (1999) 'Using behaviour management packages as a stepping stone from school to society: a Scottish evaluation of "Turn Your School Round" ', *Children and Society*, 13, 346–64.

Weare, K. (2000) *Promoting Mental, Emotional + Social Health; A Whole School Approach.* London and New York: Routledge.

Webster-Stratton, C. (1999) *How to Promote Children's Social and Emotional Competence.* London: Paul Chapman.

Webster-Stratton, C. and Hammond, M. (1999) 'Marital conflict management, parenting skills, parenting style and early conduct problems: processes and pathways', *Journal of Child Psychology and Psychiatry*, 40, 917–27.

Weiss, M. (1986) 'Children's attitudes towards the mentally ill – a developmental analysis', *Psychological Reports*, 58, 11–20.

Weiss, M. (1994) 'Children's attitudes towards the mentally ill, an eight year longitudinal follow-up', *Psychological Reports*, 74, 51–6.

West, P., Sweeting, H. (2003) 'Fifteen, female and stressed: changing patterns of psychological distress over time', *Journal of Child Psychology and Psychiatry*, 44:3, 399–411.

Whitaker, P. (1998) 'Children with autism and peer group support', *British Journal of Special Education*, 25, 60–4.

White, M. (1992) *Self Esteem, its Meaning and Value in Schools*. Bristol: Daniels Publishing.

White, M. (1999) *Magic Circles*. Bristol: Lucky Duck Publishing.

Whitmore, D. (2003) *Teens and Toddlers Executive Summary*. COUI (UK), Southfield, Leigh, Kent, TN11 9 PJ.

Whitney, I. and Smith, P.K. (1993) 'A survey of the nature and extent of bully/victim problems in junior/middle and secondary schools', *Educational Research*, 35, 3–25.

Wiencke, J.K., Thurston, S.W., Kelsey, K.T., Varkonuyi, A., Wain, J.C., Mark, E.J. and Christiani, D.C. (1999) 'Early age at smoking initiation and tobacco carcinogen DNA damage in the lung', *Journal of the National Cancer Institute*, 91 (7), 614–19.

Wight, Henderson, Raab, Abraham, Buston, Scott and Hart (2000) 'Extent of regretted sexual intercourse among young teenagers in Scotland: a cross sectional survey', *British Medical Journal*, 320, 1243–4. Also at www.msoc-mrc.gla.ac.uk

Williams, E. (2002) 'Behaviour, part 3, The Issue', *Times Educational Supplement*, 6 December, p. 17.

Wilson, M. (2001) *Mind's Respect Campaign*. CD-ROM, pp. 415–19.

Worden, J.W. (1991) *Grief Counselling and Grief Therapy*. London: Routledge.

Worden, J.W. (1997) *Children and Grief – When a Parent Dies*. New York: Guilford Press.

World Health Organization (WHO) (1995) *European Charter on Alcohol*. Geneva: WHO.

World Health Organization (WHO) (1999) *Violence Prevention: An Important Element of a Health-Promoting School*. Geneva: WHO

World Health Organization (WHO) (2003) *Understanding Sexual and Reproductive Health including HIV/AIDS and STDs Among Street Children*. Department of Mental Health and Substance Dependence, WHO. Available at www.who.int/reproductive-health/adolescent/index.html

Young Minds (2002) *Mental Health Services for Adolescents and Young Adults*. Available from Young Minds, tel. 0207336 8445 or at www.youngminds.org.uk

Young, S. (1998) 'The support group approach to bullying in schools', *Educational Psychology in Practice*, 14 (1), 32–9.

Youth Justice Board (2002) *Youth Survey 2002 for the Youth Justice Board*. London: MORI.

Zammit, S., Allebeck, P., Andreasson, S., Lundberg, I. and Lewis, G. (2002) 'Self reported cannabis use as a risk factor for schizophrenia in Swedish conscripts of 1969: historical cohort study', *British Medical Journal*, 325, 1191–202.

Index

academic achievement, 24, 27
Adolescent Self Harm Forum, 169, 171
adversity, 8
after–school care clubs, 12
aggressive behaviour, 4, 6, 17, 69, 81, 92, 145
alcohol use, see also drug and alcohol use, 111, 120–131
Alexander technique, 61, 62
anorexia nervosa, 5, see also eating disorders, 151, 164
anti-bullying policy, 9, 12, 97, 157
anxiety–generalised, 5
anxiety–separation, 5
anxiety disorders, 5
APAUSE, 64, 115
art therapists, 187
Aspergers, 132–141
Assertiveness training, 64, 101
asylum- seeker communities, 9
attention deficit hyperactivity disorder, 4, 6, 36, 64, 110, 172–183
auditory stimulae, 55
Autistic Spectrum Disorders, 132–141, 175

behaviour and education support teams(BESTS), 74
behaviour management package, 206–208
Behavioural Management Consultancies, 64, 70, 72, 73
Behavioural Support Service, 49, 58, 186
behavioural support units, 72, 186
bereavement, 142–150
BNTL freeway, 64, 127
body image, 5, 151
brain damage, 8
building bridges, 32
bulimia nervosa, 5, see also eating disorders, 153
bullies, persistent, 64, 102, 103
bullying behaviours, 35, 56, 64, 80, 92–108, 162
bullying, bystander, 93
bullying, defender, 94
bullying, participants, 93, 95
bullying, reinforcer, 93
bullying, victims, 93, 94, 96
bullying,outsider, 93

cannabis, 8, 122
Changing Minds campaign, 16, 45

Checkpoints For Schools, 46, 64, 83
Checkpoints For Young People, 46, 64, 83
Child and Adolescent Mental Health Service, 4, 42, 45, 47, 144, 184, 186
ChildLine, 80, 84, 103
CHIPS, 64, 84–85, 103
chronic physical illness, 8
circle of friends, 64, 112, 135, 200, 136–140
circle time, 64, 70, 75–79, 112, 207
Citizenship, 85, 98, 114
clear consistent discipline, 9
closure, 201
cognitive skills, 60, 64
comic strip conversation, 64, 136
community paediatricians, 186
community psychiatric nurses, 187
community, school, 55, 63
competence, 10
computer systems, 57
conduct disorder, 4, 68
conflict resolution, 39, 90
ConneXions, 3, 185, 186, 188
cooperative group learning, 71, 98
cooperative values, 64, 98
coping skills, 12
counselling, 60, 166
crime, 8, 123
criminal justice system, 6, 162, 186, 188
CRISP, 64, 83
cutting, 5, 163
cycle of change, 193, 194, 208
cycle of disadvantage, 9

De Bono hats, 56, 61
deafness, 8
Defeat Stigma Campaign, 25
delinquency, 8, 9, 68, 82
depression, 4, 14, 35, 162, 164, 165
difficulties, 193–202
disadvantaged backgrounds, 16
disaffected young people, 68–79
discrimination, 8, 13–23
divorce, 142
drama, 42
drama therapists, 187
drop in clinics, 157, 186
Drug and Alcohol Service for London, 128
drug and alcohol use, 4, 7, 8, 18, 33, 64, 111,

120–131, 162
drug dependence, 7, 14
dyspraxia, 175

eating disorder education programme, 157–159
eating disorders, 14, 35, 64, 151–160
Education Welfare Officers, 58, 186
emotional intelligence, 37, 138
empathy, 37, 38, 94
Essex School Award Scheme, 46
ethnic minorities, 6, 9, 17, 32
ethos, 41, 55, 56
evaluation, 42, 48, 195, 202, 203–213
Excellence in Cities, 3
exclusions, 6, 33, 122
externalizing disorder, 4, 6
Extra Edge Project, 168

family size, 9
financial resources, 44
flow diagrams, 42
focus groups, 42
funding, 197
furnishings, 55

governors, school, 41, 44
graduate primary mental health care worker, 187
grief, 142–150

health education, 27
helplines, 166
hepatitis, 8
HIV, 8
home school support workers, 64
homelessness, 8
hospital admissions, 7
human resouces, 44
hypnosis, 61, 62

impaired social development, 69
implementation, 48, 204
impulsiveness, 179
impulsivity, 162, 174
inattention, 174, 178
internalizing disorder, 4, 17
IQ, 37

Jenny Mosley Consultancy, 76–79
jigsaws, 42

kinetic stimulae, 55

language disorder, 175
Leap Confronting Conflict, 64, 85–90
learning difficulties, 175
learning intervention centres, 72, 73
learning mentors, 185

learning support assistants, 185
learning support units, 64, 72
lighting, 55
local communities, 30, 34
lockers, 56
loss, 64, 142–150
lunchtime supervision, 58

masculine identity, 10
Maslow's hierarchy of needs, 28
massage, 61, 62
material resouces, 44
mediation, 99
mental health, 15, 36
mental health–positive, 17, 42
mental health disorder, 3, 4
mental health education program, 19
Mental Health Foundation, 15, 184, 195
mental health problem, 3, 8, 9, 13, 25, 42
Mental Health Task Force, 9, 36
mentoring, 7, 33, 99
merit systems, 58
method of shared concern, 64, 99
MIND, 14
mind mapping, 42, 61
monitoring, 48–49, 203–213
music therapists, 187
My Life in School Checklist, 43, 51, 204

National Healthy School Standard, 3, 127
needs analysis, 40–50, 61, 94
No Blame approach, 64, 100, 112

obesity, 151, 154
obsessive-compulsive disorder, 5, 35
occupational therapists, 187
olefactory stimulae, 55
oppositional defiant disorder, 68
organization, poor, 179
outside agencies, 200, 184–189
outside inclusion, 68
overactivity, 179
overdoses, 8
Owler Brook Infant School, 32
ownership, 43, 196

parental criminality, 8
parental pyschiatric illness, 8
PATHS, 38
peer group, 10, 26, 70, 83, 95, 121, 165
peer researchers, 42– 43
peer support, 64, 94, 98, 103–107, 112, 186, 206
Penn Prevention Program, 10
personal growth, 10
phobias, 5
physical health, 13
policy makers, 11

policy, school, 45, 64, 97, 126
positive psychology, 10
post 14 vocational training, 64, 70
poverty, 8, 9
PPP Healthcare Medical Trust, 20
protective factors, 8, 9, 10, 82
PSHE, 85, 112, 114, 157, 167
psychotherapist, 187
puberty, 112, 154

racial tensions, 34, 44, 93
readiness to change, 195
refugee communities, 9
resilience, 9, 10, 35
Respect Campaign, 14
review, 202, 203–213
reward schemes, 58
risk factors, 8, 9, 10, 82
Rites of Passge Programmes, 34
roadblocks, 47, 196–202
    time, 196–197
    funding, 196
    integration, 197–198
    training, 198
    ownership, 198–199
    promotion, 200
    outside agencies, 200–201
    closure, 201–202
role models, 69, 86
Royal College of Psychiatrists, 25

safe learning environment, 83
sanctuaries, 30
schizophrenia, 8, 14, 164
scholastic failure, 69, 83
school council, 40, 58
school nurses, 186, 187
School of Emotional Literacy, 61
School Software Company, 57
Schools Psychological Service, 42, 139, 177
self awareness, 37, 38
self esteem, 63, 64, 86, 102, 111, 117, 180
Self Harm Guidelines, 169–170, 171
self harming behaviours, 5, 64, 161–171
self regulation, 37
SENCO, 185
Sex Education Forum, 114
sex education, 113
sexual abuse, 163
sexual health, 64, 109–119, 124
sexually transmitted disease, 110
smoking, 120–131

social adversity, 4
social exclusion, 8
social skills, 37, 64, 133
social stories, 135
social support, 12
social workers, 187
socially isolated, 64, 132–141
Society for the Advancement of Sexual Health, 114
solvent abuse, 120–131, 125
southwarkblack mentor and inclusion project, 7
stigmatization, 8, 13–23
storytelling, 42, 135
suicidal thoughts, 5, 17
suicide, 5, 18, 164
supervision, 69
support programmes following suicide, 167
Sure Start, 3

teenage pregnancy, 109
Teens and Toddlers, 64, 116–118
The Big Fish Theatre Company, 64, 129–131
thematic learning, 64, 71
tic disorders, 175
tiered models of mental health, 27
time management, 196
toilets, 56
Toolkit for tackling Racism in Schools, 34
truancy, 68
Turn Your School Round (TYSR), 206–213, 207

UK Observatory, 91

victims, 94, 96
victims, counter aggressive, 95
victims, helpless, 95
victims, nonchalant, 95
victims, provocative, 64, 103
violence, definitions of, 80–81
violent behaviours, 31, 80–91, 92
Vocational Education and Training in Schools Programme (VETS), 70
voluntary sector, 189
Volunteer Development Scotland, 168

Webster-Stratton, 8
Winston's Wish, 64, 147–150
Wirral Health Promoting Schools Scheme, 46, 128

yoga, 61, 62
youth offending team, 189

3 5282 00573 5991